grammarRULES!,Inc. Louisa,Virginia

I'm History

...but do I repeat myself?

Lee Knapp

a memoir

grammarRULES!, Inc.

ISBN: 979-8-9898927-0-9
ISBN: 979-8-9898927-1-6 (e-book)

Library of Congress Control Number: 2024903307

First Paperback Edition May 2024

Cover art and Layout by Peter Long
Cover Photo Credit Kurt Lauer

To Cheston, Eric, and Stephen

Heraclitus purportedly said that the one constant in life is change. But Heraclitus wasn't your mother. Past, present, future; my love for you conquers time.

"We know, in the case of the person, that whoever cannot tell himself the truth about his past is trapped in it, is immobilized in the prison of his undiscovered self. This is also true of nations. We know how a person, in such a paralysis, is unable to assess either his weaknesses or his strengths, and how frequently indeed he mistakes one for the other . . . But the price for this is a long look backward whence we came and an unflinching assessment of the record. For an artist, the record of that journey is most clearly revealed in the personalities of the people the journey produced. Societies never know it, but the war of an artist with his society is a lover's war, and he does, at his best, what lovers do, which is to reveal the beloved to himself, and with that revelation, make freedom real."

James Baldwin
"The Creative Process"
from *Creative America*
Ridge Press, 1962

Contents

A Prologue of My Past

I t was the second September after I had ended my marriage. The grass around our dream house was way past due for a mow. The only problem was the cooperation of our, I mean, my John Deere. (Even after a year of being alone, the plural pronouns persisted.) Like almost everything *we* had owned with an engine, turning the key did not guarantee ignition. I did, however, have the number of an older Black gentleman named Mr. Williams who had helped us out before. Many Saturdays, through the odd angle from the kitchen window, I had seen him coaxing the older, crappier mower to start while lying in the grass, his legs and the soles of his shoes appearing to stick out from under the shed, not unlike the Wicked Witch of the East.

Mr. Williams arrived in his '85 Chevy pickup at about six o'clock. It was the first Monday of the school year, the time when the reality of the relentless routine of the next ten months hits teachers hard. I was already exhausted. Knowing the drill, Mr. Williams drove through the high grass straight down to the shed. He bore a slight look of confusion as he exited the truck and went straight to the subject of my husband. When I revealed that we were separated, he pressed. I just answered that he had some issues with alcohol and employment. "That's a shame. Always such a nice fella.'" I nodded, then redirected him to the dead machine. After methodically hooking up the jumper cables, he instructed me to get on the mower, my left leg at the clutch and my right leg way over on the other side for the brake. As Mr. Williams revved the truck engine, he signaled for me to turn the key. Nothing happened.

Then something did. Mr. Williams left the truck and, casually leaning over me, fully rested his late-sixties/early-seventies side belly on my mid-fifties, spread-eagle thighs. Looking downward with his face away from my crotch, he uttered something about the choke, which I almost did as I tried to suppress my laughter. With a Lucille Ball look of surprise on my face, I played to an imaginary camera in the woods. Here I was, upright on my lawnmower, staring into the woods, with an old man sprawled across my lap.

The dead battery finally resurrected. Hallelujah! I pulled out what I hoped would be enough money for Mr. Williams's trouble—no one in the country seems to give you a price up front—and thanked him over the deafening noise of the engine. I engaged the deck, drove off up the hill, spinning my neck backwards over my shoulder to admire the first buzz of the yard's crew cut. There it was. Just as I gave Mr. Williams a big thumbs-up, my hair whiplashed over my forehead and my whole body lurched violently forwards, lifting me out of the foam-exposed yellow vinyl seat. Dammit. In my elation, I had hit that pesky little stump I normally avoided. Of course, the mower had not charged up enough to restart. I was stuck. I saw the old Chevy's brake lights flash, followed by the creaking of the old truck's door. He backed up, and once again, with a couple of grunts from under his big salt-and-pepper moustache, hooked up the cables, started his truck, and revved the engine. To my horror, this time *he* got on the John Deere, cranked the ignition, and just took off to cut the grass for me. Like so much of my recent life, I had not bargained for this.

It was now about 7:20, ten minutes before *Jeopardy* was going to start, a longstanding signal for the end of my workday. I desperately wanted to go upstairs with a pretty glass of sauvignon blanc, rest my feet on one of the stools my grandmother Mema had needle-pointed, and yell answers at Alex Trebek to justify my existence. While Mr. Williams very slowly crisscrossed the yard, I, to not seem lazy, picked up sticks and begrudgingly threw them into the woods like I was ten and my father was making me. My legs were getting weary and prickly sweaty in my jeans. I was exhausted. We were approaching *Double Jeopardy*.

If it isn't clear by now, I'm a white lady. I'm a white lady who was an artist in a past life and strives for a studious bohemian look, takes the greatest pleasure in life from funny turns of phrases and challenging intellectual ideas, and who raised three sons in a pretty preppy neighborhood. You see—and then don't see—women like me everywhere. Before retiring in 2021, I had taught for nearly twenty years at the very same public high school that I graduated from in the 1970s. Although, it is not the same school at all. John Randolph Tucker High is located in suburban Richmond, Virginia—the former capital of the Confederacy. When I attended, my class of about four hundred had only a handful of Black students. When I returned nearly three decades later as an educator, the school was one of the most ethnically diverse—with about thirty-seven languages spoken—in Virginia. Along with about 20 percent of Asian, Hispanic, and "other" populations who attended, Tucker now served close to an equal number of Black and white students.

Perhaps because of the tractor exhaust, or my own exhaustion, as I watched Mr. Williams cut the grass I had a mini hallucination. I suddenly imagined him as my husband. The plural pronouns resurfaced. Yes, the old comfortable feeling of marriage returned. Only in this other kind of grass-induced fantasy, as Obama's first term was wrapping up, it was something altogether new: something akin to a truly New South, a New America, *Yes We Can*. Having a partner, working together, all felt so natural. We had shared a light dinner of arugula salad and grilled salmon before going outside to garden and keep up appearances. We had a party, after all, this coming weekend. This whole "working together" was so nice. Then, just as quickly as this paradigm arose, it shifted. Mema entered the scene; she entered me.

My personal time–space continuum became disoriented. It was 1965. I was the Lady of the House like Mema had been to the many young Black men she hired to do only the very few jobs she could not do herself. To the one thousand people in the little town of Norlina, North Carolina, she was "Mizhix" (Mrs. Hicks) who ran the big white rooming house on the corner of US Number One and Hyco Street. Now in this retro dream, I was Miznap, the lady in the big yellow house across from the horse farm and fancy bed and breakfast. (Never mind that in real time and real place Mr. Williams sometimes drove up in his beautiful new SUV, a car that surely started when you turned the key.) As I bent over in the flower garden, Mr. Williams wasn't my "husband," he was my hired help. I had deliriously reverted to a time when social and basic human equality—never mind a Black president—was still a dream. Only to most of my forebears, that would have been a dystopian nightmare.

Born in 1957, I am old enough to appreciate these remarkable changes in my old stomping grounds. I spent my childhood between a *de facto* segregated Richmond and Mema's openly segregated small

North Carolina town, where the races coexisted just fine, "as long as Blacks knew their place," a common observation I heard more than a few times growing up in the 1960s. Hers was an era of matter-of-fact, unquestioned structural and personal racism. Yet I loved her so dearly. Her influence still gives me strength, especially when I have needed to fend for myself in life, to work three jobs, to cut my own grass. But I have had to reconcile this Mema with the one who never once questioned her white superiority, so blatantly displayed in her recounting of a 1921 lynching in Norlina.

As he puttered along on the riding mower and I was unnecessarily pruning the butterfly bush down to its larvae, Mr. Williams had no idea of the complicated hysterical historical thoughts I was having. Husband or help? Both roles have a root in my lifetime. Had I not returned to my old high school campus with its completely new demographic, the idea of being married to Mr. Williams may have been just that—an idea. Because something had been missing: actual, sustained, community-driven, multi-ethnic relationships on a human level. When I was growing up, most people in my old city, and perhaps many today, were scared to death of the very thing that I came to love about my old high school this second time around—as much as I did the first.

✳ ✳ ✳

To earn money for my first ever trip to Europe, I taught World History One during the second summer of my singleness. The course spanned eons of history between Lucy Australopithecus and her Early Man buddies up through the Late Middle Ages in all of six weeks. In that final unit, I showed a History Channel reenactment of frantic, desperate medieval villagers dismantling the glorious Roman aqueducts stone by stone and using them to build their meager dwellings. It was upsetting to see the destruction of such a glorious past achievement, but that glory was now literally ancient history. During my own medieval period, all of that applied to me, too. Even though my survival was at stake, I still felt—and sometimes still feel —overwhelmingly guilty about dismantling the great civilization that I thought in my early years I was building to last forever. I believed then that with Jesus's guidance, my life would follow the upward spiral theory of history we studied the first day of school. I thought my family picture would continue to be as perfect as the one we took at Sears on a muggy July day in 1989, wearing our matching colorful Ecuadoran sweaters brought back as a gift from my brother-in-law. We were all together, united in our hot woolen itchiness in the back of the store's third floor next to the toy department, the boys giggling and almost edible in their cuteness. But things *would* fall apart. But were those dismantled aqueducts any less glorious because they were later destroyed? Just because a civilization changes over time, does that diminish the beauty of its earlier manifestations? Can its influence persist without a tainted memory? That was the challenge: to resist the tendentious coloring of my own past, either with bright yellow or murky brown.

This dream house in the country was my aqueduct. It was to give life to a continuation of family, of children and grandchildren living within Sunday dinner distance. For a Southern person deeply affected by memories of childhood homes, I thought mine was next, a place where mother sits at one end of the big table and father at the other. Yet soon after we laid its cinderblock foundation, my boys lit out for the territories. That was their love destiny, though. Babies proceeded. A few years after they split, my marriage ended. So did much of my long cultivated personal identity from so many longstanding tribes, most notably my membership in evangelical Christianity, as my alma mater revealed a renewed way for me to love the world. Then I went back to the future in a way. My old school gave up something new, a second-chance relationship late in life. And just like in any story, of a person or a high school or a country, nothing would be the same again.

PART ONE
The Great Schism in my Schema

And we shall all be called as witnesses
Each and every one.
PAUL SIMON, SILENT EYES

An Inquisition of Innocence

I was the last one to slide my burgundy plastic tray off the metal-tubed conveyor shelf before making my way to the dead center of the restaurant. The older brothers, who were maybe in their late twenties, were pushing together four tables to accommodate our group of about twelve. It was a Sunday—any Sunday between 1978 and 1983—at around two o'clock at the Wendy's on Richmond Road in Williamsburg, Virginia. I was starving. The sun streamed in the big windows, speckling the straggling lunch crowd of elderly couples and young families with a halo of dusty light as they chewed and talked in hushed tones. Finally, we were all seated. Then as routinely—and loudly—as starting a cheer in front of the student section of a crowded football stadium, one of the brothers stood up and began to clap. As though his salvation depended upon it. He clapped his hands together with such vigor that his feet came off the teal, ketch-up-stained carpet. We all joined in the clapping, enthusiastically bobbing our heads and earnestly squinting our eyes before blasting out, *"Happy—happy—happyhappyhappy . . . happy are the people whose God is the Lo-ord!"* followed by an elongated, slide-whistly *"oh-oh"* and a repeat of that happy line. By now the crowd at Wendy's was dead quiet. Judging by their furrowed brows, they appeared curious to hear the answer posed by the song's theological question. "Where does this happy feeling come from?" After a teasing pause, we gave it to them . . . "JESUS!"

It wasn't over yet. We all joined hands and the clapping brother led us in a long prayer to be sure that our fries and Singles were duly blessed, if not by now lukewarm. It had been a long morning of clapping that spilled into the afternoon. First, we had our pick of Sunday School classes which began at nine with singing and clapping, followed by intense notetaking on humility, or Jonah's weakness, or sexual impurity. Then we emptied into the high school's linoleum and concrete block Commons area where we stood around making witty banter, stories from our week sprinkled with phrases like "yeah, it was like the Lord was telling me . . ." or "ain't that just like the Lord." Church started at 10:30. For the first forty-five minutes (45 minutes!) we sang praise songs and clapped, with a couple of interludes of glossolalia. For the next fifteen minutes, we heard announcements about what the Lord was doing all around the world and how we could help Him. Then it was time to settle in.

On a "good" Sunday, according to the little Devil on your right shoulder, you could be out of there in another forty-five minutes. If you truly loved the Lord, the little Angel on the other shoulder made you never think once to look at your watch. You did not care one bit that it had been nearly ninety minutes since the pastor began rebuking us, reassuring us, or prophesying the destruction of America. Afterwards, we all fellowshipped some more back in the Commons. Like the Japanese businessman who would rather die at his desk than leave work first, none of us wanted to appear to be too anxious to get the hell out of there.

Just a few short years earlier, I had been born again in my childhood bedroom, or so I was told later. By the time I was fifteen, my intense childhood addiction to the wonderment of creation turned on me in a vicious way. Reveling in all the possibilities of the moment gave way to one thought: all of those moments were going to end. So, what was the point? And everything had to have a point. Nature and Life became huge, uncontrollable mysteries that overwhelmed and paralyzed my joy. Compulsive thoughts about the meaning of life and the prospect of death, particularly mine, sent me spiraling into a yearlong depression. As if coming from grotesque figures in a funhouse, voices asked, *"Why are you here? Why bother to live at all when you are just going to die?"* It's tempting to attribute my precocious existentialism to teen angst or the anxiety of growing up in a chaotic household. But I am not ready to be typical on this point. I still believe what happened to me was a genuine genesis of my spiritual awakening.

In the same way that as a little girl I used to billow my bedsheets to feel them drape slowly across my body, a sense of peace and love finally fell over me one summer night before the start of ninth grade. My mother had recently abandoned the dog-eat-dog world of garden club politics for a more benign stint as decorating chairman for a mission-minded, evangelical women's group. The jump made for a very obvious square peg—or in her case square Sarah—in the round hole of these pious groups because of her quick temper, although that was kept under wraps at its meetings, meetings where personal prayer requests were taken. Hers were all for my brother. She had been struggling exclusively with his self-destruction, while her Sunday School class—in 1972—seemed only to care about such tangential things like war and politics, "damned social issues" as she called them, on the way home from church. Mom wanted Jesus to stop worrying about Vietnam and focus on keeping my brother out of jail. By sixteen, he had already amassed a dozen larceny charges, both petit and grand, and I guess thanks to Jesus and our really good lawyer, he had not seen one day of any punishment.

After watching me languish on the den sofa for months, not even able to muster a laugh at Lancelot Link, she invited one of her new friends who "knew a lot about the Bible" to teach a bit of it to me and a few friends. Clara was a lovely woman with a honey blonde French twist, and on her fifth visit, we were sitting around a little round table in my bedroom when a passage provoked several questions about true belief. She stopped to ask if any of us had ever prayed to receive Christ, personally. While I really couldn't have said I knew what that meant, I was ready to do anything to travel anywhere outside of my own mind. As she led me in a prayer, a strange and very slight physical sensation began in my legs and moved up through the top of my head as though the sheer weight of all that depression just evaporated. I didn't know any hymns yet, but the common reference to a burden being lifted, which for me was the burden to solve all the mysteries of life, made immediate sense.

At the time, this was truly revolutionary for me. My earlier obsession with Questions found a new channel in Answers. I may have become a bit like the little girl who responded to the minister's children's sermon question, "What lives in your backyard and runs up and down the trees?" with "I know the answer is Jesus, but it sure sounds like a squirrel." During high school my newfound faith was innocent. I pursued my relationship with Jesus by adding Bible studies and a group called Young Life to class council meetings and play practice. Once a week someone's parents would host this "parachurch" fellowship we called Club. Before it started, kids were hanging out on the front yard and some were smoking cigarettes! At a Christian group! We'd head into a family room and sing some hippie Jesus songs and have some cool young college guy or girl give a talk about love or forgiveness based on a Bible story. Jesus fit right in, in his Levi's, red and white rugby shirt, and, duh, desert boots. No one talked about who was going to Hell. We didn't judge others. We talked a lot about love. In those days, my Young Life leader would end a meeting or split a scene by raising a fist to the sky and urging us to, "Keep up the revolution!"

It is tempting to look back from this present moment when the most vocal Christians in some corners have given Jesus such a bad name, making me want to dissociate from this past spiritual moment. (Many of my very smartest students who despise stereotyping had no problem lumping all Christians together by saying "they all hate gay people" or "they're all hypocrites," to which I sometimes, a wee bit sarcastically, responded, "you mean like all Muslims are terrorists.") It is also tempting to question whether what happened that summer evening before ninth grade was a "conversion" or just an emotional release to some nice man named Jesus in some kind of admission to this invisible therapist that I was not in control. It doesn't help my clarity on this intimate moment that it was followed by forty layers of sediment, one for each year, formed from the detritus of the most disillusioning force to one's spirituality: membership. The sediment began to erode, though, once my involvement in organized, and semi-organized, religion ended after four decades. Then, quite unexpectedly, that detritus crystallized into some kind of unfettered love, right back on the very same campus—only now with its wild array of humanity—where it began.

During senior year of high school, some of my lifelong friends started having sex. Anything sexual up to that point had been silly innuendo and wordplay that we cluelessly bantered back and forth in art class. Now, evidently, some of these same people were willingly taking their clothes off in front of a boy, or *boys*, in some cases, or a *teacher*, in one case. I say evidently because I always found out through the grapevine. I don't think I was shut out of the scuttlebutt because of any sanctimonious attitude I exuded; one friend said that others respected me and didn't want me to think less of them. It was more from an inability to relate. As somewhat precocious as I was in academics, I had been carnally challenged by what I later dubbed my chronic neuter complex, developed from so many "always-a-bridesmaid-never-a-bride" relationships with boys. This amoebic juju made the mortification of the flesh no sweat. In fact, my flesh became more of a nuisance, a mere housing, if not impediment, for what I thought of as the real me, that would be the spiritual me, to emerge.

Even though I did finally have my first boyfriend who I met at a summer program, he lived two hours away. When we visited, it was all very innocent. Perhaps my reticence in that relationship and my disillusionment with my peers had nothing to do with my newfound faith in God, after all. Maybe it was a fear not of "the flesh," but a fear of what my parents, my grandmother and her sister, my great aunt Dizzy, would think. I had staked my acceptance, self- and otherwise, on obedience and achievement. I also might have feared the loss of some moral high ground with my mother that not having what was quaintly known then as "premarital sex" (not much of a threat since it usually takes another person) so easily gave. Besides, in my mind, there was a quota on squeaky wheels per family. My brother could be the juvenile delinquent filling up an impressive rap sheet: I'd take the role of good girl fulfilling my presidency of the National Honor Society.

Still, by graduation, as more of my classmates fell from my increasingly prudish moral standards, the more nervous—I mean high-minded—I got about maintaining them. I didn't think I judged them with any holier-than-thou attitude, but the first entry in my first journal kind of gives me away. Miss Perkins, my attractive and vivacious young art teacher, gave it to me on graduation night. In the front was a strip of lime green art paper on which she'd nicely complimented my sense of humor and told me to record some of it because it would take me far in life. A week later this is what I wrote on its opening page:

June 16, 1976

I am becoming aware of how very different I am from others. I have either an enormous sense of guilt or a strict sense of morality. I cannot believe the words of people and their contradicting actions. It feels as though I am wrong, but I know I am with God . . . The realization of my generation becoming just like past ones hurts. I will remain the revolutionary though . . . I should continue to denounce the ways of the world for myself and speak to others at a God-chosen time.

What a barrel of laughs! The entry is humorous and not a little pathetic. "The ways of the world" is the telling phrase; something had already begun to come apart in my childhood's more blithesome and integrated spirituality. Categories were forming as I was inadvertently searching for depth in ever-narrowing religious passages. While verbalizing it only with my Young Life Crew, I began to believe that all human problems, personal and political, however intractable, could be solved if all parties involved would just accept Christ as their personal savior. Not that love and forgiveness and humility are bad things, but the path to them had narrowed in my mind. (Although it did hurt senior year when an adult I nearly idolized for her beauty, smarts, and unmatched charm asked me about my faith: "How can you be so narrow minded?") Indeed, the downward ramp from a childhood of warm-spirited humanitarianism to an adolescent high-minded idealism to an adulthood of well-meaning dogmatism is a gentle one, nearly imperceptible. But when that ramp leads to a one-way train steered by an engineer with a questionable sense of direction, danger looms. Others may join you on your journey. Those people may challenge you inside that tunnel, and they certainly love you with great sincerity. Yet if one is, like I was at that time, so inclined on this decline, it becomes necessary to leave behind unexpressed pieces of your true soul so that you can make room for the engineer's baggage.

Enter Pastor Joe. Pastor "Kind-of-Misogynist" Joe. A law school dropout, he and a couple of graduate students and young golf pro-shop workers started the church in the early 1970s in Herculon-upholstered, shag-carpeted living rooms around the colonial hamlet. This was at about the same time that Pat Robertson was going door-to-door selling cable boxes in Virginia Beach so the Holy Spirit could speak through them for only $29.99 a month. Our leaders knew him well. By the time I arrived at the church in 1978, it had undergone a huge growth curve, meeting in ever-larger school auditoriums and gymnasiums to hold its nearly five hundred members, and Robertson was about to arrive on the national stage. Like Martin Luther before me, I had no inkling of any larger social or political movement that was about to be unleashed on my country's culture and politics right down Interstate 64 East from Williamsburg. I was just looking to be "challenged" in my faith, beginning a lifetime of subconsciously confusing faith with self-improvement and turning it into some kind of competition.

That competition was strictly in my own soul, but Joe put the winning of other souls at the top of our to-do list. I hated it in a kind of flip side of the hatred of the awkward silence. My inner resistance to evangelism, which could have created enough kinetic energy to light up Long Island, should have told me that I was misplaced in evangelicalism. So instead of trying to bring up Jesus somehow during tennis with a hall mate (Her: "Fifteen-Love." Me: "You know God is Love, right? OK. Serve"), I opted for a more subtle, organic approach. I thought that if I could just wrap my mind around my sinful flesh and squeeze it to death, eliminating anything negative about my personality, then other kids on campus would see my saintly glow, walk up, and ask: "Hey, there's something different about you. What is it?" And I would be all like, "Aww, it's just Jesus." And they would be all like, "How can I get that glow too?" Then I would pray them into the Kingdom and go brag about it to my Bible study. Counteracting my inherited maternal pathology by being "really sweet" would be tough. When I was in second grade, Dizzy asked me how school was going. Evidently I responded—at seven—"This has been the worst year of my life!" That same year, Charles Johnston stood next to me in the cafeteria line listening to my observation of some low-quality yeast rolls. He looked at the seven-year-old me and in his slow, wise-as-an-old-man, Southern drawl, said, "Lee Pearson. You are just a bag of complaints." As it turns out, I may not have been alone in this historic inner struggle with my personality and my "witness."

If I, at nineteen, had lived in early seventeenth-century Massachusetts and not a fake twentieth-century replica of eighteenth-century Williamsburg, Puritan poet Anne Bradstreet and I would have gotten along famously. Without the fame, of course, because that would be one of those fleshly pursuits she cleverly laments in her posthumously famous and revelatory poem "The Flesh and The Spirit." From where I sat each Sunday, not much had changed in almost four centuries except that Anne Bradstreet probably didn't attend church in a high school auditorium without a bonnet. I began to experience—deeply subconsciously—the same fabricated, bifurcated psychic struggle that she personified as two sisters at odds with each other over what brings real joy. At that time of so much spiritual striving in my life, I would have totally taken up for Sweet Sister Spirit who endures the taunts of the hell-bound, sarcastic Flesh:

> "Sister," quoth Flesh, "what liv'st thou on
> Nothing but Meditation?
> Doth Contemplation feed thee so
> Regardlessly to let earth go?
> Can Speculation satisfy
> Notion without Reality? . . ."

Miss Flesh encourages rebellion in her pious sister by making light of Contemplation and Meditation. In my day, we called these an individual's "Quiet Time," and it was a major emphasis of Joe's sermons. How many times did he berate us for not getting up at four o'clock in the morning to pray for hours before the day began? There was a direct correlation between how much time I (it's all up to me) spent with the Lord in the morning—always in the morning—and the hastening of the End Times. During QT, as old lights short-handed it, we were also supposed to be memorizing vast tracts of Scripture so we could foil the plans of our captors, Communists or Democrats—oftentimes hard to tell the difference—to take away our Bibles so they could expel God from America. This approach seemed to be in complete agreement with Sister Spirit, that Speculation, not direct experience, is enough for Spirit to form her notions of life. Flesh finds this ridiculous, and in doing so hints at some postmodern conceptions of experience-driven truth. The insight Bradstreet perhaps unintentionally reveals through this conceit makes me wonder if she were not just the least bit aware of her own suffocation.

Sister Spirit answers Flesh with more than a few military metaphors, reminiscent of the "battles" we Christians were in, according to Joe. She calls her sister a "foe to combat" until "I see thee laid in th' dust." Spirit's greatest honor will be "when I am victor over thee." In my day, people spoke about getting the victory over some temptation like Ben & Jerry's or *General Hospital*. With an eerily similar attitude as my high school journal entry above, Spirit answers Flesh with a nearly audible nanny-nanny-booboo that comes from knowing that Jesus likes you more:

> ". . . But my arise is from above,
> Whence my dear father I do love . . .
> Mine eye doth pierce the heav'ns and see
> What is Invisible to thee.
> Thine honours do, nor will I love,
> For my ambition lies above.
> If I of Heav'n may have my fill,
> Take thou the world, and all that will."

This poem is another of the many rhyming moments of history that Mark Twain aphorized: a poem written four centuries ago that perfectly captures my thought patterns of over four decades ago. According to Spirit, Flesh could have the stinking world because it was full of mere shadows of beauty that bore no connection to the real beauty of the unseen in heaven. For so long, I took this dichotomy to heart, so much so that my heart became impervious to the magnificent beauty in the world's diversity as a means of spiritual nourishment. It was not that this church did not revere Nature's diversity; some of them loved to go camping. I just don't remember any equal love of the variety in *human* nature.

Sister Spirit's hegemony over Sister Flesh might have helped explain most women's wardrobes at church in those days. The older women, by older I mean those in their late twenties, set the standard for female attire. A fellow former church member friend and I were discussing our old notions of the spirituality/sexuality duality as it related to cleavage. She remarked that she just didn't feel like she had really lived because the necklines of her youthful glory days had always been so high. When she relayed a story about a current church friend of hers, a very serious, faithful woman whose décolletage was always on display, I confessed that in the old days, a plunging neckline would have certainly meant a questionable eternity. This is why every time I shopped at the Goodwill, I used to laugh out loud in the $4.00 dress aisle. Without fail, while hunting designer castoffs, I would find at least two or three flower-appliqued, oversized jean jumpers. I kept laughing while I imagined wearing one to see my good friend Dianne who also went through the church thing with me. I knock on the door of her then cool New York City apartment, and she opens it to see me all be-denimed. We laugh, then play a guessing game of what saint I am from the old days. Of course, in this daydream, I would be wearing a mini-print turtleneck, maybe with little roses or polka dots on it, underneath my high-waisted, gathered jumper. If it were the holidays, maybe the stretched-out cotton top would sport pumpkins or Christmas trees. But no Santa turtlenecks. That would be a bit too pagan. The outer dress became another reflection of inner righteousness, one that would not cause the men of the church "to stumble."

✳ ✳ ✳

At the end of my sophomore year of college, a good friend introduced me to my future husband at church one Sunday. He was a star lacrosse player with a hail-fellow-well-met demeanor and a boyish, preppy, redhead look. My first impression was of his unabashed confidence, refreshing lack of self-consciousness, and lively personality, characteristics that served him well in his roles as team captain and resident advisor, described as "the best one ever" by our beloved dean of students. I was attracted to his upbeat voice, athleticism, and the sheer discipline that being a college athlete required. Unlike anyone else in those days, he unironically wore a knit stocking hat with a pompom on the top, displaying a kind of oblivious genuineness that I lacked. That summer after we met, I stayed in Williamsburg to take extra classes and got a job working in the Education Department. He called in to make sure he would be able to get his teaching license in time because of the demands of lacrosse. Before he identified himself, I immediately and weirdly, recognized his voice and we started laughing. I looked in the big book of rules and told him he probably needed to take chemistry that very summer. As it turned out, I, who later made a small business out of grammar, had misinterpreted the meanings of "should" and "shall." The professor told him on the last day of class that the course had actually been optional.

Nevertheless, we hit it off during that unnecessary summer. We played tennis barefoot one night; he rode his bike pretty far out to our girls' apartment where I made his Northern-self my grandmother's Southern fried chicken. I met a bunch of his lacrosse friends and coach at a party; we went to church, of course. Like me, he had had his own conversion experience only during his freshman year of college through the guidance of his RA. After he finally asked me on an official dinner date in late September, I became something I never dreamed of—a jock's girlfriend. I went to every lacrosse game his senior year, proudly walking with him from the field to the locker room, along with all of his teammates. In our early conversations, I gathered that, even as a senior in college, he still missed his family quite a lot, despite being very popular around campus. This struck an immediate contrast for me. He grew up with four brothers in what seemed to me a rancor-free, idyllic all-American environment. His charming and hilarious stories gave me the vision of what I wanted to replicate in creating a family. When I finally visited "his people" in Connecticut, it felt like I had been cast in a 1960s sitcom where the successful father sat at the head of the table, the upbeat mom ran the household, and the five sons cracked wholesome jokes while everyone laughed. And there was an adorable golden retriever to boot. This had not been the experience in my own nuclear family.

After graduation, he got a job teaching middle school science and coaching lacrosse at an elite private school in Richmond while I finished my senior year. Our relationship maintained its fun feeling, but it was also inextricable from our shared faith. Our deepest conversations and best letters revolved around what "God was doing in our lives," usually meaning some area we needed to have more trust or less ego. In December, on William and Mary's beautiful Crim Dell Bridge, he proposed. That spring, in true 1970s fashion, I brought my sewing machine from home to my dorm room and made my own white eyelet cotton wedding dress from a Simplicity pattern. Six weeks after I graduated, we got married on the first day of summer.

It was a simple, outdoor wedding at my parents' new place in the growing exurb way west of Richmond called Short Pump. I remember the feeling that this was my mother's big chance to show off her pride and joy—her house—to so many people at once. Unlike many brides of today, I had little input into the affair. My father built a brick-floored gazebo, or *gabozo* as he liked to call it, in the backyard from old carved posts and frilly, Victorian trim that my mother found at her favorite salvage yard. The ladies of my mother's bridge club prepared the food. Mom arranged three huge old wicker funeral baskets of flowers—blue geraniums, day lilies, Queen Anne's lace that she picked from the side of the road, and a few pricey irises and roses she bought from the nursery across the street—and hung them at the back of the gabozo. The land sloped perfectly down to the twelve-by-twelve venue so that everyone in their metal folding chairs had a good view, as did the geriatric gallery which sat up close to the left. Joe officiated, after I argued my mother down that he was not the leader of some cult.

Just as the Pilgrims could no longer hope for the purification of the Anglican Church and crossed the Atlantic in the 1620s, this college church, among many others in the 1970s, splintered away from the mere seven or so major Protestant denominations that had been shaping Europeanized America's religious history for nearly four centuries. As time went on, it was not uncommon to hear of some guy meeting with five people in his living room and calling themselves a church. I, too, credulously set sail on my own errand into this unaccountable wilderness, sure that I would grow "deeper" in my faith along with so many great friends. Still, how unfortunate that a history major would not have realized that she was caught in one of the recurring eddies of American spiritual revivalism, set spinning by an influx of scary undercurrents in our cultural life.

Joe preached many jeremiads on God's judgment on a backslidden, debauched America as it neared the 1980s. He wasn't alone. Another Virginian, Jerry Falwell, declared America's Moral Majority had been silent for too long. Christian intellectual Francis Schaefer became the evangelical movement's prophet, in large part in response to the 1972 decision to legalize abortion. Ronald Reagan became the de facto savior over the openly evangelical Jimmy Carter. How many times did Joe say from the stage on a Sunday morning, "I'm not saying you spell God, G-O-P, but . . ?" followed by peals of laughter from the five hundred brothers and sisters. Once the religious right took hold, we had agendas to fight: the secular agenda, the homosexual agenda, the public school sex-ed agenda. The most vocal church members became the political ones who presumed that to save America we must all lobby the General Assembly on pro-life legislation, or home school the kids, or campaign for local Republicans.

Joe and the eight or so elders adhered to a practice popular in evangelical churches at the time known as shepherding. It could have been described as a type of mentoring, but others might have characterized it as an intense, even extreme form of control. As a by-product, these sessions provided a network by which Joe could keep tabs on his flock's loyalty and submission. Shepherding, as well as the many Bible study groups, could reveal to Joe what Puritan reverend, ironically named Thomas Shepard, called "the spreading of the contagion of corrupt opinions" which he felt could destroy the church. Like so many church leaders throughout time, Joe thought that was most likely to happen through women, judging by how often he mentioned Jezebel as a warning in his sermons and a moniker for "rebellious" women of those times. Women maintaining their rightful place in submission to men—who were themselves in submission to God—was key to a happy family, a happy church, and a *happyhappyhappy* society. This was, as many Sunday School lessons explained, because women possessed more vulnerable and emotional personalities; they were more susceptible to that contagion of error and needed the correcting influence of the man's rationality. Dangers abounded when the man's rightful place before God and over his wife was challenged.

After five years of attending this church and the birth of my first son, an increasingly relentless inner monologue told me that, despite that annoying song, I wasn't happy. In truth, I was becoming mortified. In more truth, I was transforming into a squirming ball of self-conscious flesh, flesh that obviously needed mortification according to another of Joe's favorite shibboleths, to "rule my spirit." Teased out over time, ruling my spirit meant triumphing over an inherited, natural inner freedom with the goal of realizing some ideal Christian personality. Like the Puritans who wanted to at least look like they were one of the Elect, Joe admonished us to be vigilant in our holiness and wholly separate from "the world" in order to maintain your witness.

The problem was, I always kind of liked the world. The moments in my childhood that approached the sacred came through some kind of creation, one of my many artistic hobbies. As early as six, I would drop my books after riding the bus home from first grade and run to a hill on the next street over to collect rocks in my shirttail. The intense, aesthetic, lost-in-time feelings I got back in my tiny ranch house bedroom as I glued them into bodies and drew faces on them would be repeated over and over in my life, through five years of art in school, a few college classes, and then a small art business. It would take me a long time to see that those creative drives borne in childhood were not separate from, but deeply integral to, my adult soul. It would take much longer still to then reclaim them as gifts, gifts with spiritual meaning. Even though one of my favorite verses of the Bible reminded me that "it is for freedom that Christ has set you free," my own psychic freedom would become a casualty of a decades-long diagnoses of and prescriptions for my spiritual ailments.

* * *

Since 1636, Anne Hutchinson had been a thorn in the side of John Winthrop, the orthodox governor of the Massachusetts Bay colony. With her "ready wit and bold spirit," she challenged the church's hierarchy and power. In October of that year, Winthrop wrote in his journal that Hutchinson held a dangerous idea, "the divers opinion," that "no sanctification can help to evidence our justification." This seems to me merely a restatement of Luther's revolutionary idea that it is by grace, God's grace, that one is given salvation, not by the estimation of our works by any priest or pope, or minister in this case. Nevertheless, she persisted at her civic trial and seemed to go for broke in front of the, duh, all male judges: "Therefore take heed how you proceed against me—for I know that, for this you go about to do to me, God will ruin you and your posterity and this whole state." Later, John Cotton, her minister, who himself once entertained a more open theology, now played to the crowd at her separate church trial. He tried to lay on her some titillating potential results of her radical, antinomian teaching because she held meetings in her home with both men and women. With that same fixation on sex, a "filthie proclivity," and the corrupting power of wayward women that I heard in a school auditorium some 350 years later, Cotton implied that all kinds of debauchery would result. Anne Hutchinson, who had once admired Cotton, was convicted on the charge of "slandering the ministers" and being an instrument of the Devil. She was banished from the colony. Upon later hearing of Hutchinson's murder and most of her fourteen children by New York natives, John Winthrop purportedly replied, "Proud Jezebel has at last been cast down."

I had a similar shift in the relationship with my spiritual leader. Only instead of an austere Boston courtroom in Puritan New England, mine took place in the swanky Captain George's Seafood Buffet in Colonial Williamsburg. Looking back, it may have only been a matter of time before I, "Miss Bag of Complaints, Daughter of Sarah Who Cusses After Church," would have a run-in with this twentieth-century Cotton, a patchwork of paranoia, egomania, and just a touch of misogyny. Despite trying to rule my spirit and not be like my mother, I still could not deny my *filthie proclivity* to innocently observe situations with, let's say, an eye as to how things could improve. One of those suggestions got back to Joe. Before I knew it, the church secretary called to invite us to discuss my thoughts with none other than Joe himself. At George's Seafood Buffet! I had only been there once since its massive price had been a little out of my parents' reach at the time. No wonder I was a little excited; first about the seafood that I was counting on the church paying for, and for a private audience, a chance to be heard and perhaps impress, with the always charming, charismatic, celebrity Joe. I looked at the calendar every day awaiting the meeting, carefully planning which jean jumper and turtleneck I would wear. Once we arrived, my husband, my Richmond pastor (we now attended a satellite church), and I made small talk and clean jokes with Joe, hinting at quite the enjoyable evening to come. Almost as soon as we had all gone through the line and sat down with our steaming plates in front of us, Joe blindsided me.

His face made such a rapid transformation from that synthetic smile to an angry furrowed brow that I couldn't help but think about my favorite scene from *Tootsie* when a cross-dressed Dustin Hoffman hails the cab twice in Dorothy's high sweet voice before he abandons the sham and belts out an angry, deep "TAXI!" Only there was no humor in this scene. I hardly managed a few sentences before Joe accused me of having the spirit of Jezebel. Alright! I was in the club! After advising, no, warning me with a pointed finger, to "watch my witness" and "submit" to authority, he questioned me, like a good totalitarian is supposed to do, for names of other dissenters. He asked me about my good friend Sue, and if I had heard her making any derogatory comments about some conference. So there I was. A modern-day Anne Hutchinson with a pile of fried scallops and shrimp scampi sitting in front of her, now doomed to go to waste. I just listened, in shock, and focused on not crying. It would remain, though, as another significant incidence of *treppenwitz*—the German word implying the regret that accompanies a missed opportunity for a takedown zinger. Still, there is a dilemma for the Christian: at what point are you expected to become a chump in the name of Jesus? How do we account for and address affronts to our personhood and dignity, especially coming from an authority figure? Should I have turned the other cheek, the one on my face or the other one, for him to kiss? Oh yeah, then there is that pesky issue of forgiveness, even when events, or God, orchestrate a divine justice that can easily replace it with a kind of satisfying vengeance, as would become the case for Joe.

Joe was the Williamsburg Wizard of Oz. Only in a kind of reverse revelation when the curtain dropped; a seemingly nice person was actually a jerk, more interested in maintaining power than encouraging love. I bet he rode home from George's Seafood feeling like he had stopped a contagion by putting down a *filthie woemen* for God. I rode home accepting that my observations, my self-awareness, my judgment, and even my temperament, were not signs of rebellion, but rather my inner voice screaming like Tootsie to save me from those who had co-opted my soul. Obviously, some forty years later, my bitterness can be produced like a rabbit out of a hat. Was my mother right? Was this a cult, or maybe just cult-adjacent? No matter. As anyone who has flirted with any cultish group—religious, social, political, or otherwise—knows, the anger rests most squarely on yourself for tolerating it as long as you did. But it can be difficult to exit. Existential danger lurks right around the corner of a long-cultivated identity, ready to knife fight you in an alley, when you start to ask the question, "What am I doing here?" Or more precisely: "What am *I* doing *here*?"

Not long after being buffeted at the buffet, I had nurtured enough inner Hutchinson to now embrace, not resist, my inner antinomianism. My resistance to forced proselytizing grew, but I no longer felt guilty about it, especially as Joe encouraged all of us to become missionaries to a foreign country. The church had paid for Joe to visit something like eighty countries on short-term trips to meet with their church leaders. There were conferences to strategize converting the entire world to Christianity by the millennium. Meanwhile, I had come to terms with the fact that I was not, nor had ever been, a particularly cause-oriented person, not a good trait for an evangelical, which has more than a semantic connection to evangelism it seems. Was there not some other way to live out Jesus's commands to love God, others, and myself? A way that did not involve grand strategies for converting those you love? When Joe made this statement nearing the end of a two-hour sermon about an upcoming missionary conference, "If you are not going this year, then I seriously doubt whether you know Christ at all," I gave up. Like Huck Finn when he helps Jim escape from slavery, I thought, "All right then, I'll go to hell."

Joe would face his own personal hell after one very unlucky day.

This was in spite of the fact that "luck" was a forbidden word because everything happened for a reason. Looking back, it might have been no surprise that lust was a favorite topic for Joe's sermons. Perhaps he knew his spiritual influence over so many young female acolytes could so easily turn physical. His rock star status honed on that high school auditorium stage each Sunday might have boosted his sexual appeal past its otherwise *meh* status and given him more opportunities to give into this greatest temptation. Like two other nationally prominent J-named ministers, Bakker and Swaggert, followed much later by Ted Haggard and Jerry Falwell Jr., this one succumbed.

A super insider sister gave me the deets. Evidently, one of the more obsequious-*seeming* elders picked up an extension phone in the church office, an extension phone being part of a system of wires that connected six-pound, boxy metal phones that sat on a desk with a circular number dial and a handset connected to it by a cord, that if you picked it up very quietly, you could listen in on other conversations in the system. In a fleshed-out example of "your sin will find you out," this fourth-in-charge elder must have tuned in at the precise, most damning moment, otherwise his godliness would have told him that listening to others' conversations was a sin. It was in those brief moments that he heard irrefutable evidence of the classic tag team takedown of powerful men: secretaries and sex. This kind, and now shocked, elder was left with no question in his mind of an extramarital affair between this woman and his leader, Joe, a father of three young children married to a truly sweet and beautiful woman with eyes so big and brown they may very well have been the inspiration for Van Morrison's song. Only in Joe's case, as the carefully parsed and obfuscated storyline went, he had been told by God, probably in one spectacular QT, that this lovely submissive wife was going to die, imminently, and He wanted to have a new wife all lined up for

His special servant Joe. It would be easy to imagine, especially after my encounter at George's, that this mild-mannered elder had been given a piece of Joe's mind in the past, too. To this elder's eternal credit, he feared God more than man. Still, the disillusionment and hypocrisy left my friends and me reeling.

It took a year or so for the church, now under new leadership, to dwindle from around six hundred at its height to about fifty faithful parishioners. Joe's wife divorced him. He started selling real estate in town, put on fifty pounds, and later remarried. According to a friend who ran into him about fifteen years later who dared to confront him about all the damage he had done, Joe acted like he didn't know what she was talking about. He died at age sixty-four. His online obituary is a glowing tribute to a godly family man who traveled to ninety countries of the world, spreading the love of God. Oh, and his first wife is still very much alive.

I left this world behind with my faith intact, but with a deep longing for a normal expression of it. No more weirdness. My approach to the world, though, would remain filtered through church; my deepest relationships confined to those within.

Backsliding Away

I n the spring of 1980, teaching jobs were nearly impossible to come by. I felt extremely fortunate to have secured a position for that fall in my home county of Henrico. He was teaching middle school science and coaching lacrosse at the most prestigious private school in Richmond. Between us we would make a whopping $19K. I felt rich, even after a slight jolt a year later upon hearing about a former roommate's new business job that started her at $35K! The shift in values—in the culture and my heart—had not yet begun, but it would only take a few very short years before Robin Leach eclipsed Gabe Kotter as a worthy role model. But for us as a newly married couple fresh out of college and on the heels of a camp counselor summer job on Martha's Vineyard, the lame duck months of the Carter Administration found us in love and occupying good places, a 650-square-foot, charming but somewhat dilapidated apartment, and each our own spheres of influence in the classroom.

When I taught modern world history, we started the year with a little chart that delineated ancient, medieval, and modern history by years. The kids probably got the impression, if they even listened, that ancient history came to an abrupt halt one day in 476 CE when the barbarians sacked Rome and Odoacer sat on the last Roman emperor's throne. The next day the Middle Ages promptly began. That lasted until one fine October 12 in 1492 when Columbus bumped into a world that was new to him. So, on October 13, modern history began. In our own lives, inner and outer but especially inner, such calendar demarcations are equally as arbitrary and simplistic. If pressed, the beginning of a new historical era in my own life came at twenty-five, around mid-May 1983, in the first trimester of my second surprise pregnancy.

My husband quit his teaching job. He had thrived for four years as an educator, but as would become a reliable pattern in the decades to come, he grew disaffected with environments in which he perceived a lack of respect and appreciation for the job he was doing despite all evidence to the contrary. When we ate dinner at the school every weeknight, it was clear to me just how popular he was with the kids and faculty. On several occasions, I overheard parents raving about him. His unilateral decision to leave and enter the financial sector might have come from the prospect of providing for two children at twenty-six, a person who had dreams in which authority figures in hallways of funhouse mirrors yelled the word, "Responsibility" at him. More so, he may not have known or valued himself and his natural gifts enough to resist a changing culture that increasingly discounted them.

Young as I was, and understanding of his yearnings (and still operating under the promises of the old church's teachings about the happy family), I supported his decision. Besides, I had seen what being a stockbroker could get you if you put in your time.

Just a year before, his father had provided the family six weeks on Martha's Vineyard! A very quick learner, he was able to make a go of this new career, although after three years he switched firms, bad management and all. In the first few months at his new position, it happened: the proverbial windfall, several months' worth of income all at once. Plus, we now had yet another son to feed. I had never in my life made more than what was needed per month. But in the winter of '87–'88, I thought we were making up for lost ground and would soon emerge among the winners. We bought a used Dodge Caravan. I went to the fabric store and bought inch-high shoulder pads to sew into the sleeve seams of all my church dresses. Then in the spring, he announced to me that he had quit his job without a new one lined up.

For the next six months we survived on the remainder of the big payout and on income I made going out at night to tutor. That summer, in whipsaw contrast, my father-in-law again treated us all to a week on Nantucket. Our little gang stayed on a big screened-in sleeping porch. It was a magical week, especially at night when the sparkling blanket of stars sent jolts of wonder through the three little boys and their mom. Under those stars and seemingly alone on that small island in the town of Madaket, reassurance came. I would be returning to another period of unknown quantities and tremendous responsibilities. But it seemed my story and my problems were at once an important part of the mystery of life, yet also insignificant in its vastness. At that moment, with those three little doll babies—six, four and nearly two—snuggled up to me, a girl who thought she would never have a family, I found some peace. I was thirty years old. I may have begun to relinquish some earlier ambition, a need to make some kind of mark on this world. Who needs that when the world you made is making its mark on you?

Nantucket also became part of my personal folktale. In a little shop in cobblestoned Nantucket Town, I spotted an adorable handmade canister set. It had an unusual feature compared to all the other earthy-looking, duck motif clay pieces of the time—it was butter yellow! With tiny handmade pink roses and green leaves at the intersection of etched lines in a diamond grid! I almost fell over at its cuteness. Of course, I couldn't afford it at that point and since the cell phone camera hadn't yet been invented, I committed the image to memory and determined to make one just like it. I wasn't sure if my five years of high school art and one ceramics class in college would make that goal come to fruition, but that set haunted me. I got a bag of clay. The trajectory of my life then took a sharp turn down a long and winding, very muddy road.

For the next fifteen years, while the economy heated up and the world was moving steadily towards all things digital, my digits were elbow deep in a bucket of mud, sometimes forming cool, dirt evening gloves on my hands and arms. It wasn't like I was Dustin Hoffman (this time in *The Graduate*); some Mr. McGuire pulling me aside at a cocktail party after getting my history degree from William and Mary, whispering discretely in my ear, "Ceramics. There's a great future in ceramics." No, the clay just formed a life of its own on mine. My first show, a total misnomer for what artists know as a sale, came at a friend's sister-in-law's house off River Road, in the fanciest neighborhood in town. There, for the first time, a lady took out her wallet and gave me thirty bucks cash for a pink, black, and white teapot I called "Buttons and Bows." Boom! Just like that, I was a professional artist. According to nineties crazes, with my "home business," I guess I had become what was formerly considered an esoteric French word: an "entrepreneur." That might have been a little too sexy for my mud-based operation in the cinderblock tool room in the basement.

With generous help from my father-in-law, we had bought our first house in a leafy suburb of modest fifty-year-old Cape Cods and ranchers just before the birth of my third son. We joined the religious mainstream and attended a nearby lively evangelical Presbyterian church, a cute brick one with a little parlor and a fellowship hall and a steeple and a sanctuary and no glossolalia. This place was led by humble Greatest Generation men like my dad who were just as ready with a joke as a prayer, a place where good old middle-class folks attended and sang hymns. Whether we wanted it or not, responsibility now circumscribed our lives. So did real estate. Our little house bordered neighborhoods of prestige and wealth, which probably added to a creeping kudzu of cultural conformity and mounting materialism.

On Wednesday mornings with three boys under five in tow, I attended a very popular Bible study of nearly three hundred women at this new suburban church. There the Scriptures were taken very seriously; there was homework and small group discussion and a lecture. The old student in me revived as I tried to make the pithiest comments in class so as to be noticed by the bigwigs and maybe get a speaking gig at one of the retreats on humility. But one day outside of class, temptation arose. I overheard a couple of other women whispering about last night's television show, "thirty*something*." I was a diehard fan; I even slept in a nightshirt with that cool typewriter font. We had to keep this to ourselves since watching television at that time was a clandestine pleasure, not openly admitted among Christians or anyone wanting to keep up an intellectual facade. Each week, these bad girls and I would sneak away down the hall and stand outside our Bible study classroom. In hushed tones, before discussing faith and hope, we would dish on Tuesday night's episode about Michael and Hope. In all honesty, I looked forward to that show probably a little more than church. Employment uncertainty, stay-at-home mom identity, and marriage tension were dramatized so well by those believable characters. Not everyone was a fan. The rap on the show was that it was full of semi-affluent whiners. Boomer whiners, to boot. At last, I had found another tribe! On Abraham Maslow's famous pyramid of needs, the ones whined about on thirty*something* were near the top. He called such needs, which may have been more aptly named desires, meta-motivation, or the constant need for betterment. In other words, the lack of contentment. As the nineties began—and it would only get worse—this meta-motivation may account for the full blossoming of the narcissism begun in the eighties. And the most interesting narcissism, at least to me, was spiritual. Indeed, Jesus began to reincarnate into Tony Robbins. Many Christian book titles could have been mistaken for self-help books, since their subtitles began with "how to."

As evidence, in the upstairs closet lay probably five cloth-covered journals filled with old Sunday school and sermon notes. Some of them have church bulletins stuck in them with random ideas scratched in blank spaces along with games of hangman and sketches of army men, ephemeral evidence of my struggle to keep the boys quiet during the service. The Sunday school lessons were excellent, taught by many lay people with tremendous analytical insight into the inner life. However, it had been a long time since my childhood when I did not need to apply some layer of analysis on life and just lived in a sense of wonder. Perhaps as an ongoing, lifelong conversation with my mother about "how to" fix my brother—and more close to home—how to appease my spouse, I also developed an outsized yearning for behavioral outcomes produced by my faith. The urge was to solve life, to bend its will to my own, while supposedly submitting to God's will.

It was partially working. In those intense early childrearing years, I had arrived at a close approximation of what I always dreamed of during the days of my own ill-tempered origin family—a happy one. Our backyard was the site of regular basketball and soccer games, scaled to the size of the many elementary kids who played there. We gave up completely on any grass and threw pulverized gravel on the back half of the yard. I often looked down from the back porch to see the three guys and their dad going end to end, laughing with glee. Inside the tiny basement, we even squeezed in a ping pong table on one side; and around the corner stood the television and Nintendo my dad gave the boys, against my wishes, the year it came out. The crappy sofa and two chairs down there were all sock-feet jumpable. We had dinner together every night around the table where the kids did what I called the Tuckahoe Talk, all the dish from that day at their school. The only problem was, by then, a reliable three-year cycle of employment had been established. First came the relief of finding a new job. That was followed by success. Then a third, longer phase began, a protracted slow burn of disgruntlement and bitterness. This is when my anxiety cranked up. At the final step, quitting, if I'd gotten a dollar every time one of us, or an acquaintance said, "Well, something better is in store," the entire cycle would have been broken because we would have been rich.

The last white-collar cycle began with a straight commission, *Glen Gary, Glen Ross*, ranked-list-of-salesmen on the bulletin board type of sales job. I once attended a "regional sales meeting" with him in Baltimore. The dick-measuring money talk from the super-salesmen up front was downright laughable, kind of a real-life prototype of an episode of *The Office*. "Your life can really change; you can really have it all. Look at me. I've got a boat." At that, I got up from the banquet table and went to the restroom not knowing whether to laugh or cry. It felt like someone else's life. Some kind of primal scream, some barbaric yawp erupted in my head. My disgust for this blatant materialism, while kind of wanting some of it, made me linger in the bathroom wondering how in the world I, and he, had ended up here.

In early July 1994, my father-in-law treated us all again to yet another summer vacation on Martha's Vineyard, this time for two magnificent weeks. Right before we hit the road, my husband informed me that he had once again quit that sales job without another one lined up. Just like six years earlier in Nantucket, my life was a tale of two cities, a permanent struggle with money and the ease of temporary affluence. We stayed in one of those epic cedar shake mansions on a cliff that overlooked Vineyard Sound in West Chop, among those that first blew me away as a newlywed. This particular house had been recently used as a backdrop for a Tommy Hilfiger photo shoot—the epitome of rustic New England charm, complete with a butler's pantry and faded nautical wallpaper and worn scatter rugs. Standing on the lawn with Vineyard Sound behind me, I looked up a few times to see the boys hanging out of various upstairs windows, like a classy, cedar shake, *Laugh-In* set, all three being adorably silly. Every night Poppy, my father-in-law, oversaw our private flag lowering ceremony; every morning one to raise it. About twenty of the family celebrated the Fourth of July there. It was magical. Their great uncle set off his South Carolina fireworks on the cliff, culminating with the "Lexington and Concord," a pretty impressive amateur display that sent all the cousins into fits of random jumping on the perfectly manicured grass. Across the water we watched a seemingly endless display of colorful light balloons erupt over Cape Cod. From the yard, I later caught my Wall Street broker father-in-law in the glow of that living room. He was ghost conducting, with abandon, the Boston Pops through "Stars and Stripes Forever" in a kind of dance-when-no-one-is-looking moment. I did not want to go home.

But I had to. That August marked the start about five years of wandering through an employment and identity wilderness with the constant anxiety that accompanied it. My respite came in my clay studio as orders and show preparations kept my mind occupied and my hands very busy. I added a few of my own extra jobs so that my contribution came close to a teaching position. My patience was beginning to fray at what was either his naïveté, or willful ignorance, about the actual money needed to support a family and the needs of three growing boys.

* * *

After a good dozen years of easily fitting in to my suburban world and church, I felt some twinges of misfitting. They showed up first in the hotbed of most churches—the youth group. Two camps had emerged during the late nineties: parents who could afford to home-school their kids and those who loved that big yellow bus that took their kids from home to school. Some homeschooled to ensure a more unique, personalized education, but many others feared that public schools were becoming the tool of a liberalizing culture. It was not long before a couple of the more vocal, homeschooling mothers expressed their dislike, perhaps even fears, of non-church kids (ones that might even have gone to Tucker), being allowed to go on an upcoming youth retreat. At a meeting of about one hundred parents, either my early menopause or my inner Sarah kicked in; my face may have betrayed my disgust. In front of all those parents the minister asked, "Anybody else?" before looking at me and saying, "I'm sure Lee has an opinion." And people laughed. They laughed! I did have an opinion but kept it to myself.

My twin fears of rejection and change dampened the friction I felt over this emergent isolationist tendency among some folks at church. That is, until other influences—my growing, much too observant sons coupled with my aging, much too ridiculous father—ignited a small flame of disquiet. The older I was getting, the more I felt some paternal zombification process; Daddy's historic silliness and epic eccentricities overtaking me. Maybe I feared it; maybe I kind of welcomed it. He did not possess a mask; no gap existed between his world and *the* world. A brilliant clown of the Greatest Generation, Ed Pearson didn't care what people thought of him because he didn't quite acknowledge that other people actually had thoughts, especially about him. This was most obvious in his fashion choices. He was that guy who bought six pairs of 100% polyester slacks from the back of the Sunday paper's *Parade Magazine*; he wore powder blue, Nehru-collared leisure suits way after the two weeks in 1974 that they had been popular. He used an actual pocket protector. He was known to, in the middle of the winter, in the middle of a party, in the middle of a sentence, just step outside onto the screened-in porch off the kitchen. But before his relieved listener could escape, he returned in a few seconds and resumed his monologue—himself relieved after he'd let out that bothersome fart. People enjoyed his company because he liked to have a drink and could be very funny. He liked people, but was possessed by machines his entire life, like his TRS-80 from Radio Shack—make that *anything* from Radio Shack—where upon his regular entries he was always greeted with a *Cheers*-like "Ed!" It was not uncommon to hear Russian voices coming from his Ham radio in my parents' bedroom. All of this gave him great joy, this constant quest to see how things worked and then build them.

I once opened an essay about him with the line, "my father didn't have idiosyncrasies; he was one." I called him a brilliant clown for his ability on the one hand to build an oscilloscope in his bedroom—for what reasons I have no idea—and on the other hand, have his pants drop off his waist at any given moment. This wardrobe malfunction was caused by a completely flat butt and a front-loaded belly that my brothers and I used to jump on as he lay on the floor after a long day selling auto parts. The pants-drop was guaranteed if he ever reached up over his head, like the time he was attaching an awning over the glass patio door. From the kitchen, I looked across the den and saw him on a stepladder from about his chest down. As if on cue, just as I looked, his pants dropped around his ankles. There he stood on the ladder, continuing with the job, now only in his soon-to-be infamous pink-dotted threadbare boxers. Infamous, because this happened again once in broad daylight in a very public place, this time without even raising his arms overhead. I was twelve. We had gone to Westland Shopping Center one Saturday morning so I could buy my first Monkees album with babysitting money. He went ahead of me, already in the parking lot. I saw him round the back of his Pontiac. And boom—he was pantsless. Pink dots showing for the world to see. Witnessing this from the sidewalk, I instinctively crouched behind the blue US mailbox. It still baffles me that he fought Hitler as an eighteen-year-old, although the source of his sans-culottes tendencies, his no-waist barrel belly, had not yet become a factor. Back then he could battle fascism without fear of tripping over his fatigues.

I think my father relished being a dad in his way, and especially having a daughter, especially since he—and my mother—were ten years older than most in their cohort. At three and four years old, I would tempt fate and stand—*stand!*—next to him on the front seat of the car and put my arms around his neck while he drove the light blue, fin-fendered 1957 Chevy sedan. When I was a little older, we would sometimes go up to Peoples Drug Store's soda fountain after dinner where I'd get a Shirley Temple and he'd smoke his Panatelas. We were usually the only ones there and sat in one of the three booths at the end of the counter. He loved to imitate my mispronunciations with a unique gibberish that cracked me up. He called me his little doll baby then, but never treated me any differently from my two brothers. Sometimes we both made lighthearted fun of my mother and her friends in the *glabben* club. He was an older dad, a man who was left alone to struggle at fourteen with his Ukrainian-born mother and disdainful Richmond grandmother after his father dropped dead at forty-three while playing the organ in a movie theater downtown. My father would turn eighteen on December 30, 1941, but that did not prevent him from running to the enlistment office in Richmond on December 8. Based on his test scores and his propensity for electronics, the army sent him to college in Ohio. He spent most of 1942 there before he was needed on the battlefield as a radio operator at the age of nineteen.

I have no memory of any original words of fatherly wisdom or philosophy of life or even an "I love you" ever parting Daddy's lips, but he never refused to help me with anything I asked of him, from stretching white fake Naugahyde seat covers on my '66 VW's seats in high school to wiring my kiln for my business as a young mother. Daddy had a simple faith. He accepted Jesus into his heart every chance he got, which usually came at the end of the annual Christian Women's Club dinner. (In those circles, it's supposed to take on the first try.) Right about the time my piety peaked in college, Daddy moved from his longtime membership in the raucous, fez-wearing, Tobacco Parade mini-car driving, Acca Temple Shriners to the more serious and less alcohol-driven Masonic Lodge. When it was his turn to become the Grand Poobah, he had to recite pages and pages of their ritual from memory. Although he lacked any shred of self-consciousness, he was not immune to a lingering social inferiority complex, most likely a result of losing his father so young. He endearingly confessed his nerves to me at taking on this responsibility and leading his peers. I offered to help by "holding the book" on him, trying hard not to laugh thinking of Daddy, who resembled a fleshed-out Fred Flintstone, in a furry hat with elephant tusks sticking out at the Richmond equivalent of meetings of the Loyal Order of Water Buffalo. Daddy, though, took this deadly seriously.

Besides "geometry—the noblest of all sciences," which I remember so well because he kept starting over at that point, the phrase "the fatherhood of god and the brotherhood of man" recurred often. In my evangelical education, this universalism may have risen to the level of dangerous heresy. Yet, I tried to ignore other feelings, human ones that agreed with this simplistic philosophy, especially hearing Daddy say it. His fellowship at church did not come from sitting around a living room picking apart the Bible and applying verses to our personal struggles or creating "biblical worldviews." It was serving breakfast with the men's group on Palm Sunday. That line in his Masonic book made me question if I really needed five journals full of sermon notes to live it out? It's ironic, or rather no wonder, that my father had an actual vision of a reassuring Christ standing behind him in a steamy hospital bathroom mirror as he faced a quadruple bypass, a vision that caused him to drop to his knees right there at the sink. Even after that vision though, no self-conscious, personal piety affected Daddy's behavior even into his old age, proved by a story my brother reminded me of recently when Daddy was in the last week of his life. He had become fond of the orange breakfast drink of the astronauts and had left a glass of it on the kitchen table. From the sofa he asked my mother, "Hey Sarah, will you poon that Tang over here?"

Then there were those "let the little children come to me" reminders. After my middle son, at about twelve, harassed me one night for signing him up to help with Vacation Bible School without his express permission, he started to cry. This was highly unusual. I knew what I had to do. I had to get my forty-year-old ample rear end up the tiny Ikea metal ladder, not whack my head on the ceiling, and snuggle up to him. Vacation Bible School wasn't the issue. He confessed his remorse over losing his temper there. Furthermore, he cried because he hadn't been very "faithful" to God, which meant not paying attention in church. And worst of all, like hellfire and damnation bad, he was reprimanded for cutting up in Sunday school because he didn't know a single answer to Bible Jeopardy. He told me he felt stupid during the game, but then confessed something even worse: he really didn't care.

This was exactly how I was feeling, stupid and apathetic. I faced a maternal and personal moment of truth up there on the top bunk. Should I play the heavy and admonish him to pay more attention? What did he get angry about? Was it a public display like on the bus in third grade when he kicked the seat in front of him and said, "Shit!" because he had gotten the only F of his whole life on some science homework? Pursuing those questions would have been more about keeping up my reputation than comforting his heart. No, at that moment he didn't need a role model, he needed me. I confessed right back at him about my own questions, how it had begun to feel like a foot race that I was losing. In trying to phrase my own spiritual questions in the form of a behavior to avoid existential jeopardy, I had lost my purpose and was in danger of losing some part of myself. It was strange but very freeing, for once, to let down some façade of parental wisdom and just speak honestly. It was all the more refreshing because my confessor was my son.

No small part of my uneasiness was a growing corporate subculture that seemed to infest the suburban church in the late twentieth century. Corporate in both senses of the word: attributes shared by a whole group, and those pertaining to a large business. Both only added to my growing estrangement. When we joined, our simple church had been a telephone and letter office until, almost overnight, the staff had laptop computers and our minister was driving a Cadillac. It didn't take long for the anonymous donor to be found out. He'd been tapped by some financial guru to learn a trading strategy that *"rescued him from a normal life"* as he said in an interview. He became fabulously rich, but many more wealthy families found their way to our congregation, with many working for him. This may have accounted for the emphasis on corporate church growth in those years. Creating a semblance of the popular mega-church model was ironically propelled by breaking the congregation down into small groups of weekly fellowship and Bible study. To do this, "captains" became like mid-level managers of neighborhoods. A religious consulting firm told us to "brand" our worship as "contemporary" and "seeker-friendly." When I first heard that this firm had also focus-grouped many members, I thought it was a joke. It wasn't so funny when many of us learned how much we paid them.

There was also a lot of talk about God's agenda. And agendas require meetings. What was wrong with me that deep inside I resisted being organized, being asked to express my faith according to someone else's agenda? My inner mojo could not get with the program. I wrestled with being of any value to God, spending my days in my studio, or making lunches, or running the boys all over creation for some sports thing, doing zilch for the Lord. My guilt reached a pinnacle if I were to see these very motivated folks from church in the café area of the local grocery. I might be there trying to write, back then on a legal pad—not about God, but about me. It was usually thirty-ish, professionally dressed, tanned men, their brows furrowed locked in intense conversation, writing stuff—spiritual stuff—on *their* legal pads. To the unenlightened, they might have been having what looked like business meetings, and they were; they were just conducting the Lord's business. Nevertheless, the very best people anyone could ever know were found in my congregation, and I had so many great friends there. It was that second definition of "corporate," a group's shared identity, that caused the tension. It seemed that I was slipping into a subculture, one increasingly shaped by louder culturally and politically conservative voices.

It would be a Wednesday night program about Hollywood movies— at church—that crystallized and then freed me from some of this inner tension. Somehow the movie *Something About Mary* came up. Before I could express my disgust, an Ivy-educated, respected Bible scholar sitting next to me whispered that he *loved* that movie. I hated any raunchy sex-based humor and thought all good Christians should too. So maybe I was the one all along with the problem. On the flip side, another person said they just didn't "get" *Chariots of Fire*, one of the most "spiritual" movies of recent memory. Some big chasm opened up in my own neatly formulated notions of a WWJD (what would Jesus do?) aesthetic, or in this case, WWJVCR? And if it were impossible to know his viewing habits, how could we know anything else about his modern tastes, as some seemed to be claiming to know.

Good old grammar came to my rescue. I realized that my spiritual life had devolved into a series of adverbs, those "how-to's" that yanked at the back of the pants of a verb-driven life, always modifying the action. I also realized that the word "christian" had been egregiously misappropriated through history. Even though dictionary-approved, this is why it has not been capitalized here, despite Microsoft Word autocorrecting it unless I change it back three times. "Christian," to me, is not an adjective. It is a noun. A noun is a person, place, thing, or idea; of these, "person" best applied to me. This, in spite of my efforts to become a perfected idea, which actually has the effect of turning a person into a thing. And while no two people are the same, all people share in the human condition that defies singular descriptors. To be a Christian, then, is to attempt to follow the teachings of Jesus, which boils down to verbs: loving God and loving one's neighbor as oneself. What does the adjective "christian" actually mean when applied to a "thing" noun, particularly cultural things: christian music, christian movies, christian books, christian businesses, christian television shows, christian dating sites? Its definition can easily fall into another one of those dangerous "you know what I mean" categories. Most likely, the word had come to imply wholesome, safe for kids, proper, sexless, respectable. In some instances, it may have meant ethical and could have been used to modify a person, as in a christian businessman, rather than a businessman who believed in the claims of Christ, as in the landscaper's business card that recently assured me that Jesus was his CEO.

This line of thinking is precisely what I questioned in a *Christianity Today* piece. After I won third place in an earlier essay contest, which got me an in there, an agent who worked with a christian publisher contacted me. It seemed for a time that the sure way to make a lot of money in christian publishing was to criticize anything christian. A whole spate of christian writers was making a pretty good living by telling Christians that reading a lot of christian books on "how to" do something the christian way was missing the point. (This reminded me of my youngest son's senior year in high school when students pinned signs on their backpacks protesting some policy at school. He joined in; only the sign on his backpack said, "Backpack protests are stupid.") This agent may have sensed I had a lucrative axe to grind when he called and asked, "Do you think you have a book in you?" Nearly speechless from disbelief, I managed to squeak out a "yes." However, most of the book that came out of me did not have the same critical, corrective tone as the two magazine pieces. It didn't grind too much; it was fifteen essays of life stories with a few observations thrown in. My agent was very supportive of it, as well as my objections to writing with prescriptions, in response to the editors' repeated comments to him that the book needed "a takeaway." Another way of saying, a "how-to."

I could only write honestly. That seemed to be a problem, too. Word came down from one editor that my book (and perhaps by extension, I) was "too weird." She nixed all of my clever title choices, especially my favorite. Based on a metaphor about my son's Darwinian social struggles in middle school involving ill-fated backyard chicks we were supposed to be raising for the scary science teacher, I wanted to call it *When Chickens Flew and Other Stories of Unlikely Grace*. I could just see the cover! The editor, however, was not so enthused and told my agent, "She has to stop coming up with things like this." "Things like this" meaning like me. Later, the christian editorial board (who I wish I could have overheard discussing this) made me cut the use of the word "breast," even though it referred to a frozen one that used to belong to a chicken. It was part of a story about greed and class and fighting over discounted meat at the grocery store. There was the chicken theme again. Hmmm, in my many years of note-taking at church, had I missed some Old Testament poultry taboo? Aside from weirdness, I started to get the picture that my book was "not christian enough" whatever that meant. This was according to some editors, a few acquaintances, and one christian radio show interviewer who told me during the commercial to make it sound more christian. (Yet another *treppenwitz*: it might have been funny to drop a few f-bombs after we came back on air.) I guess I missed out on some kind of windfall by not heeding that advice. No surprise that no one made one cluck to me about a second book. The entire process was like rolling a boulder up a hill; their wanting it to be more "spiritual" and my not willing to use the lingo of that world I knew so well. I wasn't being spiteful or stubborn, just honest. Soon after, a writer named Anne Lamott enjoyed raging success by going counter goody-goody Christian, although she wisely avoided any reference to cock or poussin.

∗ ∗ ∗

In the mid-sixteenth century, some Catholic theologians attempted to adapt the strict morals of the early church to the more modern moral codes they observed all around them. These accommodating thinkers went by the name of Casuists ("Kazoo-ists") and thought it wise to judge penitents on a more individual level. A century later, the issue would divide Catholic thinkers between the Rigorists, those taking strict and literal interpretations of moral laws based on the Scripture and Catholic teachings, and the Laxists, who adopted a more liberal, progressive stance. The same thing seemed to be happening in the diocese of my head; I was a born Laxist who found herself in a more Rigorist institution. At yet another Wednesday night class, some very impressive speakers recognized a similar dichotomy playing out across the entire Christian church at the end of the millennium. Recognizing a challenge to biblical authority, they seemed to issue a warning about increasingly non-literal interpretations of the Bible, which could lead to questioning their longstanding moralities. This postmodern "threat" then lay in validating the ultimate subjectivity of any notion of an objective truth. The first big test of a formerly unquestioned tenet of faith was the issue of the ordination of homosexual priests and ministers. This alarmed—then mobilized—the evangelical church, including the one I attended at the time. It correlated with Bill Clinton's second term, no accident according to the new Limbaugh subset of evangelicals who blamed him for America's growing anti-Christian, immoral culture.

By then, conservative politics was kind of a given in evangelical circles, although never openly preached from the pulpit like during college. I only remember one—*one*—very highly regarded family being "found out" to hold Democratic preferences and others being shocked. While I shared the disgust and outrage with Clinton's personal behavior and lying, my aversion to great causes borne of fear of "other" people began to rumble again. As the culture looked like it was heading left, the church's anxiety about staying straight grew. This pugilistic stance towards homosexual ordination, as well as the ongoing pro-life issue, sent factions of evangelicalism storming back into the political world, claiming with characteristic, obfuscating niceness that their opposition was certainly not personal; it was just biblical. Oh no. Here we go again. Great causes. It felt like twenty years earlier when Joe had warned about Communists and secularists and public schools. I tried to understand the threat, but wondered ashamedly in silence how anyone could deny the existence of something that doesn't get much more personal than sexuality.

Enlightenment came one afternoon, October 24, 1999 to be exact, while working on some commission in my basement studio. *All Things Considered* aired a long interview with Mel White, a gay pastor who formerly served at none other than Thomas Road Baptist Church in Lynchburg. He had confronted his former head minister Jerry Falwell for his harsh speech toward gay people, speech that White feared would lead to violence. This was a very new phenomenon at the time, an open and rather non-negotiable statement of a homosexual identity—and a love of Jesus. He made me think for the first time about the discrimination that he and other non-straight people faced. Hearing Mel White speak so passionately and openly about his love of God, who he kept saying made him that way, touched me. It was a jolt of radical reality that pointed up just how cloistered and conformist and unchallenged my faith had been. He spoke to my own earlier yearnings—in my average white woman way—for the same brave self-love before a God of love. This was a moment, a tiny moment of testing of my true confession: I was either a spineless, unprincipled heretic, or some ancient, unedited, accepting, childhood heart was reemerging that only judged people if they weren't funny.

Roger Williams and Me

B ack in college, I got the impression from Pastor Joe that other people were considered first as targets, then as a set of behaviors to change. Joe's twisted justification for judging others—not so subtly at times—was so we could save them. I was never going to be good at it. Whenever anyone's name came up in conversation, whether of national prominence or campus notoriety, without hesitation the very next question was whether the person was a Christian. If the name were not met with a spit take, a guffaw, or the charismatic equivalent of an "Oh, hell no!" then the person was deemed either a "strong" Christian or a "nominal" one. One of the "strongest" women from the old church, blonde, with a knockout figure, happened to sit next to me once in the early eighties at a big Christmas play. When she returned from the restroom, she was nearly evangelically orgasmic. "WOW! This is exciting. There are a lot of non-Christians here. Almost everyone in the bathroom is smoking!" And these were all white Richmonders. This said nothing of the foundational principle

of a literal interpretation of the Bible that presumed the eternal damnation of billions of other people in the world, the likes of which did
not appear in Virginia too often in the early eighties.

In the same way that the longstanding seven or so Protestant
American churches splintered into countless nondenominational,
living room congregations just in time for me to land cluelessly in one
in the 1970s, by the 1990s, historians began writing about another
shift in our collective religious life that absolutely had not shifted
far enough to affect the world I inhabited. In a National Humanities
Center article, then Duke PhD candidate Joanne C. Beckman wrote,
"Americans are going to be exposed to multiple ethnic and 'Two-Thirds'
world religions as never before," and "by the end of this century . . .
Americans will increasingly encounter Buddhist neighbors, Muslim
colleagues, and Hindu businessmen. These 'foreign' religions will
no longer be simply descriptions in school textbooks or exotic movie
subjects." Her implication was that this demographic change would
challenge the orthodoxy and the culture of traditional American
churchgoers. Absolutely oblivious to me who lived five miles away,
these very families had been steadily filling the apartment complexes
near my old high school. But I was already being challenged, only in
my internal geography. Little did I know that in my very near future,
these two changes—inner and outer—would collide. In so doing they
created what Marx might have called a dialectical spiritualism, which
led to one of many revolutions in my midlife, this one blowing up the
orthodoxy and culture that had been so deeply formative and defining
since adolescence. And it started at my old public high school.

As it turns out, I may not have been the first person in history to
experience such an explosion. I suppose Jesus's early followers were
"keeping up the revolution" against mediating religious power in the
Pharisees, too. Then came Luther. Asked to recant his radical ideas,

he famously replied, "Here I stand. I can do no other. To go against conscience is neither right nor safe." He risked his life when he challenged the entire power structure of Europe, but staying within that power structure would have cost him his soul. Then there was Roger Williams. Three bullet-pointed prepositional phrases—"founder of Rhode Island," "separation of church and state," and "freedom of religion"—define him in Virginia's history standards. That was about the extent of my knowledge of him too. But in a moment of intellectual honesty, I decided to learn more. Afterwards, I wished I could have had a beer with him.

Forever, I had posters in my classroom over the lockers. One asked, "Do people make history?" and the other, "OR, does history make people?" with portraits of famous history-makers in between. I live twenty-five minutes from both Monticello and the University of Virginia. This is Jefferson country. Despite all of his contradictions, Jefferson remains on the highest altar in the pantheon of the founding fathers. Yes, he crystallized in the American imagination the idea that all men are created equal, but he did not live it out. While he made history, history did not really remake him. Roger Williams made history. His contributions are more in touch with the American psyche today, but he is overlooked in favor of those an entire century later. Some postulate that is because he was uncompromisingly devoted to God, but his personal devotion led to societal justice, like Martin Luther King, Jr. centuries later. Williams early on advocated keeping the church pure from state corruption. Religion is protected from the government today in America because of it.

The Puritans arrived in Massachusetts Bay aboard the *Arbella* in 1630. Williams soon followed. At the age of twenty-seven, his ideas about church and state had already formed in part because he had been an assistant to and greatly influenced by Sir Edward Coke. An outspoken critic of Queen Elizabeth's Scottish successor, James I, Coke disagreed with the king's revived emphasis on divine right; he would later author the Petition of Right, a landmark of individual rights equal to the Magna Carta, which would be issued to James's son Charles I. The dispute over the relative power of Parliament to the Crown, as well as one over the dominance of the Anglican Church, would lead to the English Civil War in the mid-seventeenth century, which served as the backdrop to the exodus of the Pilgrims in 1620 and the Puritans in 1630.

When Williams arrived in Massachusetts Bay, he recognized an ominous redux of the very issues he thought he was escaping. As an intellectual heavyweight and widely respected man of the cloth, he disagreed with Governor Winthrop and other leaders who believed the government had God's unqualified authority which brought with it a "responsibility" to prevent heresy among the colonists—a tenet most famously fulfilled at the 1637 trial of Anne Hutchinson and equally famously in my own history at George's Seafood Buffet. Williams had witnessed through history how political power had corrupted the church far more than the church had bettered politics. The state can ultimately use its power to punish or even destroy those who do not adhere to its preferred beliefs, even if they are perverted from true religion.

Through his experience and his interpretation of the Scripture, a seventeenth-century Williams famously came to believe in his very postmodern idea of "soul libertie," a total freedom of conscience for each believer, a believer of any persuasion. He believed that ignoring this had led to hatred and war, not to mention the pride it took to pronounce judgment on another person's or nation's soul. He wrote, "It is the will and command of God that a permission of the most paganish, Jewish, Turkish, or anti-Christian consciences and worships, be granted to all men in all nations and countries . . ." and concluded that any fighting over this should not be with real swords but with the Word of God. Winthrop and Cotton had been determined to create a more Old Testament covenant community, a new Jerusalem, with only old hierarchies of power; Williams's freedom was a very New Testament notion, one that gave value to the individual soul, one that may have well laid a foundation for the developing America and its influx of immigrants. Williams did garner a church post in Salem, and by 1635 had found a sympathetic congregation. Though warned by the powers that be, he would not cease preaching his blasphemous views there. In order to uphold the charge to root out heresy and maintain a singular interpretation of the faith, the General Court soon banished the thirty-two-year-old from the colony in the fall of 1635. Knowing winter was coming and that he was ill, the court allowed him to stay around until spring before getting kicked out. But he still would not keep his mouth shut.

This could be the end of Act One of *Roger Williams: The Movie.* Act Two would open with none other than John Winthrop secretly warning Williams that the Court was sending troops to arrest him in his home and put him on a boat to England where jail awaited him. John Cotton, the same clergyman who ultimately betrayed and convicted Anne Hutchinson, did not have the same mercy. He observed in Williams "the heady unruliness of his spirit and the incorrigibleness thereof by any church-way" which "hastened the sentence of his banishment." In other words, as I heard so often back in college, he was unable to "rule his spirit." Williams escaped in January 1636 and began a fourteen-week-long, near-death march in the wintry woods of New England. He wrote later how he never forgot the hunger and cold, but also the lifesaving kindnesses of the Narragansett, who taught him their language. During this long isolation, his prodigious imagination produced a vision of a society that was driven by his concept of soul liberty. He found the perfect place to bring that vision into being and called it Providence. But unlike most all other white men who landed on the shores of America, Williams bought the land from his Native friends.

In a 2012 *Smithsonian* article adapted from his book, *Roger Williams and the Creation of the American Soul*, author John Barry noted that since Williams had made the purchase he was lawfully entitled to be in charge. Yet he forewent that privilege and power and gave himself just one vote like everyone else. The group created a charter that had no mention of God at all. A big plot turn around this time would open Act Three of the Roger Williams movie. Disgusted that he was still preaching his heretical soul liberty, the leaders of the Massachusetts Bay Colony, which consisted of nearly 25,000 people by then, tried to take over neighboring Providence by military force. Williams knew that he had to get to England to secure a royal charter for his colony to prevent such an invasion and establish its own sovereignty. He also needed to convince Parliament, many of whom he knew well and who respected him, about his intention to separate the new colony's government from any religion. He boarded a boat bound for London that was in the midst of the bloody English Civil War, which was being fought, in part, over the right of the king to maintain his dominion over Cromwell's insurgent Puritans. Williams lobbied everyone he met for the colony's charter with its emphasis on soul liberty, asking that Rhode Island would be an experiment in allowing majority rule to decide religious matters. The first would be to sever the state's control over worship. Parliament miraculously agreed.

Before returning to America, Williams wrote a kind of manifesto of these ideas, not unlike Luther's *95 Theses*. It was called *The Bloudy*

Tenent, published in July 1644 to the outrage of Englishmen of all allegiances during their civil war. It has a lot to say to culture warriors today who mix religion with politics and who interpret Scripture tendentiously. In it, Roger Williams imagined an entirely different political foundation from any that the world had tried up to that point, one based on the sovereignty of the people. His ideas greatly influenced John Locke's contract theory, which influenced Jefferson. At that time though, these early ideas of a secular government established by the people themselves were much too radical. Parliament ordered all copies of *The Bloudy Tenent* burned. Williams returned to Providence with his value of a free conscience renewed, an idea unattainable in the religiously polarized culture of England at the time. In Providence's charter, there is not a single mention of God. This is so radical to me, a person who has seen the regrettable backslide of a spiritual movement into the dirty world of power politics over the last fifty years to the point some believers cannot separate the two.

* * *

When I heard that Randall Balmer, the insightful intellectual and critic of the religious right was giving a lecture at the University of Richmond, I did something rare. I rallied my energy after a long day of working in the studio, general housewifery, making my standby hamburger/mushroom soup/sour cream/egg noodle-dinner for three teenaged boys and a husband, and left home at 7:15 for a lecture. A lecture! At a college! No doubt what I heard would have at first disturbed Roger Williams for its eerie historical rhyme, but then cheered him for Balmer's critique. Balmer also warned about the dangers of using religion to define citizenship and national identity. He gave me permission to keep up my own wall between church and state by lamenting the fusing of evangelicalism with the Reagan Republican party. Like Williams, he criticized current religious leaders for unabashedly entering the halls of power as welcome guests, not as advocates for the poor. And the greatest resonance of all would surely have come with Balmer's warning from the example of Williams's own people, the Puritans. Their ultimate demise—in a larger First Amendment, freedom of religion culture—came from a "homogenous theocracy." Boom. There it was. My years-long disquiet in two words. The Puritans, when faced with "competition" from Quakers and Anglicans, not even the many world religions as in America today, retreated from politics. Retreated! In doing so, as Balmer wrote in a June 23, 2006 article in the *Chronicle for Higher Education*, they "reinvigorated religion in New England . . . in an utterly transformative event known as the Great Awakening. The lesson was clear. Religion functions best outside the political order, and often as a challenge to the political order."

That took care of my "theocracy" complaints. Still, the old student in me tended to rely on some outside validation to the spiritual equivalent of my early menopause question, "Is it me—or is it hot in here?" I needed a footnote, a citation, about the "homogenous" part. I got it. Mr. Balmer labeled evangelicalism a subculture. He used the same notion of "circling the wagons" that pervaded the era of the youth group that bothered me. As though he had been a silent guest with Joe and me at George's Buffet, he targeted many "leaders" for their intolerance of dissent and vindictiveness after being challenged on what they considered orthodoxy. He explained Christianity "was still a subculture in the 1980s, but it was no longer a counterculture. It had lost its edge, its capacity for cultural critique." Again, validation of my hippie Jesus. What, if anything, is his message but countercultural? Perhaps, super-cultural? Just as I had slipped into the back of that small U of R auditorium before his talk, afterwards I slipped out of the hall and my threadbare identity as an evangelical.

Roger Williams realized that there could be no political freedom, at least not the type that America built its nation upon, without the more radical inner freedom, soul liberty, being guaranteed—not a homogenous theocracy, but a heterogenous democracy. Williams's acceptance of nonconformist beliefs and his promotion of a free soul found full incarnation in his lifelong relationships with the Narragansett and Wampanoag, peoples with whom the English could not have been more different. In the very beginning, when he was still teetering around the edges of the colony's authority, Williams set out as a missionary to the Narragansett but soon gave up on baptizing any of them. In a 1990 book entitled *Exemplar of Liberty: Native America and the Evolution of Democracy*, authors Donald A. Grinde, Jr. and Bruce Johansen make the interesting point that the political systems of Native Americans had an important influence on the future of democracy in Colonial America. Chapter Five is dedicated to examining the unique role Williams played in establishing a relationship with the tribes and learning from them, but unlike some other colonials, never pretending to become one of them. They write that Williams believed that the Natives of America "were just as godly, even if not as Christian, as Europeans," which, of course, caused a great uproar among the church elders. Like me after giving up some kind of soul-winning angle with people, a universal feeling of friendship and appreciation replaced the power dynamic that can taint some evangelicals. Concerning Williams, Grinde and Johansen observe the following:

> To Williams, religion seemed to mean less a professed doctrine than possession of an innate sense of justice and morality, and

he saw that capacity in all people, Christian and not. From observing the Indians, he learned that such morality was endowed in humankind naturally, not by membership in a church or adherence to a doctrine . . . Where Puritans often saw heathens and devils, Williams saw people, usually friends, with intelligence, moral sense, and a workable political system based on consensus. Such people had the intelligence and the right, Williams reasoned, to judge Christianity for themselves, and to decide without coercion, whether they preferred the Christian doctrine to their own traditions, making the decision "according to their Indian and American consciences, for other consciences it is not supposed they should have."

Ultimately, Williams's soul liberty would lead him to believe even more radically than Luther. He seemed to embrace a line from Luther's contemporary, Erasmus, "O the singular care of Nature that in so great a variety of things has made all equal!" Roger Williams's radical heterodoxy emerged when *he* was the unexpected immigrant, a stranger in a new land, encountering the cultures of those who occupied New England *first*. They had to tolerate him! My reconsiderations of a lifelong religious orthodoxy were sparked by encounters with a wholly unexpected influx of immigrant cultures on *my* Virginia turf.

The first year I returned to teaching, I had a Pakistani kid named Abdul in one of my classes. He was a technology whiz library aide, a member of the robotics team, and otherwise general slacker. Consequently, at the interim for the second quarter right before the holiday break, Abdul was failing most of his subjects. But he succeeded at having one big, bright, endearing personality. His family was full of professionals both here and in Pakistan, including two uncles who were doctors back home. He came into class one day after getting his report card in homeroom and shoved it in my face, saying, "You see this Ms. Knapp? You see this?" I backed up and focused on the column of four Fs and said something like, "Not looking too good there, Abdul." With a kind of grinning, alarmed look, he finished dramatically, "This is the reason that I have relatives, as we speak, getting on planes in Pakistan and coming to America. My uncles want to see what is wrong with me. They are going to lay into me about this!" I laughed at his hyperbole until he assured me that he was telling the truth. In 2003, these men, boarding planes on a mission, could have easily looked suspect and dangerous, and yet they were on a mission to rescue their brother's kid, and maybe strike a little fear in his soul. I was brought up short, not so much on the international fears of the time, but over my longsome indifference to the vast similarities among the cultures of the world, which were inextricably linked to their own religions. In Abdul's case, what love, what sense of family, what humor this child obviously had known.

My own three sons have had each of those things, too. From the moment they were born, these were my primary aims. They have endlessly fascinated me as separate creatures and souls with more personality and intelligence than the law allows. I wanted them to thrive. Well, as this shameful epiphany reminded me, Abdul must have been the same focus, just from halfway around the world, and in his case, from uncles with coarse dark hair and olive skin. Again, as lame and ethnocentric as this sounds, I had in my mind that all uncles were blonde and olive-toned only after a week at the Jersey Shore. Now this previously foreign world had names and flesh and context, which made it even more appalling to hear after the holiday break how Abdul and his extended family were detained in an airport for eight hours because they were perceived as a threat to our national security. Maybe the airport officials knew about his report card, a widespread threat that knows no ethnicity. Of course, his family missed their plane and had to drive twelve hours home from Michigan. He told this whole story with that same grin, with absolutely no trace of anger. Any American I had ever known until then would have hit the roof, caused a scene, threatened to sue.

Kosal was a Cambodian-American. His junior year, he was one of five select students to receive an award, a gold plastic party favor loving cup with the number 3 Sharpied on it, signifying he had survived me as his teacher for all three years of high school history, as my course assignments kept changing. When I first had him in ninth grade, I thought that if ever a fourteen-year-old could be labeled Zen, it was Kosal. He was a preternaturally placid young man who maintained and revered his Buddhist heritage. He was also a talented artist and poet, gifts that presented in various creative assignments I tried to slip in throughout the year. At the end of his sophomore year, when he was in my modern world history class, he chose Cambodia for his short project on an area that experienced some kind of upheaval in the recent past. Kosal gave a thorough presentation on Pol Pot's horrors. Then I casually, maybe a little thoughtlessly, asked him if any of his information possibly came from personal experiences of any family members.

The next few minutes may have been the most gripping of my teaching career. Kosal would soon blossom out of his quietness and love to laugh, especially junior year when he was part of a group of wisecracking, good-natured, multinational jokesters who insisted on calling the young Cambodian Chinese. But he was deadly serious as he answered my question with a detached monotone, all the while staring at his computer. He recounted how his parents were able to escape earlier, but his uncle was left behind and found himself in one of the infamous killing fields. Kosal haltingly told the entire class what must be seldom spoken family lore of how his uncle lay still among the dead bodies as the soldiers walked among them randomly stabbing people to be sure they were dead. His uncle knew what they were doing so he braced himself as the bayonet slid through his flesh, Kosal shared, somewhere in the top of his back. His uncle didn't flinch.

The class was in total silence, a pretty long time for fifteen-year-olds. I felt like crying. Some of my own adolescent humanitarianism and heightened sense of justice and cynicism over power-crazed adults that I first experienced in these very school walls had perhaps been reignited. I was a forty-six-year-old, middle class, white American woman sitting among the rows of a veritable United Nations of tenth graders in a classroom where, decades earlier, I sat among my all-white classmates, very possibly while this was happening to Kosal's uncle. I broke the silence by asking how his uncle got away. Kosal explained that he waited long into the night to be sure no Khmer Rouge were still patrolling and ran towards the sea to risk his life on a boat to make it to safety and freedom. This uncle now lives with Kosal and his parents in a brick rancher in a neighborhood near my old middle school.

Farid was a handsome Iranian student who seemed not to have a care in the world. In his senior year he put that into effect and kind of disappeared. We all thought he'd dropped out, but as it turned out he just had a little Iranian Huck Finn moment and lit out for the territories, traveling America for six weeks instead of sitting in government and English class. As I learned a couple years earlier in my class, it wasn't the first time he had disappeared. During a discussion about the persecution of the early Protestants, a normally uninterested student asked, "Ms. Knapp, do you really think we have, in America like, you know, (using air quotes) 'freedom of religion?'" I started to make some intellectual reference to the Constitution, when Farid raised his hand and opened my eyes to what others are willing to do for their beliefs.

As it turned out, there were other members (besides Seals and Crofts) of the Bahai religion, including Farid and his family who practiced it secretly in Iran where Islam was the only religion allowed. He told us about one family dinner that took place when he was in seventh grade; it started out innocently enough with a recounting of each person's day. When it became his sister's turn to speak, she shared how her friend wondered if she was going to attend the assembly at their mosque that evening. When Farid's sister, then in the fifth grade, told her classmate "no," because they were not Muslim, the classmate got up immediately and whispered something to the teacher. The teacher left the room for a while. As Farid relayed this to our class, another memorable and rare hush fell over them. With a wry smile that obviously tried to hide the painful memory, Farid told how his father, right there at the dinner table, got up and immediately began making plans to sell his lucrative grocery business and get their papers in order to come to America. It took two weeks. They left on horseback!

In these three different stories, religion wasn't the dominant factor; family was. And of course, love. This is nothing revelatory, nor should it have been for me. Yet during my formative years, the most outspoken evangelical Christians seemed to claim some corner on the market of "family values." Furthermore, all relationships must be approached as attempts at fulfillment of the Great Commission. This made me the center, the power center, of the relationship. I was the seller looking for buyers. Instead, as I had already thrown my hands up in a kind of resignation or failure to make my quota or to even try, these and countless other children of all faiths started to appear to me more as individual works of art, gifts. I just began to revel in them. Don't get me wrong as I morph here into Polly Anna, a now retired Pollyanna. There's still plenty of jerkiness, smelliness, laziness, etc., in the teenage, or adult, human condition, no matter one's race, nationality, class or ethnicity, gender, eye color, height, or religion.

* * *

Infidelity in our marriage was never even a remote possibility, or should I say threat, but another version of "the wife is the last to know" was. I had already faced about ten "I have to tell you something" employment conversations in nearly twenty years of marriage. Yet in the middle of so much uncertainty at the hands of another person, I could not imagine leaving or even threatening to if he didn't buckle down. We had three kids. I had made a commitment to him before God. The entire context of my life's story fell within the parameters of a larger identity, an extremely appealing and fun circumscription. Financially, even with the unpredictability, I could not have made it on my own without his contribution, or so I thought. Throughout his twenty years from about age twenty-five to forty-five, the ones where most people establish at least a general career, he had careened through about a dozen or so jobs in almost every sector of the economy: education, business, blue-collar labor, and government. I kept thinking that the next situation would be the answer, that he would finally realize his ideal, that his unhappiness was a matter of circumstances, not an emotional pathology.

He would much later confess to having what he and an armchair psychiatrist might call delusions of grandeur, of wanting to live a larger life than is possible or practical. This condition can be characterized by ill-advised risk taking, an imperviousness to facts, and impulsivity, all of which surfaced once on a device known as an answering machine, a faux-wood, boxy, radio-type mechanism that recorded phone messages that could be played back later. On it was the voice of a realtor from Charlottesville. Why was this person calling us, especially since he represented a real estate market an hour to the west, and especially since our youngest had just entered the stellar high school his brothers attended? Although, I had nursed a hazy dream since childhood to one day have some kind of place in the country, having grown up in stereotypical suburbia. I was torn when I heard that message about a piece of property—angered at what seemed to be the next avenue for his unilateral decision-making, but also intrigued. What had the guy found? After an unpleasant confrontation about sneaking around behind my back, he agreed to show me the three properties that just he and the realtor had seen several times already.

The choice was clear: the one with the single-wide trailer and beat up shed that also had a beautiful mountain view—if the future house had a full basement. I ensured that view by setting a ladder against a tree and climbing up about nine feet. Plus, the property was only minutes from the main highway and similar distances from Richmond and Charlottesville. But my naïveté reached even higher levels than that ladder. I still trusted him with our finances—me, the girl who wrote down every purchase in a tiny green spiral notebook, a long dead money control freak borne of making my own disposable income since fifth grade. But he had been a broker, as his father and both grandfathers before him. And there was no saying "no" to his delusions that everything will work out, just have faith. I had made some futile attempts early on, fewer and fewer as the years piled up, to have budget discussions. However, until this vision of a country place took hold, we somehow managed the roller coaster of income with the help of Visas, Master Cards, and lots of store credit cards, as I discovered—oh, and Discover—to pay bills.

Never mind that even post-Clarence the Angel George Bailey himself would have thrown us out of his Savings and Loan if we had come asking for a mortgage. A regular mortgage, that is. Not a sliced and diced, tranched-up, mortgage-backed security, CDO, I-have-no-idea-what-I-am-talking-about loan. Nevertheless, in a very concrete—and two-by-four and Sheetrock—way, my personal history again intersected with American history. Around the time we started construction loan shopping, just about anyone with a pulse was qualifying for loans of any kind. In the same laughable way that we made no "financial assessment" of our own ability to afford a big house, the MO of the supposedly smart, and ultimately criminal, financial companies of that time did not base decisions on anything real either. Ironically for our rural property, the first mortgage company to tranch it up was Countrywide. Like us, the country itself suffered from yet another widespread delusion of grandeur. If it is too good to be true, then . . . That's how my dream house got built—on some financial wet dream that would turn into a national nightmare a few years later.

Maybe delusions of grandeur are contagious. I either consciously or subconsciously ignored the very tenuous financial aspect of this entire venture, signing at all those yellow-highlighted Xs for loans and credit lines that he and a willing banker thrust in front of me because of my own inherited pathological obsession with houses. My mother before me, and my grandmother before her, were driven by this same vision-creating condition. My mother had built her dream house in her fifties that finally satisfied her lifelong craving to make those country house magazine pictures she stared at come to life. More significantly, I had been deeply affected spiritually, as in gathered deep inner strength from, my grandmother's very earthly ten-bedroom tourist home, to which she had devoted most of her time, talents, energy, and scarce extra income. The beauty she created there instilled a sense of self-reliance and inner pride that I would need soon enough. I had high hopes that my new place would follow in that tradition. I wanted its beauty to create the same spiritual effect on my family, not knowing what would happen to my family.

While building the house, some old Protestant guilt resurfaced, just for a couple of days. Despite the many huge homes that I had visited belonging to former church friend folks, I wrestled with what seemed like the ungodly materialism involved in building and then furnishing the new place until I didn't. Maybe Sister Flesh and Sister Spirit could come together and agree on a few things after all, like that adorable pink Formica retro kitchen table with four red vinyl chairs that I bought at a secondhand store. Not everything had to be practical and justifiable. In fact, the entire idea and execution of this house in the country did not fit either of those conditions.

* * *

The abovementioned quote concerning Roger Williams: "Such people had the intelligence and the right, Williams reasoned, to judge Christianity for themselves," became flesh right in my classroom sometime around 2008. And although we are talking about different Indians [sic], this was the gist of my encounter with my former Indian student, and now friend, Arnatha after she had heard about the concept of the Trinity. This tiny girl with a wicked sense of humor and big potty mouth who once bragged about teaching her mother to cuss ("You are fool of sheet, Arnatha," she imitated) did not hold back her puzzlement.

"So, Miz Knapp. What is this crazy thing called the Trinity?"

"You mean in the Christianity sense, trinity?"

"Yeah. Like how can God be three things? That's nuts. I mean Jesus, God, which is it?"

I probably stood there looking a little dopey in a wide-eyed, freeze tag pose while a flashback of quickly turning notebook pages of sermon notes and Sunday school lessons paralyzed me for a second. This would have been one of those "opportunities" for which all of those old journals and church bulletins had prepared me. Instead, the moment was more academic. Nothing particularly monumental seemed at stake. I gave her the standard analogy about water, steam, and ice all being H_2O but coming in different forms. She wasn't buying. For just a split second, however, a cultural chauvinism did flash through my mind. How does anyone not know Father, Son, and Holy Ghost? Still, I just listened and tried to put myself in her shoes while casually sharing my faith background and concepts.

When she was a senior in college, Arnatha and another former student surprised me at the end of school one fall day. In catching up, she shared that her father had recently died. After an earlier semi-estrangement, they had renewed their relationship soon before his long illness took him. She then shared a dream that seemed very real, one in which her father reassured her of his deep love for and pride in this wildly fun, highly talented, beautiful young Zoroastrian Twiggy. We shared a few tears, but overall, Arnatha was surprisingly matter-of-fact in the retelling. We walked out on to the sidewalk and shared a few speculations on an afterlife. I told of my grandmother's calling the names of her deceased husband and brother as though she were seeing them, as did my father-in-law. This wasn't the typical high schooler's spooky take on death; we were three women equally sharing the heartaches and mysteries of living in this world. Besides being one of those great joys of teaching, seeing the development of a child into an adult, this conversation somehow compounded my own sense of individuality by sharing such a universal emotion with two young women whose cultural and religious background could not have been more different than my own.

On one of the high holy days for any teacher, the last day of school, a similarly powerful spiritual discussion broke out about what happens to us when we die. Stephan, a handsome young Black student who sported some long locs, showed me and three other boys a black and white video by some sour ex-evangelical, homeschooled kid. He was all pierced and tatted up, dressed completely in black and positioned against a black background. He was making many of the "what kind of God would allow" arguments. He went on to name equally troubling examples of hypocrisy and Christians behaving badly. I remember that this occurred in 2011 because one of the guys around my desk was Egyptian, and we had watched the Arab Spring coverage in class earlier that year on his eager requests. He was also a Coptic Christian, a vulnerable minority at times in Egypt. While viewing the video, he expressed how he hated when people confused Jesus with religion and its flawed adherents, and reminded us of how God forgave the two criminals who were hanged on a cross next to Jesus without even knowing who he was, and that God allows anyone he wants into heaven! Stephan relayed that he was a total rationalist, countering people's end of life stories of visions of heaven as just the last functions of an imaginative brain. Although at that point I had not been to church in well over two years, I was honest about my background with them but felt zero urge to persuade them of anything. This was all so natural.

These discussions, just a couple among so many, happened in what would be called a secular environment, a public school. Yet they had come to embody a sense of the sacred to me. If we believe in the sacredness of each person, then any environment will do, even those "debauched public schools" feared by so many radio preachers. Roger Williams believed that God does not need any particular institution to spread His will, and later in his life worshiped at no church at all. Here was yet another couplet of Twain's rhyming history with my own twenty-first century experience. Williams discovered the mere friendship with his Native neighbors as a kind of spiritual expression. This was my discovery with my students. I think it is called love. Unrequired love, volunteer love. It was more Golden Rule love and less the Great Commission love of my college days. Perhaps my interpretation had been flawed; it seemed there had to be proof and results of love, somebody "came to Christ" instead of me bringing Christ's love to my world without expectation or condition. This type of faith honors the two commands in one: to love my neighbor as myself; to love my self, my entire self. Which keeps bringing me back to the essential tenets of my own faith tradition: a source of inspiration in Jesus and the Scriptures; a belief in an animating and selfless love that assures me of my own worth; some larger force that created my ego, but then tempers that ego as it searches for meaning in achievement and for justification in moral perfection. I can go for a Jesus who fleshed out the Scriptural ideals of a sacrificial love, of turning the other cheek, of our individual worth.

My early hopes for my own city on a hill, my upward spiral of history over the years gave way to a downstairs-bound Slinky of crisis management. My personal life became wildly unpredictable and run on short-term plans. I wanted control, desperately. I wanted those Answers, but only ended up with another whole list of Questions. But I had to throw my hands up in surrender to a kind of beautiful chaos. I found myself closer to God through Anne Bradstreet's Sister

Flesh, not the author's intent I am guessing. Sister Flesh mocks her heavenly-minded Sibling for ignoring the world and dreaming of things "beyond the Moon/And dost thou hope to dwell there soon?/ Hast treasures there laid up in store/That all in the world thou count'st but poor?" Sister Spirit ends the debate with "If I of Heav'n may have my fill, Take though the world, and all that will," only after Sister Flesh challenges her, and me, with "Come, come. I'll show unto thy sense, Industry hath its recompense./ What canst desire, but thou maist see/ *True substance in variety.*" (Italics mine.)

True substance in variety. My spiritual life actually gained substance when I allowed my heart to be open to God Monday through Friday from 8:45 a.m. to 3:55 p.m. and not just on Sunday mornings. Indeed, whenever I braved the sidewalks when classes were changing, I just shook my head at the unclassifiable variety of biological traits and ethnicities of this mass of international and homespun teenagers, not to mention their equally unclassifiable ridiculousness. Milling past their conversations, laughter, the rare fight, or exchanging a few private jokes with former students, some "yo's" or wassups" in my purposefully fake urbanspeak with some of the guys, and high-pitched, two-syllabled "hey-ey"s with the girls, I occasionally got a very familiar feeling from doing my art. I loved going down to the basement studio in the morning after a final firing the night before. I slowly opened the kiln lid in anticipation of seeing those previously dull colors now brilliant under the glass coating. Each teapot or sculpture, which started from a little spark of my imagination that I willed to life from a lump of moist clay had, through a miraculous scientific process beyond my control, transformed into a shiny, bright, colorful vessel. I was at once proud and in awe of my creation and wondered "did I make that?" On campus, while negotiating my way to the faculty restroom through the masses, I sometimes wondered,

"In whose imagination did these kids begin?" Is their diversity just an accident of biological science, or is there some forethought, some miraculous loving force of Creation willing them to life, a force that gets my same sense of awe and surprise at its equally colorful vessels?

Back in that Wednesday night church class on the eve of the new millennium, a summary of Jean-François Lyotard's ideas mirrored those of Beckman in that he wrote of the decline of modernism as the world became more of a global village. More communication with "foreign" cultures had the unexpected effect of casting a skeptical eye on Eurocentric narratives. For me, because I grew up in the American South, it took a lot longer for such skepticism to root. It would be the early twenty-first century when the global village finally sprawled far enough to reach the sidewalks of my old Virginia high school. Though disorienting, I am not ready to say that the interaction with world cultures made me completely forsake my own tradition. In fact, besides reading like the speakers docket at the UN, the list of kids assigned to in-school suspension every day reassured me of some concept of original sin. As idealistic as I want to be, I am also not naïve enough to think that merely embracing diversity for its own sake is a replacement metanarrative. No, I think perhaps it is the suffix "-centric" in Lyotard's above observation that hit closest to home. It is frightening to relinquish the myth that we are at the center of anything except what we have so carefully, but tenuously, constructed as our "lives." At Tucker, any centrism, whether ego- or ethno-, or any grand narratives, succumbed to simple daily narratives, tiny moments of human encounter.

But is this enough? Is this enough to bind society together without a mystical and time-honored shared religious belief, especially when we don't all share the same ones anymore? More importantly to my centrism, are these moments enough to bind me together? Do not I need a worldview, a thread of universal truth to hang on to? Perhaps the notion of some inner anarchy is a suitable substitute if the goal or byproduct is openness to the mysterious outer world. Especially since such anarchy and openness are essential to the nurturing of the creative process, a process borne of inner liberation. The Russian philosopher Nikolai Berdyaev wrote of the bottomless chasm of inner freedom possessed by the person of faith, precisely because she is created in the image of a limitless God. And God, according to Berdyaev, found greatest expression in human personality. He believed that the personality has been formed from both a cosmic and earthly origin, from a distillation of both countless, historical chemical reactions as well as immeasurable emotional encounters from eons of life. In this way, are we not all, literally, a part of one another? He believed this essential personality is destined for some "super-conscious" reality where the physical body will no longer be needed. As long as we are in this body though, we must be careful to guard not only our own inner freedom, but that of others. Both express the boundless imagination of Creation's infinite beauty.

PART TWO
The Fall and Rise of My West End Civilization

What is the point of this story
What information pertains?
The thought that life could be better
Is woven indelibly
Into our hearts and our brains.

PAUL SIMON, TRAIN IN THE DISTANCE

Mother, Tucker

After getting married on the first day of summer in 1980, we enjoyed a one-week honeymoon before heading straight to Martha's Vineyard to work at an elite community entertaining the kids of some pretty wealthy and powerful Northeastern types. We returned the next summer. *Duh*. One afternoon when my duties had ended for the day, and while my new husband was off teaching sailing, I strolled into Murdick's Fudge in the more relatable town of Oak Bluffs. Goshdarnit, I was going to treat myself to some dense, overly sweet chocolate to celebrate a successful morning of making yarn babies and egg carton caterpillars with those one-percenter kindergarteners. The candy lady carefully slid the two decadent squares into a classic white bag. Savoring them one pinch at a time, I sauntered contemplatively up the sidewalk and window-shopped. Ooh . . . what's this? A secondhand jeans store?! I'd been wanting another pair of overall cutoffs since it was 1980 and I hadn't developed any historical fashion perspective.

I was the only person in this smorgasbord of denim until a kind of stocky, dark-haired guy and a very tall woman with long, kinky hair entered. She was singing. And she was really good. I stopped the rapid sliding of hanger hooks across the steel rod and looked at the entrance. Oh my God. There stood Carly Simon and her pal John Belushi, both at the height of their fame. I would have given anything for a flux-capacitored DeLorean at that moment so I could grab my iPhone's camera from the future. I overcame my starstruck panic and thought: *Autograph*. Paper? I reached into my straw purse. The Murdick's wrapper would have to do even though it was smeared with fudge residue. I tore off a small clean corner. Carly Simon was deeply engaged with and towering over the bald-headed owner (I found out later) of this head shop. I could hardly stand looking at her intimidating, Diana Ross-like presence. But Belushi looked right at me. Thinking of my teenaged brothers-in-law, I humbly asked for his autograph. "Make it out to Stu and Chris," which he did, and also wrote, "Stay Cool."

What happened next served as a kind of portent of my status in the looming culture shift towards all things affluent. I returned to my big in-law family who had rented a nearby house for a couple of weeks. Everyone was on the capacious front porch. I excitedly relayed my celebrity sighting story and then gave the young guys the storied white triangle. Hindsight. After thanking me in amazement, they evidently took it upstairs and laid it on the dresser next to their bunk beds. The final Saturday of vacation arrived, which meant a massive cleanup. In the boys' room, my mother-in-law swooped her left hand across the dresser, scooting the multitude of candy wrappers into the awaiting trash can below. The signature of the soon-to-be late Mr. Belushi included. As it turned out, my chance at fame and fortune would be just as fudged up.

I had begun the 1980s like my wedding dress pattern—in Simplicity—but as the decade went on and I kept popping out sons, I developed some pretty outsized internal fears for their safety as well as unfamiliar outsized external expectations for our material success. Both of these, I thought, could be obtained through an affair with an older man. Yes, Ronald Reagan seduced me. I—like 489 out of 538 electors in 1980—suffered some kind of Thermidorian reaction from the heat of his Hollywood charms. He never fought in a war, but he was another Greatest Generation father figure, a babysitter-in-Chief. Yes, not only would Ronald Reagan protect and defend my three toddler sons in the backyard sandbox from the multitudes of lurking Satan worshippers and kidnappers, but he would also prevent the boys from someday becoming Communists, or suffering a nuclear winter, or worst of all, enduring date nights at Applebee's. My first stint of teaching ended with the third son, as did a degree of my inner contentment. As the decade closed, my teacher-self quickly drifted into some long ago past.

The elementary school zoned for our little ranch house neighborhood also welcomed kids from the big houses along beautiful River Road, parallel to the James west of Richmond. This darling school seemed stuck in a time warp from the day it opened in September 1947; it could have been the set for one of those anti-Commie government films made in the 1950s. Its halls and playgrounds were filled with curly blonde hair, tiny khakis and tiny golf shirts, and pastel dresses and matching hair ribbons on all of those adorable Dicks and Janes, including my three little Dicks. From then on, my fate was sealed; I would propel through life encased in an airtight 1984 Dodge Caravan canister, careening inside greased, pneumatic-tubed roads that sucked me between my suburban ranch house, my suburban grocery store, my kids' suburban elementary school, my suburban evangelical church, oh, and a giant brand-new suburban soccer complex since that sport had just begun to delimit childhood. My minivan thoughts were occupied with grocery lists, improving my backhand, decorating some corner of my house, my lady book club book, Oprah, or some overwrought essay for my women's writing group. If I wasn't in the Caravan, my ear was epoxied to the corded phone making tennis mom calls, church mom calls, or calls with friends about church, or tennis, or other moms. These were squeezed in between hourlong calls with my mother—at least three times a week—most often about my psychopath brother.

And if not in the van or on the phone, I was alone in my base-ment art studio, fulfilling commissions and listening to NPR. Except that once a month, I climbed into the Caravan's maroon driver's seat covered with my dog Mabel's white hair and dotted with that embarrassing, ill-placed stain of melted chocolate. It was time to do battle with the crowds at the new Costco on Broad Street. This took me "across town," really only about five miles north, but a world away—and in the opposite direction—from the River Road neigh-borhoods I had come to envy, ones full of huge brick Colonials and those new "transitional" McMansions on two-acre lots, eight times bigger than the one our little rancher sat on. But fighting the hoi polloi was a necessary sacrifice in order to maintain that sweet 40 percent chicken nugget to Little Debbie ratio in the boys' cellular makeup. At Costco, I could get great deals on giant, thick plastic bags of thick plastic chicken nuggets, or maybe a three-gallon jug of maple syrup, or some Pacific salmon sold by the yard.

My quest took me by my old alma mater of J. R. Tucker High and a cut-through street surrounded by about eight to ten apartment complexes of varying qualities. A few times I saw some kids heading towards school, clearly late or skipping, along the sidewalks of busy

Parham Road, some with dreadlocks and sagging pants, walking slowly with that hyper bowlegged gait adopted to keep their pants up, I would later learn. I would also learn, not so much in time but in experience, that each of those kids had a name, a story, a unique personality. Like Mercedes, a young Black woman who I once saw on that same stretch walking to school. I would come to find out when she became my student that she possessed a deep personality and giftedness in art. But at that time in my life, that dear girl would not have registered in my consciousness.

After the boys reached high school, one of their friends from River Road once commented to me, "You went to Tucker, Mrs. Knapp? Man, it's kind of ghetto now." *Ghetto?* Perhaps his upscale world made the leap to stereotyping that swift. I should have challenged him on his racist implications and ignorant misconceptions. But I didn't. My world had changed so much, my awareness had become so singular, like that kid, that I was the one who was ignorant about my old school. My feelings for Tucker in those years were mere nostalgia, a warmth in thinking of its place in my past, but a cold indifference to what it might have become.

* * *

Duping the bank, I mean buying the piece of land in the country, was the first step in a multi-part plan to build a house on it. The second was selling our little brick rancher that had appreciated beyond our dreams as the kids went through school. The third was renting a small Cape Cod nearby so my youngest could finish his last three years of high school. I moved my kiln from my basement to my mother's basement in her house in Short Pump and set up a new studio in her lawnmower shed. I dubbed this new shed-studio my "She-dudio," where She Do. I laid black and white linoleum tile squares on the floor, painted the far wall with chalkboard paint, and set up my big canvas-covered table and tall orange swivel chair. Behind that creaky, slatted, rough-hewn door decorated with an old scythe (one of dozens of Mom's old farm tools nailed to that shed and a dangerously low beam in the "great room" of her *Country Living* wannabe house) stood about a hundred and fifty square feet of me. It was like a fort in the woods. I spent many days and even nights in Mom's backyard plying my wares. I am sure that at night she could see the light emanating from the slats of that ill-fitting door to her tractor shed while she sat in her second-floor, TV-watching perch at the back of the house, wondering where she went wrong. Actually, I think she liked me being there in her line of sight. During the day, as her knees failed her, she would drive her red Chevy Malibu thirty feet down the yard, blow the horn, and roll the passenger window down so I could talk to her, again, about how my older brother had threatened the life of his wife and daughter.

The tricky, nay terrifying, part of working there was transporting my labor-intensive clay house replicas that had taken weeks to build and paint from the yard to the house. I used my car to drive the big piece of plywood holding the creation now in its delicate greenware stage the thirty precarious yards from the Shedudio to Mom's basement laundry room where the kiln stood. I sweated through sliding the utterly dry piece, usually about eight-by-twentysome inches depending on the client's neighborhood, from the half-inch thick wooden board on which I constructed it on to the slightly less than half-inch thick octagonal kiln shelf. Then I had to spread my arms over my wrought creation, grab the edges of the heavy shelf and lower its fifteen-pound mass ten inches down the narrow walls of the kiln without my wrists breaking through the houses' side walls or my knuckles getting scraped on the kiln's bricks. A lot was riding on that transition—a hunk of our monthly expenses and my sanity. I could not have said so at the time, but the fragility of those keepsake clay homes foretokened the same condition of the very real one we were about to construct. In only a few weeks of getting our credit-default-swapped, highly questionable loan, he informed me that he had quit his latest, and by then, maybe thirteenth job.

This is what sent me one late night in September 2003 to dial-up the Erol's internet connection on our old Gateway computer, which would open a whole new gateway in my life. Where do those small hints in our minds originate? From what source do sometimes life-changing whispers come? How does an idea materialize into action? Are they part of some divine plan, or fate, or just random coincidence? The momentous whisper that night nudged me to look at jobs on my county's school website. Why? It didn't make sense: school had already started, my license had lapsed long ago, and we were embarking on building a house fifty miles west of town. In the tee-tiny downstairs bedroom office of the rental, I saw, along with listings for a custodian and a bus driver, a part-time history position at, aww . . . how quaint . . . my old high school. The ad made note of some kind of new provisional license that would require only one in-house free class to become a legit teacher again (very different from the few thousand dollars I would have needed for classes in the past), hinting at shortages to come. In my own unilateral employment decision, only one for getting—not quitting—a job, I sent in an application. I got an email back the very next day to set up an interview. I think they were desperate. The next night, I joined my writer friends at our monthly meeting. After revealing my job search some of them warned me, in all kindness but from their perspective of stable incomes, not to take the job. Teaching is just too consuming, they said. It would interfere with my writing. Little did I know that it would actually give me something to write about. I listened with gratefulness, but I wanted to build that house.

Three days later I was called into the same principal's office where I never was called during high school. Even during the interview, I wasn't sure I wanted to take the job. As I listened to the details, I sort of thought it could be fun; every student daydreams from their seat in class about giving detentions and writing on the board. Although for most people, those daydreams usually end sometime around the ninth grade. As I listened more, a sudden *what a loser* refrain began in my mind, something akin to pre-Clarence the Angel George Bailey's gripes in *It's a Wonderful Life*. Sitting in that office, a nearly two-decade tinnitus of angst intensified into an ear-piercing crescendo of questions: Why had I not traveled far from home? What about that big world out there? What difference had I made? They ended with a timpani drum and cymbal clash of "why, in my mid-forties, am I still struggling so much with money?!" Being wealth-adjacent over the years had warped some ancient part of my essence. I might have been an unwitting, or witting, victim of my own aspirations too, aspirations of joining the upper middle—or for those two days in the eighties—the upper class, while forgetting my just barely middle-class roots. By the new millennium, it seemed teachers, particularly female teachers, had joined mothers in the "justa" category of existence. I'm "just a teacher" or "just a mother." My resumé had been *justa* both of those. In fact, in those days of no-fault, credit default swap-'til-you-drop, before everyone realized that at some point you have to actually work for a living, teaching had already come to be considered charity work. It was still respected, but not without a tinge of puzzlement as to how anyone could work for so little money. "Those who can" were out there making *real* money.

Before I knew it, I was shaking hands with the principal and the chairman of the history department. He was a stellar person and dedicated teacher who looked almost the same as when I graduated twenty-seven years earlier, still wearing khakis, short-sleeved poly-blend shirts, and a tie. He ushered me out of the office and led me up to what would be my classroom—a classroom! It was an uncharacteristically capricious decision. At the time I was not one given to whims, nor having to be somewhere, much less pee, every day when a bell rang. I would be less than honest if I didn't say that I might have had a small amount of trepidation about my safety. Would anyone listen to me? Would my classroom be a nightmare? Why did that one neighbor ask, after learning where I was going, if I had my bulletproof vest ready?

It had been fifteen years, fifteen very busy years during which I had transformed from high school graduate to mother of three. After leaving the classroom once my youngest arrived, all of my relationships were with people who looked like me. Then the Clark family moved in two doors down the hill on our all-white street in an all-white neighborhood in a nearly all-white district. They had an older daughter, followed by two boys whose ages intersected my three. When the little boys first met, they would exuberantly epitomize the theory of my future country neighbor and lawn mower helper many decades later. Over the years, Mr. Williams and I gradually shared a few personal facts and stories. One day, I told him I'd spent the whole day cleaning my windows, but that it wasn't too bad since they were the kind that tilted out into the room. He stared at me, and then began a kind of mumbling reminiscence evidently involving his wife. I stood more as spectator than dialogist as he recounted "yeah, she done wanted 'dem tiltin' windas. All I heard about for months, tiltin' windas. (Frustrated pause.) She done tilted 'em once." But he returned to the present and, as usual, asked me yet again about my former husband. Mr. Williams became a little thoughtful before turning philosophical: "The people in your race seem to be able to be friendly with your exes. That's not true in my race." Whoa. We had never crossed the conversational line into larger cultural matters. Despite the stereotyping and questionable truth of his statement (my older brother and his threats with the .45 he kept on his front seat), I just listened. His words came haltingly, as though he were testing my reaction, as though he hadn't known too many white people with whom he could express himself. He finished up his thoughts with this final truism: "I mean if you take a little white baby and a little Black baby, and you put 'em in the floor together, they gonna' play. They ain't gonna' know any difference." I told him that I had seen this in action.

When the Clarks moved in, my three little boys stood around me on the front yard, while Marlon and Michael stood close to their mom, Corinne, as we made a few connections. Then Corinne said, "So boys, introduce yourselves." Marlon was about six, wiry, and even then possessed a deep-throated, infectious laugh beyond his years that he employed often. My middle boy, Eric, was about the same age, as tow-headed as they come, and already had a well-developed sense of cool, interrupted by his own moments of wackiness. Marlon slunk forward first. "Hey. I'm Marlon." Eric stepped up, hand extended on my urging. "Hey, I'm Eric." Marlon took his hand, and before the moms knew it, the handshake turned into a good-hearted takedown, the two of them rolling around on the yard wrestling and laughing. I think my three-year-old jumped in for good measure as my oldest busted out in his famous giggle, while Michael observed with his soon-to-be-familiar serenity.

Up into my forties, I fancied myself progressive and certainly superior to the daft guy in my old Sunday school class. He introduced my neighbor, the dad of the Clark boys, as a guest speaker in a Sunday School class at my all-white, suburban evangelical church at the time: "I want you guys to welcome my good buddy. You know, I don't even think of him as being Black." I nearly slid out of my folding metal Sunday school chair. I knew why that was so wrong; I had heard someone like Michael Eric Dyson or Henry Louis Gates, Jr. explain it on a talk show along with the "some of my best friends are Black" faux pas. On the other end of the spectrum, a few very proudly liberal Christian friends, making them at the time very counter-cultural among the Christians I knew, would twist themselves in knots so as not to label a person as "Black" or "African American." I suppose in their minds making any distinction made one prejudiced, as though "they don't see color." But as several young Black students reassured me a decade or so later, something did not hit me right about that self-conscious omission. Are not both approaches denying an essence of a person's identity and experience? It was just a theory at that time though, a time when my interactions with Black people, or any "minority" population, amounted to the monthly family Bible studies we shared with the Clarks, general neighborliness which included being invited to a few of their extended family get-togethers, and a whole lot of basement and backyard boy bopping. Still, those were with just this one family.

It would be fair to say that in those days I was open-minded in a fairly narrow world. I wonder if the many other white people who were friends with this family somehow used them to prove something about their inner attitudes. I look back and wonder if I did, too. In a 2020 book called *Upswing,* authors Robert Putnam and Shaylen Romney chart the nationwide descent from newfound progressive postwar ideals of the 1940s to a much less socially conscious, more individualistic ethos by the late seventies and eighties. So I wasn't alone! I was not the only idealist turned solipsist, leaving behind Pete Dixon in *Room 222* for Alex P. Keaton in *Family Ties.* During this deceleration of demand for social change, however subconscious and unintentional, the authors note how many whites admitted to being comfortable when a few Black people inhabited their orbits, but not too many, mind you. When I returned to my old campus, this was not an issue. Far from discomfort, I sensed some rekindling of an old self, a relaxation of my strivings, and a fascination with this new, fun, wildly diverse slice of America I had no idea existed—right down the road. They would teach me that numbers of this and that "type" of kid really didn't matter. Tucker rekindled my belief in the preeminence of individual character to the point that rendered those questions—appropriately—academic.

The very first few minutes on the job from my newfound teacher's desk, I noticed a rather tall, curvy Black girl having an intense conversation with a rather skinny white boy with a prominent Adams apple right outside my classroom window. I heard the emotion in their voices and wrongly assumed that one or the other had said something insulting, and they were about to go at it. That got my attention. I dreaded that I might have to do what I did my very first year of teaching—break up a fight. As I tuned in more closely, I heard her saying in her delicate voice how she really wished the boy had called her and her friends last Friday instead of going off with some other group without them. Sweet. This scene and so many more like them to come could be a bit jarring and disorienting to me when I had the time to allow my mind to wander back to my own high school days on this old campus. But it didn't take long for such openness and acceptance among the students to create new norms in me. I often found myself grinning, if not straight giggling, at this crazy array of kids and, from a 1976 perspective, what then would have been rare friendships. It had been nearly two decades since my teaching career ended. I couldn't have known it then, and despite those pre-Clarence the Angel rumblings, I was meant to be at this school, as surely as I was the first time around.

* * *

Like Heraclitus's river, John Randolph Tucker may have looked like the same high school I attended in the seventies, but there had been a major redirection of its flow. When I was growing up in the early 1960s, Tucker anchored the last developed outpost in the western-most end of Henrico County, which hovers like a limp bowtie over its knot, the city of Richmond. A good fourth of the western end of Henrico County remained rural, blending seamlessly into other rural counties heading west to Charlottesville along the two-lane, forest-lined state route 250. The western outpost of Henrico had the laughable name of Short Pump. In 1978, when I was a sophomore in college, my own parents would buy some land and build a house there. My father would joke about living in "beautiful downtown Short Pump." He'd imitate a traffic helicopter by beating on his chest and reporting that a cow was holding up Farmer Jones's wagon. Their friends at the time, all lifelong Richmonders, thought my parents had lost their minds moving so far—a whopping eight miles west—into the country.

When I returned to the classroom in 2003, Tucker still drew from the same neighborhoods like the ones I grew up in—modest brick ranchers and Brady Bunch split-levels built in the 1950s; however, many apartment complexes were built near the school. Meanwhile in Short Pump, Broad Street became six, even eight, lanes in some places. Its rural nature was replaced with fake-nature-sounding street names like Heather Grove or Deep Creek or Harvest Glen in developments of big brick houses with geometry-defying roof lines. This growth eventuated in three, and soon to be four, new high schools. To a degree, the farther west the school, the less diversity of its population. That would be the opposite for Tucker as time went on. Still, in the 1970s when I came through, the neighborhoods and the schools were overwhelmingly white.

J. R. Tucker High School opened in the fall of 1962 and boasted a sprawling campus. It was if its architects were prescient about the freer, more natural ideas to come later in that decade. A welcoming courtyard with mature oak trees formed a center for the auditorium, the gym, and a low-slung office, clinic, and library. As you walked between this admin area and the gym, to the right you would come upon eleven stand-alone, one-story, rectangular academic buildings each consisting of eight classrooms, separated by big rectangular plots of grass spread across twenty-nine sloping acres. In the spring and fall, the sound of riding lawnmowers competed with my lessons, but it was worth it for that smell. Those grassy areas were connected by a grid of broad sidewalks, which were "protected" by less than rainproof, leaky V-shaped canopies. (We sometimes jumped up from a wall by Cafeteria Two and walked the whole campus on top of them when school was closed.) The close connection to the outdoors spoke to a sense of freedom, an emphasis on an almost militant individuality and equality that lingered when I returned. These hippie buildings allowed for a little communing with Nature in between classes, a little chasing of each other around at lunch, and a major appreciation for the beautiful landscaping lovingly cultivated by generations of PTAs, students, and teachers. The whole campus was filled with azaleas, daffodils, irises, dozens of crape myrtles, holly trees, and dogwoods, including three I helped plant on the third ever Earth

Day outside what would later become my classroom. In 1973, they were small, pliant, budding saplings; by 2003, they had grown into thick and gnarly, deeply rooted trees. I gazed at those trees every day, remembering my youth, contemplating how that same process had repeated itself on me.

I came through with an exceptional group of kids—at least in our notion of exceptional. While many of us ended up at good Virginia universities and a Duke here or there, nobody went to an Ivy League school. Like me, many were the first in their families to even attend college. We rarely competed past the regular season of any sport, except once or twice in baseball or basketball. No, we weren't exceptional in those traditional metrics; we were just exceptionally funny. At least *we* thought we were. We competed, good-heartedly, to be the last one to lay down that final witticism, pun, or word play that rendered everyone speechless with laughter.

One Saturday morning in the seventh grade, my good friend Nancy and I were lying in my iron double bed after she had slept over. We were going back and forth, playing around with perverting the words to famous commercials of the time, perhaps inspired by the classic Carol Burnett skits. I think I came up with the winner, a juvenile bastardization of the famous Mattel Toy slogan, "You can tell it's Fart-ell, it smells!" (You can tell it's Mattel, it's swell . . .) We rolled around on the bed in what may have looked like writhing pain, we were laughing so hard. In maybe tenth grade, during the troubled days of Nixon's second term, we girls sat around the lunch table in Cafeteria Three going on a riff using the name of the cookie that Lisa Cunningham had brought for dessert. "I regret that I have but one Lorna Doone to give to my country." "Ask not what Lorna Doone can do for your country, but what your country can do for Lorna Doone." Holding up her fingers in Tricky Dick's signature victory signs and shaking her jowls, Reneé may have won the slam down with, "I am not a Lorna Doone!" To this day, damn fifty years later, when I see those cookies in the store, I grin.

At lunchtime during our junior year, five or six of us played a boxed game of Password in Mr. Whitten's room while we ate, taking turns being Allen Ludden. While "diversity" then at Tucker was limited pretty much to maybe eight Black students, we did have a decent number of Jews. One of them was my Password partner, Louis Gary of the Gary Triplets, who possessed a superior, rapier wit. That same year, those of us on the Class Council (I was class treasurer for tenth, eleventh, and twelfth grades, deciding early on not to challenge the guy who would be our president from eighth to twelfth grade, David Cocke. We often called our high school years The Cocke Dynasty) got the idea, probably from Mr. Whitten, to raise money by showing old—as in 1930s—Marx Brothers and W. C. Fields movies in our 1970s auditorium for a dollar a ticket. This required Nancy and me to drive my '66 Bug to Willow Lawn Shopping Center, midway to downtown, to rent the giant, heavy, steel gray 16 mm canisters for the school projectors from Browning's Ideal Pictures, a kind of brick-and-mortar Netflix. Those canisters actually made the back tires of the VW sink a little into the pavement. I still remember the scene where W. C. Fields puts a cello and a string bass behind a door, only to come back in the morning to find five little violins around them on the floor. And maybe the most I laughed in high school, besides watching *A Night at the Opera*, was while writing the senior talent show with a few classmates in our modest living rooms across the West End of Richmond. It's what I imagined it would have been like to write for that brand new show called *Saturday Night Live*. We were the Class of 1976, so we called it 120 Bicentennial Minutes (mimicking the series of short television history spots), a few of which depicted the

Founding Fathers in a skit as Mafioso: Thomas Jeffersonio, Alexander Hamiltini, etc. In another skit, Louis Gary strung together random bits of famous American speeches and delivered it as though he were drunk. It brought down the house. Yeah, there's no mistaking it, we weren't just white; we were straight-up Lorna Doones.

In 1970, high school began, unbelievably, in seventh grade. Kids from twelve to eighteen shared one campus. In my first year there, my very preppy, conservative-looking, middle-aged English teacher had us read Donne's Meditation XVII, *No Man is an Island*. After we discussed its notions of the interconnectedness of humanity, she played Paul Simon's *I Am a Rock* as a contrast. I was enthralled. First of all, by a teacher playing a current song in class, like it was English or something. Then by Paul Simon, an affair that lasted and only intensified over my lifetime. But more deeply, that lesson—given in Building Three just two up the hill from where I taught for over twenty years—lives in my mind as the beginning of some kind of academic and aesthetic awakening, of chasing feelings of my own deep connection to humanity, and craving, almost like a drug, that sensation of your brain wrinkling up with little electric jolts of insight. We were young, but not unaffected by the turmoil of the times. Our senses of justice awakened early.

As elementary school kids we saw other young people fire-hosed and beaten on television, and the looks of intense rage on the faces of uniformed white men who ordered or condoned it. In rapid succession in those same years, we witnessed three young and handsome leaders gunned down before our eyes. We cried together along to the words of *Abraham, Martin, and John*. For many of us, that put us in conflict with our fathers. Unlike our parents who fought a clear-cut struggle against the evil forces of fascism, we absorbed a less Manichean, more critical mindset about domestic injustice. We had a true yearning to change the world and a sincere belief that we could. I remember a small subset of us girls staying up all night at Jamie Dowdy's seventh grade pajama party. We weren't talking about boys or teachers; we were arguing about the stupidity of the Vietnam War.

But we were still normal, goofy preteens. We little seventh graders were relegated to Building Two, at the highest point on the rolling, outdoor campus. In front was a huge, grassy hill that ended up at the butt end of the library and clinic. As twelve- and thirteen-year-olds, we sometimes ran out of class, holding our books tightly to our chests (no self-respecting high-schooler used a backpack then; those were only for Boy Scouts), and took off rolling down that hill. Then we would get up and try to walk to our next class all dizzy and drunk-like. I'm sure the juniors and seniors way down in Buildings Four through Eight took great joy in laughing at us. But all of our juvenile silliness took place under very serious, very adult, rising storm clouds of fear and outrage.

Incremental, Monumental

After nearly fourteen years, desegregation required by the Supreme Court's decision in the *Brown v. Board of Education* ruling had been slow to take place in Richmond, a classic understatement. Richmond had adopted a more voluntary plan of "school choice." The burden of desegregation had fallen on the shoulders of Black parents who could apply to any Richmond City school they wanted, but transportation was up to them. Richmond City neighborhoods were still highly segregated, so even though the city was 70 percent Black and 30 percent white, the city's individual schools did not reflect that. The more progressive goal was to fix that. In March 1970, while I awaited my big entrance into my suburban high school in the purposefully separate jurisdiction of Henrico County, the NAACP decided to forego this former voluntary plan and pursue cross-town busing within the city limits of Richmond. The idea was to create a de jure "unitary school system," instead of the de facto dual one that persisted.

Enter Judge Robert Merhige into my childhood consciousness. He was notorious, according to my parents, in his role as an Eastern District Court judge. Mehrige believed the de facto segregation remaining in the city of Richmond had to be remedied with judicial action. The surest way to fully implement the Fourteenth Amendment and the provisions of the Civil Rights Act of 1964 was to disrupt the entrenched patterns of segregated housing by busing children outside of their zoned districts. (Evidently, Mehrige would soon need police protection at his home in the city.) It wouldn't be the last time I heard the honorable judge's name cursed inside my house. "That damned Judge Merhige! He can't tell people where to send their kids to school! Interfering in our city! Goddam social engineering! Who is he, a judge, a goddam judge from NEW JERSEY, to tell us what to do!?" My father yelled these kinds of things into the open pages of the *News Leader* as he held it in the air in front of him quite a bit in those days. This activist judge, it bears repeating *from New Jersey*, threatened to upend the traditional makeup of Richmond schools. After sustained protests and enraged editorials decrying Judge Merhige's overreach and the Supreme Court's 1971 validation of the busing plan, white families took action and fled to the surrounding suburban counties in record speed. By the fall of 1971, Henrico County grew so much that a new concept called middle school began. I would spend that one year exiled from Tucker in one. Since Richmond was an independent city, the court's action did not affect my education, but my parents and many others distrusted Merhige and the legal limits he would stretch to "socially engineer" the school system. They feared the slippery slope to some forced integration. Their hunches proved to be correct. To them, something more "ominous" was in the wind.

Such a great number of whites left the city of Richmond that the ratio of Black to white students there became more and more uneven.

Many residents worried that this accelerating white flight would bring a widespread decline of the city's tax base and vitality. But they were not willing to consider the three jurisdictions of Richmond, Henrico, and Chesterfield as an area of "common interest" and assent to combining. (Recently, in light of the Richmond monuments controversy, I found it ironic that so many letters to the editor about keeping the monuments in place came from county residents who really should not have had an opinion. Yet they still claim Richmond as "their" city.) At the time, Governor Linwood Holton, Judge Merhige, and Richmond-born Harvard Professor of Social Psychology Thomas Pettigrew formed a trifecta of targets for anti-consolidation. Pettigrew had already drawn anti-busing ire for his belief in an optimal 20 to 40 percent Black population in a school to avoid both tokenism and white flight. As Richmond's white population in its schools dropped below those figures, the Richmond School Board and several Black plaintiffs saw no other solution for a unified school district than to combine Richmond's schools with suburban Henrico and Chesterfield County systems. Judge Mehrige agreed with the Black plaintiffs. On January 10, 1972, he ordered the consolidation of the city and county districts. If my father had been upset over the earlier ruling to bus other people's kids within the city, he was downright apoplectic at the prospect of the three of us having to be bused into that city, the one where he grew up. I clearly remember him standing in the kitchen yelling about this and being puzzled by his ire. On January 11, 1972, some serious shit hit the county fans. It spread out to other cities all over the country, even Northern ones. Once again in matters of race and education, all eyes were on my hometown of Richmond, Virginia.

During my one year in the new middle school, from January to June 1972, the Fourth Circuit Court of Appeals reviewed Mehrige's ruling on the consolidation of the three school systems. While parents in the two counties nervously awaited the fate of their suburban schools, we eighth graders at Tuckahoe Middle were preoccupied with some serious business of our own. We had a talent show to put on. Two of my long-time friends who were in chorus with me that year, Susie and Kimberley, decided we would enter as The Supremes. I had long been fascinated with, and really overwhelmed by, Diana Ross's beauty. My feminine fate, inherited from all the Egerton-Hicks women who ever walked this earth, was set by about fourth grade with a short waist and hints of the hips to come; the first to hit three digits in my class when we got weighed by the school nurse, recorded on the index card she handed us and that I would hide in my science book. We three girls decided that Kimberley, one of the few Black students in my class, would be Diana Ross, not for the obvious reasons, but because she was by far the best singer. Susie and I would sing back up. We were going to perform, what else, *Stop! In the Name of Love.* Microphones would be involved. We met at my house one day after school to practice. (In the realm of interpersonal relationships, my parents had no problem with this, which made my father's ire all the more puzzling.) Our killer dance moves included putting our left hands on our hips and our right hands up for "Stop!" held through-out "in the name of love." For "before you," we followed with three quick motions: air-writing the letter "B," holding up four fingers, and pointing to the audience for "you." Then, to indicate "break my heart," we—obviously—held out an imaginary stick and broke it in two before swinging out hands in to clutch our hearts. During the refrains, we rolled our forearms over and over to emphasize Diana's plea to "think it oh-oh-ver."

Our little trio confidently stood in my front yard of the little quar-ter-acre lot that stood at the top of a hill of the main drag through the rancher neighborhood. After a lot of giggling and goofing around, we finally got serious. Kimberley stood up front and Susie and I took our places behind her on the grass and started our routine. At least two cars slammed on their brakes, came to a screeching full stop at the crest of the hill, and glared at the three of us. They were not stopping in the name of love. It didn't take me long to figure out why they were upset. The second time it happened, I kind of walked towards the road and the woman driver while mustering an angry, puzzled look on my fourteen-year-old face, but the lady quickly drove away. This may have been another seed of my preoccupation with race and injustice, but it was also, sadly, the extent of my physical confrontation of it. I was dumbfounded at the stupidity of that lady's prejudice, but more so concerned at how it could have hurt Kimberley's feelings. We went on to perform in our white hot pants and go-go boots on that hot Tuckahoe Middle School stage in the spring of '72 and killed it.

A few months later as eighth grade was wrapping up, the Fourth Circuit Court of Appeals made its decision on combining Richmond, Chesterfield, and Henrico Counties into one district. The whole nation followed the case, and Virginia found itself with some formerly strange bedfellows in many northern cities' school districts who decried busing and other such consolidation plans. On June 5, 1972, the court observed that the city and the counties had indeed created "unitary" school systems in which *de jure* segregation, created and enforced by governments, had been eliminated. It reversed Mehrige's decision in a 5–1 split and criticized the judge for overstepping the jurisdiction of the states under the Tenth Amendment. Parents were jubilant. While the court agreed that Blacks had been victims of discrimination in housing practices in Richmond as well as the outlying counties, it held that school systems and school authorities were not responsible for its correction. Judge Mehrige felt that they could have been. Consolidation would have been a kind of retroactive remedy for the discrimination of the past, mostly in the historical, unlawful, and unconstitutional housing practices that led to segregated schools in the first place. He believed that integration, albeit at that time a forced integration, gave "each race a substantially greater opportunity to develop realistic attitudes toward the other race, productive of friendships and positive social behavior." Almost a year later, as I was finishing up a stereotypical freshman year in high school, fraught with cheerleading rejection and girl gossip, the Supreme Court affirmed the Fourth Circuit's decision that there would be no consolidation or busing. Neighborhood schools were maintained. I wonder what was lost in my adolescent life because of that decision. How would my experience have changed? What relationships did I miss out on that I have seen among my students over the years? Truly, what bonds of trust and friendship, what "realistic attitudes and positive social behavior" were never allowed to form generations ago, bonds that just might have changed the trajectory of Henrico County, if not the entire country?

* * *

Like my own teaching experience with many students thirty years later, Mr. Whitten taught a bunch of us history in ninth grade then again in eleventh. He surely witnessed me and many of my classmates cross over that beautiful brain bridge from the emotional jungle landscape of the middle school amygdala into the shining city of the prefrontal cortex, laid out in a grid of rational avenues and analytical streets of coming adulthood. Mr. Whitten had always led us in pursuit of all things funny, but as we matured, his eight-year age advantage and Vietnam-shaped experience gave voice to and became a role model for our idealism. He once put Bobby Seale's "Seize the Day!" on the chalkboard. He never shied away from asking us to think about history, not just memorize it. Once, responding to one of my many questions about racism and American hypocrisy in his US history class, he casually dropped the somewhat new phrase "white guilt."

That notion startled me, at least as I understood it at the time. It made me second-guess the reasons that I had had so many arguments with my father over his use of the n-word. Until then, I had a more detached tone in the inner narration of the national drama I was just learning. Perhaps, because of my brother, my perspective was one of spectator, not player. The phrase "white guilt" brought me center stage. *Had* my earlier, more visceral and more innocent, reaction to the incident with Kimberley in my front yard lost its power once an authority figure laid some label on it? Did that label obscure the experience and make its effects (which had to do with Kimberley) less important than its causes (which had to do with me), not to mention its solutions? Was I kidding myself that this growing preoc-cupation with theoretical Black people emanated from a burgeoning sense of outward justice, or was it my inward, subconscious sliver of collective guilt, my piece of the American psychic pie? Was my sentimental fascination with the "other people" in my city coming from a self-serving need to absolve myself of some sort of historical complicity in slavery and all the other injustices that followed? Was it merely "exoticizing," as recent students railed against?

I don't think so. I still believe it was, at that time, a more genuine outgrowth of my nascent belief in the notion of radical individuality, of feeling free to be yourself. I also hated to be misunderstood and then judged, which may have been a subconscious reaction to my mother. At worst, that can lead to some need to unnecessarily justify yourself to others; at best, it leads to not letting others define you. Contemplating the lack of psychic freedom and social respect for

Black people would bother me more as a teenager than examples of institutional racism. This preoccupation might have been what drew me to another student who I met at a statewide summer program in 1974 called the Governor's School. Fifty boys and fifty girls were chosen from across the state to study at Mary Baldwin College for a whole month, living in the dorms and getting a real taste of college life. Margaret was a sweet, funny, smart Black student from Richmond. While there, she and I really bonded with a couple of other girls from the far western part of Virginia. I don't know. Maybe I did purposely sidle up to Margaret at the program because she was Black, but she was also a vivacious light, possessed of both a raucous laugh and a calm spirit, among some of the fairly accomplished, but not very funny, nerdsters there. That she was different from me in our color and some of our experiences didn't matter when we were sharing a joke or dwelling in the sweetness of shared intellectual space in our Psychology class, at our meals, or walking around charming Staunton.

Once back at home, we wrote a few letters back and forth, a letter being a piece of paper on which you write sentiments and ideas and send in a stamped envelope to a metal box in front of someone's house. We made arrangements to get together before school started. My mother drove me to her house in a predominantly Black section of what is known as the Northside. I remember walking around a nearby park and laughing and talking about current issues like young girls who may have both been a wee bit precocious are prone to do. We could share our "psychic freedom." What was totally missing, though, on any real level, was an awareness of how Margaret and her family members must have had to negotiate every last social, emotional, and political interaction in the white world of Richmond. Just living in a city, a majority Black city, whose greatest public art towered over its signature thoroughfare in a can't-miss display of white supremacy-historical-revisionism-on-horseback, was a constant reminder of who was in charge.

(Fifty years later, in my highly advanced, justice-minded classes, the fate of the bronzed Civil War generals on Monument Avenue became an all-consuming topic of discussion. These kids had been in nearly all of their classes together for three years by now, so they were like a family. During one heated class discussion, a highly respected class leader and accomplished young Black woman student expressed her very personal emotions about the statues. She said that she was made to feel inferior and excluded every time she rode down Monument Avenue. A conservative-leaning white friend of hers had been defending the monuments with that same specious argument about erasing history. Yet at that moment, she really heard her friend. She said to the class, "Wow. I have never thought about how the statues could make Black people feel. I love Sarah, and I don't want her or her family to be hurt, so yeah, we need to find another place for them." Let's just say it was a moment, one that perhaps my summertime friend Margaret and I could not have shared so long ago.)

Margaret and I eventually lost touch, but during my senior year—totally unexpected and way beyond the bounds of my reputation and neuter complex—I had a kissy-face affair with my Black boss. He would end up enlightening me, just through sharing as friends, about what Black people faced, more so than had been the case with Margaret. It all started behind the curtain of the shoe department at Sears. The summer before, my mother spotted the employment office for the venerable old store that boasted riding mowers in the basement and lingerie above, just in case you ever wanted to cut the grass in a teddy. Along with three other department stores, Sears would anchor a brand spanking new indoor mall near us called Regency Square. I interviewed with a tall, kind of dashing, Midwestern-type executive in an excessively boxy 1970s suit, Mr. Hall. He hired me on the spot to work in the shoe department where I'd earn partial commission. It was all very exciting to be part of the grand opening of such a cool place. But then it wasn't. After all, it was a job that required me to spend from five to nine-thirty a few nights a week and some weekend hours fitting bratty, fidgety kids, or stinky-feeted teenagers not much younger than I, or the occasional old man, one of whom put his socked foot up on my lap one evening and said, "How big do you think it is?" I kept track of all my commissions and mall expenditures in a two-by-three-inch green spiral notebook, down to "minus $.35 for Coke." As much as I was beginning to fancy myself as a kind of intellectual, I will admit to a little thrill with every brogue, every Converse, every Wallabee I rang up on the clunky old NCR register.

But those thrills were hard to come by. Most of the time, especially on a weeknight, there just weren't any customers. So many more hip shoe stores like Thom McAn or Kinney beckoned from the mall. Working in the farthest western anchor store, and in the department closest to the parking lot, I could just barely see the entrance to the big open mall just past Sears' Men's Department. It seemed like Oz, unreachable, full of dreams coming true and wishes being granted; only without me. I was stuck in the little carpeted area of six rows of chairs, spending a lot of my time carefully placing the metal shoe measurers at equal intervals under them, sometimes slipping off my clogs and checking the size of my knee-socked foot just for fun. Shoe Department fun. Many nights, I could almost hear the hum of the fluorescent lights I was so bored. Like in ninth grade English class when I wrote the numbers one through fifty down the side of my paper and scratched off each minute, I all too often watched the second hand of the clock that hung over the cosmetics counter spin around until the blessed 9:30 p.m. came and I could punch my timecard.

But then there was my department manager. I'll call him Joe. He was a super cool, young, maybe early thirties, Black man. He was very trim, had distinctive sideburns, a tiny bit of hair that flared out on the sides that if it were to get out of control would definitely speak "clown," some big round eyes, and a killer smile. Joe walked with a kind of *Saturday Night Fever* vibe, as though he were listening to "Stayin'Alive" on his transistor as he walked around the gleaming linoleum of Sears or out to the mall for his dinner. He wore slightly heeled shoes that made his gait even more syncopated and made the bell-bottoms of his polyester plaid pants flare exactly right. Oh, and he always wore one of the four-inch-wide ties of the day, probably bought next door in our Men's Department or at the long time Black men's clothing store downtown, Freeman's Men's Shop. Joe was very jovial, talkative, and when I was scheduled with him, we had fun. He had fun with everyone, except I did notice that Joe's demeanor became a bit more serious and a little hesitant when the big boss, Mr. Hall, came by. But around me, he was both silly and a competent boss. I started to look at the upcoming week's schedule for my hours first, then to see if he were going to be on then, too.

One of those nights when it was just the two of us, maybe in March, I took one more of about a dozen "trips to the back" to get another size or style for an indecisive customer. Down one of the stacks of suede platform boots, Joe followed behind me, making fun of the woman out front who had no business wearing suede platform boots. Then all of a sudden, he leaned in and kissed me. For kind of a while. I cannot say that I was alarmed or scared. It was more like kissing practice. With a professional. From the perspective of an old woman, and as a teacher of young girls, and in the spirit of female liberation, that scene should make me at least wince or at most get outraged at this older guy taking advantage of a high-school-aged me. But I kind of liked it. Maybe for once I wasn't analyzing life, I was just experiencing it. My body was involved. However, *I* believed that Joe came on to me, not from any particular sexual attraction, but because of what a fun and nice young person I was. Gee whiz.

By the middle of my senior year, my tight-knit class, like the seniors I observed, began a gradual "breakup," all of us subconsciously pivoting to the future, anticipating college, some coupling up, some also working jobs. The ties that bound us began to loosen in some cases and fray altogether in others. So to be out in the world in this little part-time job became a small breakout for me, a laboratory for developing some new soft skills of relating to more than just my teenage peers. At eighteen, my subconscious white guilt may have seeped into my soft-skill goals and created some self-conscious effort to do something about America's racism—at Sears. It wasn't so much some early iteration of a white savior complex, but it was the seed of idealizing, and then nearly idolizing Black people. In my limited experience of interracial relationships, I was yet to realize how that idolatry was equally problematic in the goal of psychic freedom and true human equality. I recorded a very little bit of this curiosity, this nascent mission, in my new journal.

July 2, 1976

Before I forget, Lucille A. Foreman created a bright spot in my life a few days ago. I saw her again today. She was an elderly black woman customer with whom I talked and laughed. I really gave a gut laugh, too. She was so sweet and I hope to remember her as to how to be natural and friendly with a stranger.

July 30, 1976

*The old janitor at Sears evoked some feelings from me. I
wanted to take his picture as he sat on the curb waiting for
the bus as he does every night after closing. A black elderly,
slouched-over man, he pushes his trash bin throughout the
store, sliding his oversized shoes across the tiles. I look at
persons such as he, especially black, and it fills me with a
curious, paradoxical feeling. I have that sadness for him that
makes me want to have shared his life up to that point to
relieve part of the guilt I may feel for taking for granted my
advantage. I also always assume such persons have had a bad
life. Impossible. The standards are perhaps different. Then I
guess I begin to feel happiness for the diversity of mankind and
feel that powerful love for him. That muffled, "how you dis
evening?" is all it takes to share a bit of humanity with him.*

Those interactions were in front of the curtain. A little earlier that
summer, it seems my relationship with Joe became deeper, moving
along that fascinating spectrum of connection from stranger to
friend, unlikely pair that we were. Every once in a while (like most
of the time) when there wasn't much shoe traffic, Joe would leave the
department to our overly zealous colleague Mike's singular ambition
and we would go on break together. My regret now is that I left out
some of the specifics that the adult me is really curious about.

June 23, 1976

*I began to understand some things today. I need to listen
more carefully and examine all meanings of a statement.*

This results from a conversation with Joe. He has been very special to me and is a good person, not merely a novelty. I learn through him about myself. Our talk this evening about things brought us closer as friends. We can really laugh and have a nice time. His being black does play a part and an important one. I'm curious. His separation from his wife has impressed me as to the actual feelings involved in it.

Ruh roh. Reading it as a divorced grandmother and teacher of teenage girls, I can't help but zero in on that part. Midlife crisis? Teenage girl working in your department? Ego boost much? Although, I read between the lines that it was an actual friendship. My own innocent, first boy relationship had run its course. I broke up with him on America's bicentennial, July 4, 1976, a date that would recur in my own future saga of independence.

On one evening we worked together, a couple of guys came into the department wearing plaid wool hunting jackets, today's camo equivalent, looking for some work boots, one of our specialties. Of course, Mike jumped on the sale as Joe and I looked on, me lamenting not being able to record that nice commission on two pairs of those Spice Tans size 11s in the little green book. Joe smiled at the, let's say, pretty "countryfied" dudes whose plaid collar may have been hiding a certain primary color around their necks. Only his smile seemed forced and not accompanied by that usual gleam in his eyes. After they left, he pointed at one of them walking away toward the mall's big friendly opening. "See that guy on the right?" I said, "Yeah, you know him?" Joe answered, still grinning, "His brother shot my cousin." I was so shocked that I am not sure I even heard the story behind it, if there were one. I wonder how common this perverted notion of family connections in the South may have been. But I weirdly have always remembered the last name of the guy. I still see it on a raised, lit company sign when I exit the interstate a little early in route to my companion's house. It sits at the end of the highway ramp where I have to wait at a red light to turn left. I stare at that sign and each time I think about Joe. I think back on my Pollyannaish youth when I had such high hopes for the power of love to transform society, and I would even say such crazy things out loud—a lot. But when I see that name, a very white sounding name by the way, on the old sign on that roadside some forty-five years later, the hope for such a transformation in the face of such enduring cruelty is suffering. Not long after this encounter with those two guys, I wrote a poem after another food court break with Joe during which he must have really opened up.

July 21, 1976

Joe and I ate lunch together from which I obtained a lot of insight into black background. He felt frustrated and pretended many times. I wrote this poem in thinking of him.

> *Injustice*
> *Imposed inferiority claims untapped greatness*
> *How sad such situations,*
> *How acquiescent such reactions.*
> *Injustice lies in the hollows of insecurity.*
> *Pretending suffices not for reality.*
> *But it sometimes eases the pain.*

Then I add my typical didactic coda of those days:

Break from the shackles of the past
However binding, However resistant the soul.

That summer Joe and I hung out a couple of times outside of the mall. We both played tennis and thought it would be fun to hit the ball around on a mutual day off. I remember thinking how strange it was to see a Black man sitting in the VW's passenger seat instead of Nancy or Donna. We arrived at some public courts in the heart of the city, on the "wrong side of Broad Street," as most longtime white Richmonders, including my grandmother, called it. It was a traditionally Black recreation area called Brookfield Park, one of the places Arthur Ashe played tennis growing up. Several of Joe's friends were also there. I felt completely comfortable because I trusted Joe. I guess we played some tennis and had some fun because he made everything fun. I never did anything I wasn't supposed to do, drinking or smoking—anything—in the seventies. But I did have a light-hearted, platonic relationship with an older man, an older Black man. My father would have flipped out if he had known about my tennis date. Or worse, that I accompanied a Black man to a party one night where I was the only white person there, and definitely the only eighteen-year-old. Strobe lights pulsed over the dancing bodies of all shapes and sizes to the beat of the music. My memory is that I was greeted with a certain nonchalance and welcomed into the spirit of the dance.

Readjustment

B uilding a house is a lot like having a baby; nobody wants to hear about all the pain and suffering you had to endure. They just want to see the finished product. Meanwhile, forces outside of your control have taken over your life. In the case of my house, the gestation period took more than eighteen months. Over that time span, we took our third son to college where he would join his brother who was a senior. My oldest son had spent one year after college in Virginia and then shocked me by announcing he was moving to Portland . . . Oregon! It felt like a bad omen. The excitement factor of the new house dropped by one-third in my heart. I cried so hard when he left. The tyranny of the urgent, the chaos of the building process, kept my mind off the sudden empty nest, which was part of the motivation for moving in the first place. I just had not factored in just how empty I would feel.

In the three years since selling our suburban house and building the dream house, we lived first in what my middle son dubbed Apathy

Central, the tiny Cape Cod rental house in Richmond where my youngest finished high school. Then it was on to what he might have dubbed Ennui Acres, a nasty rental house in rural Louisa. During that time, like the spouse who finds, say, someone else's jewelry on the dresser, I started to find empty bourbon bottles under that country rental's back porch. Yet, like that suspected affair, I was in denial. I convinced myself that this drinking habit was a temporary and somewhat contained problem. After all, I had seen my father suffer through a five-year bout of alcohol abuse before he got a handle on it after firing a troubling employee. I kept telling myself this change, this massive relocation of our lives, the kind of change he had been clamoring for, would be the catalyst he needed. Still, one night after a loud, scary fight, he drove down the country road taking out the rental mailbox in the process. I felt so alone. I missed my boys intensely. I went outside. Amid those hundreds of acres with no one in sight, under the light of a near full moon I let out a howl, screaming at the top of my lungs my anger and frustration. Still, I held out hope that after such a dragged-out process, once we got into the real house, I would see a sea change in his attitude, and we would build our own foundation for a new start.

Only a few days after getting that long-awaited certificate of occupancy for our dream house, I drove the forty-five minutes home after staying for parent visitation night at school. I walked in to find a smoldering log on the fireplace hearth and him passed out on the living room floor. More and more, I could not trust him there alone. But those incidents were contained within our walls. That is, until I got a call from a local sheriff late one night. During yet another break in between real jobs, he was returning on a Sunday evening from an ersatz business trip to New York. He stopped the old '82 blue Mercedes an hour from home on the side of a multi-lane divided highway to relieve himself. It just happened to be right in front of a county jail where cops are coming and going all day and night. He might have been in midstream when one of them drove up and nailed him for driving under the influence. Then it was a just a short hop across the highway to board him in the austere concrete rural facility, most likely filled with dudes who had never worn a button-down Oxford, especially one made of 100% cotton.

I was awakened by an unfamiliar, and at that time, disorienting, stilted recording asking if I would accept the charges. I did. They ended up being like dynamite charges. That phone call lit a match to my fuse that would very, *very* slowly reel out across the coming five years of more of this chaos. I did not foresee the end yet, only the heightening dread of that smoldering wire exploding my future expectations and my past identity. Years of aiding and abetting, of making excuses, of prioritizing his happiness over mine had worn me out. My nerves had stretched out so far that I never realized I was constantly nervous. So hearing his slightly intoxicated, more than elevated voice insist—even demand—that I come get him right then did it. Something flipped inside. I could not believe that he really expected me to get in the car after 11:00 p.m. on a school night and drive forty-five minutes on very dark, unfamiliar country roads so that he did not spend a few uncomfortable hours detained there. Like my mother never realized with my delinquent brother, the solution to his problem was not my problem. Any initial trickle of empathy ended with a swelling tsunami of apathy. Is this how it happens? In an instant? Did that phone call prompt a long overdue self-assertiveness, or was that the moment my heart went cold? Do they necessarily go together? He was still demanding me to get over there when the sheriff interrupted and brusquely informed me not to come, that he would be staying there. I jumped back under the covers and slept better, there alone in the country in this too-big house, than I had for weeks.

Miraculously, in the midst of the national financial crisis, he had reluctantly taken a job at a nearby private military academy where students and teachers wore uniforms and were called by their rank. Those of us who knew him better than he knew himself were thrilled that he was back in his natural habitat, a middle school classroom, especially at this quirky school where he would teach about thirty total students. I had a renewed hope that he might even retire from there in about fifteen years. In that case, it would have just been a twenty-five-year detour from his true calling of teaching. Our combined incomes as teachers, like our very first three years of marriage, covered the bills and then some. But it wasn't nearly enough to take care of the massive accumulated debt that he had managed to conceal from me until I got a call from MasterCard. At my school! The secretary transferred the collection agent to my classroom—while tenth graders were staring at me! The amount was so big that the only recourse was to declare bankruptcy. I actually felt relieved, smiling broadly while we walked hand in hand to the courts building on that fine, sunny June day in 2009.

Because of the '08 collapse, we were not alone. It was like taking a number at the deli counter. On a few nights that summer, I fell into the habit of looking around my house at some of the Chapter Eleven goods there. I loved my, or American Express's, living room rug, a thick wool number with a black background and a huge multicolored floral, organic motif that cost them $500 on Overstock. That love was—at times—overpowered by my moral bankruptcy and shame at it being an ill-gotten gain. Credit scores had not yet made it on to the list of identity-defining numbers like income, weight, GPAs—nor were they the subject of so many jingled ads to come. I had no idea what my credit score became, although I assumed it was probably lower than my math SAT.

* * *

That same year in the fall, a speech was given at the October pysch-up assembly we called Senior Convocation, one I will never forget. The seniors filed into the gym in their caps and gowns while the other three classes watched and hopefully caught the vision of graduation. One of my previous year's US history students, a preppy, smart, athletic young Black man, now the class vice president, spoke to the whole school. When I taught him, he was so excited to tell me about attending Obama's inauguration with his family as seated guests. Now on that fall morning, he beautifully summed up his appreciation of our campus. He subtly contrasted us with a couple of nearby, let's say, less than heterogeneous high schools, one whose obnoxious soccer fans once yelled something at our newly immigrated goalie about being an orphan and laughed their heads off. My student knew many of those other school's kids. Alluding to our rather pitiable—to outsiders—status, Brennon said, "This is why I love Tucker. We have diversity. Other schools have very little experience with people not like them. We will all go into the world and be much more open because we have had all kinds of friends. This is a huge advantage."

A perfect example of Brennon's point, among too many to count, involved a preppy-dressing, Italian-heritage, all-American blonde great baseball player who had chosen not to go to his more homogenous, zoned high school so he could be in the advanced IB program. During an ethics council meeting in my classroom, he and a friend were paying no attention while trying to suppress some seriously unethical giggles. The friend, who had an unmatched giggle, was the daughter of Sudanese immigrants who wore a headscarf at the time. On the surface, they couldn't have been more different: boy/girl, white/Black, Catholic/Muslim. But having been in every single class together for three years, they had become like brother and sister. Just then, I noticed a young African American guy, a "regular" student as we call the kids not part of this advanced group, walk past the classroom. He saw my student through the window and his face lit up. They were baseball teammates. They *also* shared a lot in common. He popped his head in the door, and these two jock dudes shared a cool handshake and a big smile.

For many years, I was the debate club sponsor. We called ourselves the J. R. Tucker Debate Society and Culture Club since "team" would have implied we knew the actual rules for debating instead of kids yelling at each other once a week in my classroom. This duty merely required that I open my door during an activities time slot after lunch and throw out a topic, sometimes adopting Mike Myers' Linda Richmond character's accent: "Affirmative Action is neither affirmative nor action. Discuss amongst yourselves." Kids just started yelling at each other. It was awesome. It was a pre-iPhone, so pre-brain-sucking equivalent, I suppose, to "posting." They hoped to win these "debates," as one student thought, by saying something so good that the other person couldn't think of anything to say back. I told them that did not count as a victory on a real debate team, but it would sure come in handy in marriage. Once, in a heated discussion of that affirmative action topic, one of the mainstays of the club, a young Black man who possessed Ralph Lauren model good looks and ardent Republican politics, argued vehemently against it saying that financial success without any special consideration was the greatest equalizer. Bubbles, a six foot two and every bit of 250 pounds, proudly biracial, camouflage-wearing hunter dude from a country family, disagreed. He took the empathetic tack. In a statement that seemed to sum up what I found upon my return, he entreated us in a sincere and plaintive tone: "Man, you gotta' walk in someone else's shoes to feel their pain."

Those kids had no idea of how unusual, and perhaps even threatening, these interactions would have appeared to many old Richmonders. When I was growing up, Virginia was a state whose loudest voices gloried most in its past. Virginia: the mother of presidents who birthed the father of the country. You get Virginia history three different years in school. It's the *Old* Dominion for a reason. There had not been much talk of a New Dominion here until November 2008 when the state went full blue and elected Barack Obama. That was unthinkable for many old timers who believed that the "real" Virginia is rural and conservative, meaning white. I encountered some of these folks, a group of clearly over-seventy old Richmonders sitting behind me a long while back at Panera. I was trying to grade some papers. They were lamenting the pitiful state of the school system. "No one speaks English anymore, parents don't care, nobody can read," and on and on. I so wanted to go up to their table, lean into their faces, and reassure them that there's no need for worry. In fact, if I had been equally inclined as they towards rampant generalization and could have mustered some righteous rudeness, I would have informed them that it's often their sweet little peachy grandchildren whose class rank is way below those they lament. I could have told them our social studies department folk tale about the Sudanese Lost Boy who apologized to my colleague for getting a B on a test. Or the Honduran kid, still learning English, who I saw in the quiet teacher resource room quoting the entire preamble of the Constitution to the government teacher for extra credit. Or the countless advanced Bosnian, Indian, and Chinese kids who I got to teach who may very well be operating on their knees, eyes, and, perhaps, hearts one day.

Those folks and their attitudes are among the living. But what about Virginia's long-dead racist codgers who tried their damndest to keep this "race mixing" from ever happening? The most notorious being Harry Flood Byrd, Sr., longtime Virginia senator, architect of Massive Resistance, and head of the infamous Byrd Machine, the same man who had a local middle school named for him, one that fed into Tucker. At a March 2016 meeting of the same school board that had chosen the school's name fifty years earlier, the main issue was changing that name. Some objected, praising the former senator for good roads and low taxes, sure reasons to maintain a school's name for a diehard segregationist. Many others disagreed. One citizen reminded the board of the original context. "Harry F. Byrd Middle School opened just after the collapse of Massive Resistance ushered in a white flight to Henrico County," he said. To bastardize one of my favorite Randy Newman songs about Karl Marx, "If Byrd were living today, he'd be rolling around in his grave." Because, just like nearby Tucker, integration had happened naturally. Nearly 20 percent of that middle school's students are Black and many nationalities attend.

But Harry F. Byrd did not have to prevail in Virginia. Our state-mandated pacing guide allowed only a day or two to teach Reconstruction. I ignored that, lingering in that unit to get the kids to contemplate many of the big "what ifs" of that pivotal time. One of the biggest being a short-lived political movement in Virginia known as the Readjuster Party. The Readjusters. Its name, while actually a reference to how to deal with post–Civil War debt, at first made me laugh. I imagined that the platform of this political party called for universal attitude readjustments. Members had to swear an oath to readjust their presumptions. Readjust their alliances. Readjust their racism. Yet, if the Readjusters had enjoyed a more lasting success in post-Reconstruction Virginia, all of those changes may have happened by now, and Harry Byrd would never have ascended. According to a wonderful entry by Brent Tarter in the *Encyclopedia Virginia*, the Readjuster Party was a coalition of poor whites, Democrats, and

Republicans, as well as African American Virginians. As opposed to the Funders who wanted to pay back Virginia's creditors in full, the Readjusters sought to reduce the principal and the interest rate on the state's debt in order to provide for a new system of public schools for both Black and white communities. During this short-lived historical window, many Blacks won local offices and election to the General Assembly as Readjusters. This was 1879! In 1881, its candidates won all three statewide offices.

The Readjusters' strategy emphasized economic fairness and de-emphasized race. The party seemed to work miracles in state government, both practically and socially. In their short, approximately six-year existence, they raised taxes on corporations and reduced them on farmers and small businessmen. Their accomplishments included a budget surplus after years of crippling debt; doubling funding for all public schools; eliminating the poll tax and the barbaric whipping post as punishment for African Americans; and creating Virginia State University for training Black teachers. This was change on a pace arguably never seen in the post-bellum, post-Reconstruction South. However, a distinction between public and private spheres of equality persisted. While these late-nineteenth-century progressive whites assented to Blacks participating in civic affairs, they maintained an unstated belief in social barriers in private affairs, like education and marriage. Their opponents, the newly formed Democratic Party, ran against them in the General Assembly elections of 1883 on the singular issue of reassertion of white supremacy. They brought this unspoken distinction to the forefront, warning that if Blacks gained more political rights, what was to prevent them from using that to seek social equality? This fear led to a renewed effort to simply eliminate the few public rights that Blacks had gained during Reconstruction and the short-lived Readjuster coalition. They succeeded. The election of 1883 would put an end to any "what if," alternate course of Virginia politics and open the door to white supremacist rule that would lead all the way into my high school years.

For its Twainian, rhyming quality regarding some recent trends in American political life, the story of Byrd's rise to dominance is a cautionary tale about protecting democracy. This old Democratic Party seized complete control of Virginia politics through notorious, sometimes laughably corrupt, methods of voter suppression, thanks to a new constitution adopted in 1902. Not only did this constitution's suffrage clauses eliminate about 90 percent of the Black vote; nearly half of white voters were also disenfranchised. Ironic for its mythological place in the story of democracy, Virginia, for the better part of the ensuing century had the lowest number of adults participating in elections than any other state; a measly 10 to 12 percent. These Democratic plutocrats liked it that way. They saw themselves as the only qualified conservators of the Old Dominion, the saviors of Southern society from the likes of what the Panera folks feared. This well-oiled, anti-democratic political machine enjoyed complete control of the state. That is, until the Supreme Court ordered schools to be desegregated in the middle of the century. Maintaining the utterly segregated, completely inequitable public school system then became the greatest rallying cry for Harry Byrd, and evidently a reason to have a nearby middle school named in his honor in 1971, the year I started eighth grade.

I was born in the loudest reverberation of the baby boom, November 1957, an Eisenhower girl launched six weeks after Sputnik. As my mother grew more pregnant with me, she and my father would not have escaped the news out of Arkansas that fall. The standoff between segregationist Governor Orval Faubus and federal district judge Ronald Davies over court-ordered integration headlined every front page of the country's newspapers. They could not have missed that single, powerful image of Elizabeth Eckford who got separated from the group being virulently cursed at by a fifteen-year-old Hazel Bryan. A defiant Faubus had used the state's National Guard to prevent the nine Black students from entering while claiming he did it to preserve law and order. Eisenhower ultimately had to send the 101st Airborne to ensure the Black students were finally admitted. All suffered aggressive attacks in the halls of the school. On the day I was born, the fourteenth of November, one of the nine, a young woman, was pushed coming out of an assembly. A young man named Jefferson Thomas was pushed so hard by a white student that he fell to the ground. I have to wonder about his name. His mother with such a last name must have had some positive association in her mind with the third president when she named her son. Perhaps she was hanging on to his famous words, while ignoring his deeds, of all men being created equally, and hoping that for her Jefferson.

This is the moment in Virginia history that Harry Flood Byrd orchestrated the strategy known as Massive Resistance, the unified, statewide stance against integration. The plan formed Pupil Placement Boards that created extralegal, subjective, bogus criteria as obstacles to Black parents who wanted to register their children in the local school. After that, Massive Resistance employed three strategies, which, when announced, were met with cheers and, unbelievably—or not for the 1950s—*rebel yells* in the General Assembly. First, then-governor Thomas B. Stanley would outright close any school that was ordered to desegregate by the federal government. Second, the state of Virginia would discredit, harass, and hinder the NAACP's legal efforts and any Black parents who brought lawsuits forward. And finally, the editor of the *Richmond News Leader*, James J. Kilpatrick would become the head of what can only be called a propaganda commission. He and Byrd hoped Virginia would lead the way, as they did in the Civil War. As though that war had never been fought, he employed antebellum legal arguments, like interposition and nullification—essentially states' rights—to defy the Supreme Court's decree to desegregate public schools.

Every history teacher is grateful for a few invaluable resources of the video variety. In US history, the 1987 PBS documentary *Eyes on the Prize* depicting every major event of the Civil Rights movement almost taught the unit without me. Its genius is in mixing archival footage with interviews with the real people who took part in its campaigns. I usually made the kids fill out a chart of the event, the year, and the significance as we went along. They were into it. Again, this was before the dissipation of engagement and disappointing distraction by way of "smart" phones. It was also before Standards of Learning completely lowered the standards of learning. I remember the attentive, almost devout, quiet in a wonderful class full of "regular old kids" in 2010, several years before Tucker would house three specialty programs for out-of-district, academically advanced students. When we watched the second episode called "Fighting Back," which included the story of the Little Rock Nine, you could have heard a pin drop. In a class nearly equally divided between Black and white students with a decent percentage of Asian and Hispanic kids, all were respectful and, seemingly to me, in disbelief. When the film shows the military arriving on campus, some kids of all races looked at me with a *WTF?* expression, as if to say, "Really? The army? Just to go to high school?" In those moments, and in many more in the coming years when the discussion of race and violence arose, particularly involving the Klan, I was sometimes nervous about emotional outbursts from one side or the other; that Black students might turn on the white kids, who in turn, may feel unduly guilty by association with their skin color. Never happened. This was the beauty of dealing with young people. There were times, though, that the Black kids showed signs of trauma, not unlike Jewish kids when we discussed the Holocaust. This is the big dilemma in how real a history class should get.

After the video ended and kids were packing up their things, one of my all-time favorite students approached me. Jimmy was a youth preacher in a huge, well-known African American church in Richmond. He was tall and lean, and possessed a slight baby-doll face and an old soul and didn't have a mean bone in his body. We had already formed a bond due to his good questions, big heart, and easy laugh. He came up near me, just smiled and was kind of shaking his head side to side, clearly still moved by the documentary. His eyes displayed that burgeoning intellectual curiosity that I saw so often in juniors. Perhaps still seeing the traumatized but brave Elizabeth Eckford in his mind, he asked in all innocence and rather haltingly, "So, Ms. Knapp. So, I mean, just what was it, like what specifically did white people hate about Black people?" I was stunned. It was a simple and profound question. I looked at him wide-eyed as vague memories of angry dinner table tirades during the sixties and seventies about food stamps and welfare and busing whirled through my mind. I wanted to tell him that I had been asking that question myself since listening to those conversations during my childhood. I choked on my response and ultimately evaded the question until the bell rang. Staring in Jimmy's face, so full of unbounded enthusiasm, so entranced with our new president Obama, so self-confident and popular with all the students, I couldn't bring myself to dredge up that past, or in any way incriminate my people in it.

Particularly, my father. He was a mirror of the old post-Reconstruction mindset of a private vs. public estimation of Blacks and their equality. Daddy could not have run Auto Electric without the constant presence of Devron, a trim, calm, meticulously dressed Black employee who ran the warehouse. Devron was the Jerry Rice of Auto Electric—cool, precise, always a clean uniform. Then, in the mid-seventies, Daddy hired a young Black man named Tony who gave the veteran salesman—and Danny DeVito look-alike—Shorty Carter, a run for his money. Each Christmas, my mother threw a really nice party, like three-copper-chafing-dishes nice, for the ten or eleven employees and their spouses of this auto parts equivalent of *Cheers*, eccentric characters I encountered during my middle school summers when I worked upstairs in the office with the old lady bookkeeper Miss Utley. Of course, the two Black men were invited and came to our house with their wives. I remember those parties as being fun, although in retrospect I wonder if they were at all uncomfortable for Devron and Tony. (Although Black people, as I learned from reading Baldwin, have highly honed skills in dealing with "whites in the wild," as one of my Black students hilariously put it once.) Still, in private, those transactional relationships, however warm they might have been, did not often translate in the white mind to public policies like voting rights, equal education, or fair housing.

However much I respected my father's part in history, his mechanical genius, his absurdly silly sense of humor, and his almost genderless, genuine treatment of me, I could not understand the outbursts of prejudice, as we said more often than "racism" in the seventies. Also, like I am guessing was the case with other World War II veterans, he used what seemed to me at the time "nicknames" for the foreigners he fought, just like the comedians of that time did. Yes, Daddy referred to the "Japs" and the "Chinks" and the "Krauts" until his death. He bought an auto parts store when I was in fifth grade that sold AC/

Delco and GM products, and even before that, the only cars we owned were Chevrolets. He warned me often, not of boys or drugs, but of Toyotas. It almost killed him when I bought my VW Bug with the $200 I saved from babysitting. But his most intense outbursts were aimed at Black people, occasionally when watching Walter Cronkite during the height of the civil rights struggle, but more often when reading the Richmond newspaper.

In the *Richmond News Leader*, editor James J. Kilpatrick aroused the fears and stoked the anger of his readers like my father about the desegregation of public schools as ordered by the Supreme Court. I remembered him most from the SNL parody of his *60 Minutes* testy, debate segment with liberal columnist Shayna Alexander. "Jane, you ignorant slut!" was a favorite line around the lunch table my senior year of high school. But like my student Jimmy, I wondered, what did Kilpatrick fear from the mixing of school children? What justification did he offer for his attitude towards the "Negro question," by which he meant "the fear of integration and of a revolutionary Negro ascendancy"? I found far too many—what can only be described today as outrageous, but at the time perhaps standard—answers than I cared to read in an extended essay Kilpatrick wrote called "The Southern Case for School Segregation." Almost every third page has my penciled-in "OMG" in the margin. In the first chapter, "Evidence," Kilpatrick exalted a kind of oligarchy with a drawl, Southern rule of the few over the many, a conservatism borne of the Cavalier class and long executed by the Byrd Machine. He explained:

the one reality most often shunned: the inequality of
man ... The South holds small enthusiasm for egalitarian
doctrines based up on the infinite perfectibility of man
... implicit in the conservative faith is a high respect for

individual variations, for class, order, and rank . . . the
privileges of birth and office and position—these too are
long ingrained; they persevere. [1]

He derides liberalism as being of the masses who cannot be trusted
with democracy. More astonishing is his blatant racism. He wrote:

Here and now, in his own communities, in the mid-1960s,
the Negro race, as a race, plainly is not equal to the white
race; nor, for that matter, in the wider world beyond . . .
has the Negro race, as a race, ever been the cultural or
intellectual equal of the white race, as a race. This we take
to be a plain statement of fact . . . [2]

The failure of the Negro race, as a race, to achieve equality
cannot be blamed wholly on white oppression. This is
the excuse, the crutch, the piteous and finally pathetic
defense of Negrophiles unable or unwilling to face reality.
In other times and other places, sturdy, creative, and
self-reliant minorities have carved out their own destiny;
they have compelled acceptance on their own merit;
they have demonstrated those qualities of leadership and
resourcefulness and disciplined ambition that in the end
cannot ever be denied. But the Negro race, as a race, has
done none of this. [3]

---

1   Kilpatrick, James J., *The Southern Case for School Segregation* (New York: Crowell-Collier Press, 1962), 39.

2   Kilpatrick, 26.

3   Kilpatrick, 97.

Kilpatrick took issue with liberal anthropological studies that even in the 1950s were claiming race was just a myth, evidenced by how often he qualifies his statement with "as a race." After quoting a professor about how the Caucasian is superior in traits required for "civilization," he explained that the average white Southerner just kind of "knows" this from generations of observation and unfounded stereotypes. In doing so, Kilpatrick gave these whites all the reasons Jimmy wondered about to hate Black people. Oh how satisfying it would have been to invite Mr. Kilpatrick onto the right side of history at my old bicentennial campus after I returned in 2003! This new generation of Virginians would have scared the living daylights out of him. I would have liked to see that. All of his fears as well as those of his Massive Resistor cronies had come true. But as it turned out, as is to be expected from fearmongers, there was nothing to fear.

In just six years after I returned to the classroom, massive growth towards Short Pump transformed that funny-sounding rural area into massive suburban sprawl. That created a need for not one, but two, new high schools in that short span. That meant redistricting, the time when real estate values vanquish personal values. County redistricting meetings quickly became very rancorous, with many worried parents slamming Tucker. It always baffled me since the staff does not change when a school was redistricted. A "good" school—a shiny indoor one—can have crappy teachers, just as much as the reverse. Still, the disrespect created a beautiful response from dozens of alumni, students, and teachers on Facebook, all extolling their love of the place. After the final maps were drawn, some said Tucker was "taken advantage of"; others said "screwed." Unlike every other school district zone with a fairly square-ish shape, ours became like a snake, extending the length of a forsaken commercial strip of Broad Street that had small, run-down homes and apartment complexes behind it. With each new map, fewer white neighborhoods remained. We emerged with about a 40–40 Black-brown/white split, with the remaining kids from dozens of different nations as world events dictated.

My alma mater had long ago become a kind of Ellis Island in Dixie. Very soon after I graduated in 1976, a huge contingent of refugee Vietnamese kids came to live at the wonderful Boys and Girls Home near Tucker, a group home begun by one of my classmate's dads in the sixties. For years, there were more Nguyens than Smiths on campus. They were followed by a big group of Cambodian students, then Bosnians, including Elina, who could make *the* loudest shushing sound that always brought the class to silence, a girl who never left my classroom without making my day by loudly yelling the greatest: "We love you Ms. Knapp!" They were soon joined by Sudanese kids, Indian, Pakistani, and Afghan students, a few Saudis, and most recently, an influx of immigrants from Central America, including Miguel, a precious young man from Honduras. He had an amazing, nay, preternatural ability in American geography even though he was still learning English. (I learned later that geography is drilled into young students there.) It didn't matter what it was—river, mountains, states, he knew the answer right away. Miguel sat in a row of desks behind where I would stand at the projector. We were learning about the French and Indian War. I showed the class this cool picture of Fort Duquesne, a.k.a. Pittsburgh, where you can see the two colors of the rivers coming together to form the Ohio. True confession, my forte is history; I am not great at geography and at that moment, I couldn't remember the rivers' names. I told the class to hold on, I'd Google it. No need. In his quiet, nascent English, Miguel's disembodied voice casually offered up from behind me, somewhat nasally yet perfectly, the tongue twister: "Monongahela and

Allegheny." I burst out laughing as I spun around to thank him. In those moments, I sometimes wondered about those old panic-stricken coots in Panera. What would they think if they saw Miguel walking along the street? Who knows? But I bet they couldn't name the capital of South Dakota.

I think back to the busing-era sociological guru, Dr. Thomas Pettigrew, who suggested a 20–40 percent optimal minority racial percentage to avoid white flight or tokenism at that time. This ended up happening, some would say, organically at JRT. As an example, a group of four sophomore Asian girls, East and South, "befriended" me by coming in a lot of mornings before classes started. They were a riot. One morning, Indian Arnatha and Vietnamese Terri announced their goal to stop cracking on the other's ethnicity. To make it interesting, they would charge each other a quarter per infraction. Terri exclaimed in feigned disgust, "She owes me $1.25!" Those girls later invited me to the movies to see *Slumdog Millionaire*. Arnatha sat next to me and filled me in on some of the cultural details of the story. I couldn't help but remember coming to this same classic, ornate old Richmond movie palace a few times in the 60s and 70s for an annual spring ritual: the screening of 1939's *Gone with the Wind*. For white Richmonders then, it was a place to see and be seen; everyone dressed to the nines. Before the movie started, Eddie Weaver and his "renowned organ" emerged from beneath the floor and ushered in the packed house's trip to the Old South.

One particular IB world history class ended up with just fourteen ninth-grade girls at the end of the day. They were pretty much evenly split between Asian, Indian, Black, and white, and none had gone to middle school with each other. It didn't take long for me—sister, aunt, mother to all boys—to revel in this happy circumstance, or for it to resemble a pajama party as much as a classroom. We had so many wide-open discussions about race and feminism, there in such a safe space for them as young teenage girls. They often ended up sitting on top of their desks, cross-legged, elbows on knees, a position my arthritic knees so envied. It was so open and non-threatening. I don't remember laughing as much in any other class. I'll never forget when four of them wanted to practice their English project. We projected the words of Maya Angelou's "Phenomenal Woman" on the wall while one girl played the guitar. These girls of different backgrounds sang those powerful words to their own catchy, original tune while doing a little dance routine. It was so touching. And perhaps the funniest thing I was ever asked during my teaching career came in that advanced class. A tall, thin, hilarious Black girl in all honesty asked me once, "Ms. Knapp, just what is a country club? I have heard that term a lot but have never figured it out." Before I could answer, she mused, "Country club. Hmm. I picture a bunch of old white people in overalls square dancing and chewing on straw. Is that it?"

Rather than an assumed disrespect for, these kids possessed a presumed appreciation of each other that came from the security they felt in their own unique identities. It was another example of my oft-repeated revelation about diversity, accurate or not, that it comes from the kind I saw at Tucker. A good, healthy diversity is proven by how intensely unique it allows, or even forces, its individual members to be. Including to whom you are attracted. I remember an endearing student named, I'll say Jalen, a smart Black kid who had trouble with attendance and dabbled in some light drug use. In my economics class, I had given an assignment about creating demand that required them to pick a celebrity to endorse their product. He called me over to show me a picture of Reba McEntire on his computer. At the time she was in her fifties and only two years older than me. Jalen looked at me and then longingly at the flame-haired country star before declaring, "Man, Ms. Knapp, she is hot."

* * *

A week before our twenty-ninth wedding anniversary, we took a really fun trip to celebrate that milestone, plus the graduation of our last son from college, and the declaration, euphemistically, of our "personal debt relief"—all in June 2009. The sheer insanity of what was about to happen was amplified by the normality of that vacation. We revisited our days of innocence on Martha's Vineyard, swung through Connecticut to see old friends, and visited his brother's family and attended a real adult party at their beach club. This was notable since, at home, our married social life had dwindled to near nonexistence. We stopped by New York on the way home and did lots of touristy things like a Circle Line cruise and the Top of the Rock. There was so much compounding of our life together on that trip, so much reinforcement of my own identity through a thirty-year shared history of people and places. We had more than a few laughs, and for once in a great while, I felt relaxed, almost normal. No doubt this was partly due to a reprieve from a daily schedule dominated by food (all done by 5:30 p.m.), alcohol, and a bedtime two hours later. I almost caught a vision of a better future, one where his unilateral decisions about ours was over. Now in our early fifties, we had circled back around to our origin story of the union of two happy teachers. It provided ample, if not too much, extra income and summers off.

I was still completely in, still struggling exclusively with his struggles, still thinking that the Berlin Wall had fallen and the Cold War was about to end. It would take a bit longer to realize that little by little, incident by inexplicable incident, I had actually fallen into my own quagmire. And like all American wars of my lifetime, missions can start to creep beyond their original purpose, purposes that oftentimes get lost in imperceptible and incremental expansion. My marriage mission had crept into some thick jungles of criss-crossing vines of maternal, spousal, and survival instincts.

Cafeteria Fair

On January 26, 1972, during my eighth-grade year spent banished to the middle school, and only a couple of weeks after Judge Mehrige ordered the consolidation of Richmond, Chesterfield, and Henrico Schools, a debate took place at Virginia Union University. Then Vice-Mayor Henry Marsh and Roy Innis, the leader of the Congress on Racial Equality, took opposite sides in a discussion about the merits of integrating schools. Innis, representing a healthy faction of Black activists, now opposed the NAACP's longstanding push for integration. He argued that this implied "blackness was bad," that it would lead to the "whitening of Black minds," thus hindering the advancement of Black culture. He even went on to lament the whole idea of an interracial society. "Let's face it. Black and white lifestyles are basically different." Decades later, in April 2014, on the sixtieth anniversary of Brown, *New Yorker* contributor and NYU professor Jelani Cobb summed up the dilemma with a question Black people faced at that time, and no doubt still do: "In a hostile society, is it better to be isolated from those who view you with contempt or in close proximity to them?" Yet other Black activists worried that moving back toward a voluntary separation with the Black community's control over its own schools ultimately would not be beneficial. They feared that the financial support of white taxpayers would wane. As far as cultural benefits, critics of Innis thought a purposeful resegregation of white and Black students into separate schools would allow racial myths to perpetuate, preventing interactions that would challenge such myths and stereotypes.

During the first convulsion of Richmond's statue controversy in 1993 that placed Arthur Ashe's statue on Monument Avenue with many Confederate generals, I came across an interview Ashe had given to Charlie Rose. Rose seemed to be goading the tennis great into speaking ill of his past in "segregated Richmond." Ashe said that despite the racism, he was also helped by many white people there who were interested in his future. Yet another public-private morality failing on the part of the white people, but Ashe ended by saying he loved Richmond, and he was most definitely proud to be a Virginian. I was stunned. How could any Black person who grew up in my city be able to say that? This even-temper, combined with Ashe's initial lack of participation in social protests, were sometimes attacked by other civil rights leaders as being accommodationist in the vein of Booker T. Washington. Sociologist and veteran civil rights advocate Harry Edwards was quoted as saying, "we thought he was an Uncle Tom!" In *Citizen Ashe*, Rex Miller's and Sam Pollard's beautiful 2021 documentary of the tennis champion, the same Edwards owned up to his misjudgment. He recounted Arthur Ashe's response to such accusations by saying he had spent a lifetime defying white peoples' expectations and stereotypes, and I'm paraphrasing, he wasn't about to spend the rest of his life trying to live up to the expectations—and whatever stereotypes—that other Black people tried to lay on him.

Some of the most gripping presentations I witnessed by Black students echoed Ashe's emotions in that they all concerned the limits placed on their identity from all sides. The first year I taught the Theory of Knowledge class, I had to guide them through this then required Presentation. It starts with something that makes you question the truth of a situation or comment followed by an analysis using common knowledge issues like methodology, bias, interpretation, limitations, etc. A vivacious young Black woman had her real-life situation at the bus stop, where all real life happens, of course. Two younger kids zoned for the majority Black high school waiting for their bus saw her reading *A Tale of Two Cities*. They asked her, "Why are you acting so white?" This simple, and all too common, question shook her to her core. She then used the classic *Fresh Prince of Bel-Air* episode when Carlton isn't "black enough" to join the fraternity as support. During one of our one-on-one meetings for this assignment, she shed tears. This touching moment shone a light on my own psychic privilege. Two years later, another young Black woman whose general sweetness was spiced up by wonderful moments of a little fire and a lot of grit, stayed after class to finish a conversation about colleges. She expressed her inner dilemma of how to answer some of the essay prompts, particularly the ones that assume "hardships," including race. This young woman told me that of course her race had defined part of who she was, but that she did not want to be seen as relying on that or using it in any way to take away from her achievements, which were notable. She was merely expressing what everyone wants: to be known by and compete with your resumé, by your individual life. I told her I was sorry that she had to deal with that extra layer of anxiety, one that I never knew applying to college, or ever. I hated to see any student not be able to express their individuality both within and apart from any cultural expectations.

After the failure of Judge Mehrige's educational revolution, about thirty-five years of cultural evolution changed my old school. When I stepped foot back on campus, the fears of Innis and others did not seem to have materialized. Most of my early eyewitness observations of the students and subsequent honest classroom discussions dissipated them, given the amount of time and propinquity to do so. So when the accusations of "summoning your inner white girl," or "being a Karen," or "acting Black" or "not being Black enough" or "Asians are only good at math" have arisen, we were able to challenge those phrases as just more promotions of stereotypes, those "racial myths." We asked, what are the concomitant adjectives for any identity group? Any that come to mind seem to set one at the controls of a "you know what I mean" digger machine, boring deeper and deeper holes of presumption. The students, especially those of color, take most issue with these labels when laid on their long held notions of themselves as individual people, and also an identity as a burgeoning adult. However, our presentation rubric, and good thinking, requires a counterclaim.

In this case, the counterclaim is generated by the stalwart Theory of Knowledge precept of perspectives being shaped by both personal *and* shared knowledge. Therefore, what are the limits of the phrase, "I just want to be myself?" Kids over the years have concluded that in the realm of shared knowledge, or cultural knowledge, some overarching labels do have ultimate validity. It *is* justified to lay some kind of language on a common lived experience, whether privileged, minority, middle class, upper class, poverty, ethnicity, urban, suburban, education, etc. But that language, in turn, has descriptive limits in a fluid, diverse community. Those limits can create psychic and cultural expectations on one's lived experience that no one should have to clarify. As one of the ninth-grade Black girls in that all-female class answered simply "I'm just Lisa," when asked by her peers about her identity label. It stopped the conversation. For about fifteen seconds, high school girls and all.

In addition to the Presentation, each IB student had to write a high-stakes essay on one of six epistemological topics. Many of them often chose the one that spoke to this private/public origin of identity: "Labels are a necessity in the organization of knowledge, but they constrain understanding." Discussing this dichotomy with the students made me wonder if our current hyper-hyphenated taxonomy as Americans helps our mutual understanding of our shared humanity? In our suffocating narrow identity culture, is it possible for a white male, let's say one who suffered from deep insecurities, to speak to an Asian woman about her deep insecurities? Or have we gone too far down the path of "you cannot possibly understand what it is like to be me?" to the point that even our art could be ghettoized? To the point that the other's humanity is discounted? The seniors who wrote on this, especially the ones who took psychology, all acknowledged that it may not even be biologically possible to combat all the various biases that cannot help but organize taxonomies of people. Although, one girl offered a pretty original solution. She wrote that we should actually use *more* labels, the more the better, in order to know something or someone; that is the real necessity. This Venn diagram approach may more accurately categorize a fact, or a person, into their rightful place within important groups that do not constrain us in understanding them as a fully realized concept or human being. It also creates more diverse overlaps, more areas of commonality. Maybe replace hyphens with plus signs. Perhaps the diagram would also include circles of stand-alone adjectives severed from personal nouns or pronouns, like "kind," "hysterically funny," "ambitious," or "insightful." (A real-life example of this occurred while students filled out a mandatory survey during my last year of teaching. While the class was quietly bubbling in their names, a student named Michael—see below—yelled out, "Ms. Knapp, they want to know my ethnicity. I don't see 'Sexy' listed here.") This kind of Spirograph-ing of ourselves and our groups makes it much more difficult then, at least among the diverse young people at Tucker, as well as the American people, to disentangle and sort them out, or their culture, into a monolithic expression.

Innis's long-ago claim that Black and white "lifestyles" are just too different also begged a few questions for me. Among the "regular" kids at least, it was difficult to label their culture—music, movies, or even ways of speaking—as "typical," whether Black, white, Asian, Latino, or Indian. Taylor Swift seemed as popular as Lil' Baby. "Sexy" Michael, I'll call him, a raucously hilarious, tall athletic Black student with high energy and an old soul (he was the only kid to laugh at my corny Dad jokes, like "you have a face for radio") once proudly told me he loved all kinds of music. He proved it when he first asked me to play Ennio Morricone's "Gabriel's Oboe." Since showing "The Mission" in my long stint of teaching colonialism in Modern World History, that song became a haunting favorite of mine, too. It came to be a joke in class, though. During every test, Michael would yell out, "Gabriel's Oboe!" I obliged and immediate calm overcame them, and me.

During the annual senior awards ceremony held each spring, the top ten students were chosen along a sliding scale for good grades and school spirit. One year, as I watched from my seat in the freshman section of the gym's balcony, I noticed how the honoree lineup represented an almost perfect distribution of race and gender. The last student named was a very popular kid who was disabled and in a wheelchair. The lift was readied, and Ms. Allen cranked him up to stage level so he could roll across the stage to get his medal. The art teacher who was sitting next to me leaned in and remarked, "That's Tucker for you."

It is now. But she had no idea, like I do, how vastly different this Tucker gym looked from my Tucker gym close to fifty years ago. Sometimes, especially at pep rallies, I was haunted by the images of the ones of my day: super peppy, pig-tailed cheerleaders doing their white-bread, clappy cheers and modest jumps in short plaid kilt skirts and white cotton sweaters with an orange and blue megaphone appliquéd on them, while the white jocks strutted out to get their seasonal recognition and adoration. Then I would return to the present and see the multi-shaped, multi-race dance team in their Lycra outfits thrusting their hips and shimmying their chests; the Step team, mostly Black girls in coveralls and boots rhythmically stomping, jumping, and clapping while sporting faux mean faces at the senior boys of all races in the bleachers who are trying to get them to laugh; or the occasional Salsa performances by the Latin Dance Club. It may have looked like I was really enjoying myself there, living in the moment, and I was. But I cannot deny that the grin I shared with all the teachers, along with an involuntary headshake, also spread across my face because of the past, a distant past that never would have seen this coming. In Richmond, Virginia. Although, there was one obvious bridge between these two scenes: teenagers are perennially full of pep, and it is easily rallied.

Pep rallies are a tradition at Tucker, as they are at any high school. The South, Virginia, Richmond had been places that arguably valued tradition more than other regions of the country throughout our history. That is what made it, and perhaps makes it still for some, so difficult to see it disappear. Tucker High School is still Tucker, but its population does not resemble the school I knew hardly at all. The tendency to hang on to the old traditions is strong, though. It is supported by defining memories of a vastly different life. The fear of losing your roots, your familiar surroundings can paralyze your very sense of reality, much less identity, if you are unable or unwilling to make room for change.

Sometimes, teaching a microcosm of the world's populations with countless traditions between them, a crotchety old person's voice comes through my head, wanting to remind them that this is *my* high school, *my* home, *my* country. You are welcome to it, but it is still *mine* more than yours. Where were you when I was riding my bike to Westland Shopping Center to get French fries after school at W. T. Grant's, back in the corner where they had a little diner? Remember that? I don't think so. Where were you when my friends and I, at that same shopping center, joked about ordering ice cream at High's by choosing a stain color on the old lady's apron? Not here. Where were you when we tore Danielle Antonelli's pantyhose right off her legs in Cafeteria Three after she showed us a run in them? Somewhere else, I imagine. And by the way, where would you have lived since the county's development ended with Tucker and all the apartments you inhabit were woods? Huh? You have no idea of how it used to be. Other times, like I did so long ago as a newlywed in New England, *I* felt like the stranger in my own strange land. I am the immigrant, only this is my own backyard, a backyard I never left. I thought of this at Back-to-School night sometimes. All of the international parents who have actually experienced an epic loss of tradition, painful disorienting change, and even sometimes trauma—these parents were looking to me to help their child adjust and thrive.

Leave it to Karl Marx to recapitulate my experience of change. He wrote that when new social circumstances (the changing demographic of America) coincide with what he called an individual's "self-change," (my expanded notions of community), then we have ourselves a revolution. And in this revolution, according to Marx, "the *educator must himself be educated*." There was no organized revolution; it was more serendipitous. After the innocence of a couple of rare childhood interracial friendships collided with the harsh realities of my American history education, the hypocrisy of it all taunted me in those tumultuous, but idealistic, days of middle and high school. Some crazy unconscious onus fell on me, as though I alone could make it right. That burgeoning preoccupation with racial unfairness ended up in a near deification of Black people, another form of objectification. It was a mere intellectualized abstract, finding its only activism in a good-girl rebellion against my father, a short relationship with my boss at Sears, and a near obsession with Southern history reflected through my grandmother's town. But decades later, that rarity, that sampling, that abstraction, transformed into a very real, very flesh and blood new norm in the synecdoche of my old school. I did not have to train as an activist. I just had to teach all of the kids assigned to me at my old public school a little of our shared history. It could be said that it was a little disappointing because of how boringly normal the revolution turned out to be. For the most part, I found a wonderfully mundane atmosphere composed of many unique particles, defying the gravity of preconceptions. Sometimes you go looking for exciting differences and all you find are reassuring commonalities.

I remember asking my preppy Black Republican stalwart of the J. R. Tucker Debate Society if he thought his Class of '08 would ever have a reunion. My tacit implication was that *their* Tucker class couldn't possibly be as close as *my* Tucker class had been, back in the day when everyone had blonde, dirty blonde, or mousy brown hair, and a big majority of us had started first grade together. In other words, we had deep roots and were all alike. This is not unlike the specious argument some students—and pundits—make about how socialist policies work easily in Scandinavian countries because of their racial homogeneity. As soon as it came out of my mouth, I was ashamed for thinking that their many colors and backgrounds would prevent them from bonding as Tucker Tigers. Before he could even answer with the equivalent of a "hell, yeah" to a teacher, I realized my stupid assumption. He didn't pick up on it. One of my young colleagues, a Spanish teacher, was also Class of '08. In the teacher mailroom one day in 2018, she showed me some pictures on her phone of their very well-attended tenth reunion. I picked out lots of familiar faces, Garrett, Kosai, Elena, all looking so mature, pretty and handsome, and above all, happy. They were having the time of their lives.

The single most hilarious student I have ever taught, Damon, may have given me some kind of clue as to a connective tissue, a running bond between the past, present, and hopefully, future of this changed school, and maybe this changing country. A really sweet and careful, diligent student, he was in my first full year class in 2004 as a sophomore. It took me until November of that year to finally place his voice. He sounded exactly—exactly—like Tim Meadows of SNL fame and was equally as funny. Everything he said just sounded funny. He went on to do standup around town. In my desk forever had been his creation, a white mitten with black-Sharpied "shoes" on its pointer and middle fingertips, a big Sharpied smile across the hand with two giant craft store googly eyes above. Damon dubbed him Clive, the Break-Dancing Glove, the narrator for our epic French Revolution puppet show. This was the highlight of my teaching career, complete with a mini guillotine a kid built at home where we placed a ketchup packet under the unfortunate Charlotte Corday puppet. It perfectly exploded when the "blade" was dropped and her popsicle stick neck broke in half. And we got it on film! Act Five's group, charged with summarizing Napoleon's years, had a musical genius who wrote an original classical score to accompany a stop-action film, including toy soldiers set up across one of the vintage classroom maps of Europe. It even snowed one day and they filmed the Russian campaign outside! Damon's Clive would tell the camera, for instance, all about the Reign of Terror scene coming up in rhyme. Then Damon, from under the table, his hand extending up into the old puppet theater I found at a thrift store, would spin his wrist around a few times and break-dancing Clive would end up in a happy looking stance, his two shoe fingers casually crossed like Fred Astaire, his pinky and thumb spread out as if to say, "ta da!"

After I had Damon, he and a few of the others from that awesomely fun class would pop their heads into my room to say hi. We also shared a few good, deep talks, too. A couple years later when he was a senior, I had duty in Cafeteria Three during his lunch. I often waved to him and some others then carried on small talk with whomever I had duty that week. But this one day, I couldn't help noticing the table full of guys sitting with Damon—white, Black, Asian, Hispanic—but that wasn't the point. He must have been on a roll. The dudes were shoving their chairs back from the table, literally losing part of their lunch, in convulsive laughter. He just calmly kept delivering, straight-faced, whatever routine he must have been exploring, not stopping to laugh. I was jealous that I couldn't join them.

And because I remembered my own bouts of hysterical laughter in that very same place, those very Formica tables, in that very same cafeteria. Seeing that ethnically diverse group of silly minded guy friends bent over in hysterics, made me think back about thirty years when it was my silly minded all-white girl friends riffing on those Lorna Doones. It makes me wonder. Is there some kind of enduring effect of a place, a school cafeteria—a country—where the characters of whatever decade both shape and are shaped by its unique vibe? What was the vibe of Cafeteria Three? Was there something about that cafeteria, that place of communion, where kids of all types have broken pizza and chicken nuggets together since 1962, or back then, spaghetti and Salisbury steak? Is it possible that its linoleum and concrete produced some magical dust (besides the asbestos) that cast a mysterious force over those who entered, making them feel free to be who they are, free to belong and to be accepted, and then to contribute their best jokes and genuine friendships? Some may have seen a run-down, dimly lit, Venetian-blinded old school cafeteria, but I saw history. It is a history that has had way more to do with the inner spirit of the place than any outer demographic change.

I like to think that maybe some of us old timers, some of the early funny Founding Tigers, laid a Foundation of Cool, a kind of cool that came from knowing who we were, despite being the Rodney Dangerfield High School of the West End. Like those other Founders, we first Tigers were ridiculously homogenous. But our pride, especially in light of the superior reputations of other schools, was in our creativity and self-assuredness and genuineness. It seems *that* lasted into a future where these new kids' origin stories are wildly different than ours, but who seem to love to laugh with each other as much as we did. I also like to think that some of what I gleaned from my idealistic 1970s there when we could only yearn for equality helped me enjoy it even more when that equality showed up on *my* old campus, as just a new generation of Tigers.

A public school is based on random boundary lines, and Tucker's are particularly random. That students are thrown together simply because they fall within those same lines is a rather absurd idea. What they share in common is mere geography. I think of some of the nearby boundary lines that contain a more mono-cultural school population, say more like the old Europe, the France or England that Americans left behind. These geographies make more sense to the pattern-seeking, categorizing brain. Tucker's population appears to follow no discernable pattern at all. Kids from several dozen countries and cultures join together as friends and form lasting bonds just from four years spent together at a public high school. Indeed, the absurdity of that cafeteria, of that gym, those pep rallies and honor assemblies mirrors the whole idea of America itself. America the Absurd. America the Beautiful.

PART THREE
A Renaissance in My Late Middle Ages

The bedroom breathes
In clicks and clacks
Uneasy heartbeat, can't relax
But then your hand takes mine
Thank God, I found you in time.

PAUL SIMON, LOVE AND HARD TIMES

Alohas

A coconut bra and grass skirt lay in a cellophane wrapper in the walk-in closet of the extra bedroom for months. It would not be inaccurate to say that I kind of hid them there when my just-turned-sixty "boy"friend brought them back from his trip to Hawaii. With a little snarling Elvis lip action and jokey bedroom eyes, he handed over the long, crunchy bag illustrated with palm trees and a shapely cartoon Hawaiian dancer. I grinned. Then my eyes widened with fear—the same fear that had followed me into dozens of dressing rooms over dozens of springs carrying a dozen bathing suits over my arm. Certainly this gift was just for fun, destined to stay in the cellophane for everyone's safety. Or was there an implication, God forbid, of modeling it? An Endless Summer wave of anxiety washed over me while I laughingly accepted the gag, then promptly placed it out of sight. Yes, of course it was a gag. Which was what I predicted the reaction would be if I ever wore it.

One evening after work a few days later, while looking for something in that closet, the shapely Hawaiian lady dancer on the wrapper caught my eye. Then she slyly whispered something to me from her healthy cartoon body image, *"Just try it on."* Standing in the closet looking at that coconut bra surrounded by lengths of tawny grass, the fake lei, and bonus fake flower for behind my ear (not that that would be the focus if I were to wear this getup), I took her dare. Besides, it was just we girls. I ripped open the bag. First out was the polypropylene coconut bra. It would require conjuring up all of my 1971 macramé skills to adjust the twine along the top's limited square inches (these cups must have come from the coconut tree's training bra species) so that it would not only cover but somehow defy the findings of Isaac Newton on my bosom. After several tries I discovered that if I leaned forward just a bit and spread the coconuts out wide down the horizontal twine, quickly tied it around my back, then the verticals tightly around my neck, I was in business. That is, as long as I didn't laugh too hard, or sneeze. Taking a chance on a nip-slip laugh, I gazed in the upstairs bathroom mirror and raising my hands high over my head, rolled my hips from side to side, stretching out my torso as far as possible in an attempt to simulate the hula dancers I'd seen on Hawaii 5-0. In reality, I was trying to simulate slenderness. All alone in that bathroom, I failed on the laughter front, my left boob promptly popping out of its coconut. However, as in only a very few, very rare exceptions in a lifetime of body hang-ups, I did feel a twinge of what I long perceived other women knew more instinctively—a kind of feminine power. I quickly retreated, though, into my lifetime self-image of functionality. I threw away the crinkly cellophane but saved the paper tab with Little Miss Sexy Skirt as a reminder of my new companion's sense of humor.

Months rolled by. It was now fall. I went into that closet to grab a blanket. There she was, my little be-grassed alter ego. I grinned at her.

She issued a snide little dare to my sense of humor and self-respect: put on her outfit for my faux-Polynesian benefactor who lay across the hall in my bed. I argued back in my mind that he had probably already forgotten the souvenir that he "stuffed into my suitcase just for you" and any expectation of its demonstration. Yet she persisted and got into my head, which was where I'd spent most of my life. Maybe it was time to do a little redressing. And while I was at it, maybe redress some of my past notions of physical attraction. It had been almost a year and a half since I dared to imagine a life after divorce and this most unexpected, later in life affair began. Still, the refrain that began in the silence of my car after we first went to JJs Bar as colleagues returned as I took off my flannel nightgown in that closet: "*What is wrong with me?*"

At my age, this sexy stunt represented something patently, and pathetically, novel. Back in high school, often, by which I mean regularly, some boy or another eventually got around to wondering if . . . uh, if, well, you know, homecoming dance coming up and all . . . if I would maybe see if one of my cute cheerleader friends would consider going with him. Just check. Like don't be too obvious. While listening to the heart cries of these guys, I would stand there in the cafeteria or on the sidewalk all eager to help, not feeling quite like one of their male friends, but certainly not fully female either. This may have been the genesis of my aforementioned historic, and somewhat exaggerated, neuter complex.

The neuter complex presented as a twisted, fairly naïve by-product of a healthy ego and sense of self, unself-consciously bestowed on me by my parents. In other words, in the body-mind-spirit trifecta of human attraction, my assumption was that the primary motivators for everyone were of the latter two types, which were my fortes. The reason I had attracted good friends of all genders was because of "personality"; positive feedback came from humor and "deep thoughts," not outward appearances. If I were to walk away from a group, I would have been thinking how I left them laughing; not about how I looked from the back. It must have been some kind of developmental issue. I never seemed to get what some girls understood at various points during high school, or middle school for a couple of girls: that they had a different body shape than boys, a shape that they *knew* drove those boys crazy. On the flip side, I do remember the first time I noticed, and then studied, and then kind of admired the anatomical difference of men's hips. Specifically, Andy Griffith's hips. I was in fourth grade. In between my laughter at Barney's antics, I'd find myself staring at the lower half of the Mayberry sheriff in his khakis in wonderment.

I also suffered from a lifelong relentless comparison to other women that began in high school among four or five friends with "perfect figures" who, in reality, were probably only fifteen to twenty pounds lighter than me except for those two weeks junior year when I had mono and couldn't swallow. When I caught a glimpse of my emaciated self in the reflection of the doctor's office door, I had an evanescent glimmer of the perfect girls' regular mirror experiences. It could have been the old, vitrified door glass, though. Some of those girls grew into women who understood sexual power, and how it leads to emotional bonds, not the opposite. Then there are the rest of us. Like my country-haling-turned-suburban neighbor down the street once said at the bus stop in reference to some gorgeous kindergarten mom in our cohort, "Yeah, about the only thing I have in common with her is a vagina."

Adding to the neuter complex was my early puritanism, the appliqued jean jumper sect of puritanism formed in some kind of Bible study where coconut bras were not often worn. So, from puberty to my late fifties, I had been swinging between, and clenching tightly to, those perfectly timed trapezes of religious sexual hang-ups and secular body image hang-ups. If I let go of one of them, the other one swung up just in time for me to wriggle my sturdy body around and get hung up on them. This required a focused anxiety and epic self-consciousness, both of which landed me always safely on one of those safe platforms, perfectly safe. So here I stood at fifty-six trying to come out of my literal closet, to let go without a safety net, all of those metaphors that involve risking decades of insecurity, to be confident enough to show myself, to be seen as a way of giving. Not to mention, just have some fun.

It was a late fall evening, past dusk, which created a fuzzy camera filter effect in my bedroom, the single greatest factor in my decision. Plus, I knew that my companion would have already taken off his glasses for bed. The challenge was on: I tied the itchy grass skirt around my thrice-1980s-childbearing hips; shoved my boobs (most of them) into the polypropylene coconuts; put the lei around my neck; and, what the heck, added the pink silk flower behind my ear. I raised my hands over my head and sucked in my stomach. *What is wrong with me?* I made my big entrance, almost completely sober, stopping about ten feet from the bed, the fading light from the bathroom window behind me, which I hoped was creating a fantasy silhouette. The hands and hips took over for *at most* ten seconds before I burst out laughing and raced over to kiss him. Running out of the room to return to where I belonged, in my flannel nightgown, I heard, "That was worth the $16.99, alright."

* * *

For my fiftieth birthday in November 2007, my husband and my brother organized a nice dinner party. About twenty good friends made the trek out to the country on a cold November night and hid in my basement to surprise me. My mother did not attend. For months before my big day, she was still feuding with my younger brother over, what else, money. They had some lame agreement that he would pay her basic expenses as remuneration for buying my father's failing auto parts business years back, a business my brother then made extremely successful and sold at a windfall profit. Yet she demanded more and more in the form of "extras," a word that could have become a Chardonnay drinking game we played during my after-school visits on her back porch. Another source of their friction was her unilateral financial decisions. Whereas her old friends thought she had moved to the moon in the mid-seventies, thirty years later she was sitting on property a mile from the swanky new Short Pump Town Center and at the butt end of massive development. This had increased her land's value over five hundred percent. Knowing she had more equity, she refinanced several times—without my brother's knowledge—and bragged about cashing out. We would all pay for that later. So on my one fiftieth birthday, she was not there to witness me being the center of attention for once.

Whenever I think of that birthday party drama, even though I can still get a little bitter, I purposely shift to a more intimate memory of my mother being at my house the year before. That in itself was highly unusual somehow, those rare occasions when she made the forty-minute trip into my domain. I was able to see her more purely then, as someone between my guest and my mother, our relationship less encumbered by a past in which I often felt at once indispensable and yet ancillary to her real priorities. Yet on this occasion, the first Fourth of July in my new house, she came to visit. After making her favorite dinner of grilled salmon (which she always over-pronounced like the author Rushdie's first name—Sal-Mun), Mom and I moved on to the front porch. He went on to bed around 7:30, as was his habit. She sat in an old metal glider she had given me, and I rocked in Granddaddy's high-backed chair.

It was dusk. The mountains across the road were glorious in the fading summer light. In some unspoken generational, familial, geographical mandate about front porches and rock-able seats, we talked. Like we had done in my childhood bedrooms, over phone calls during college and young motherhood, and on her blue-gingham back porch in my middle age. Sometimes we hashed out family problems, but as she entered her eighties, we often revisited troves of family history and topics that ranged from the religious to the philosophical. Her narcissism and temper always loomed under the surface, but that had greatly waned as she aged. For the most part, we enjoyed each other's company like with no other. She maintained her natural curiosity until the end, once at age eighty-nine asking my youngest, "Stephen, so tell me what is this cap and trade?" Another time she inquired of me, "Now what do they mean by an 'app'?" This night she sat with her legs crossed in front of her on the glider, quite a feat after knee replacement. At eighty-four, sitting like that, even with her pure white, teased-out perm, her impish essence shone through.

The sky had grown dark by nine o'clock. In the middle of our routine conversation, we both noticed a spray of red lights across the road behind the tree line of the fancy bed and breakfast. She raised her torso up to see over the porch railing. Then we both stood up to catch the free show. Far enough away to miss the sound but close enough to see, the little explosions of blue, green, white, and red hung in the air in the dark silence of rural Virginia. I had rarely seen Mom just enjoy life: she didn't ride a bike; she never got her bathing suit wet on vacations because she never learned to swim (so why did I need to? I begged her for lessons—at fifteen!); she didn't read books or listen to music. It had always seemed to me that life, to her, was found solely in the realms of close, satisfying friend relationships and intractable family ones. With her, I fell somewhere in between. But on that night, we stood side by side, on my porch, at my house, and she put her arm around my waist. Uncommon for us, we simply enjoyed the view of something outside of the two of us.

* * *

Only one week after our renewing trip through New England to celebrate our twenty-ninth anniversary, on yet another Fourth of July, the great unraveling of my history began. It started with his excuse to go to Lowe's to get some tomato stakes. It was urgent. No matter that it was early afternoon and the white wine had been breached. I begged him to wait until morning, but from the upstairs window I saw the gold 240D spewing its blue diesel cloud out of the driveway. Decades of anxiety trained me to generate thin rationales: it was only six miles round trip. Gardening was a good hobby; what could possibly go wrong? Maybe he was right in his longstanding criticism, "you worry too much." Which I did after he did not return for over an hour. I called his flip phone. No answer. It was a painfully beautiful Saturday. He had left a golf tournament on television upstairs. I noticed it as I stepped out onto the balcony from that room. From my high perch on that Independence Day, I gazed across at the blue mountains whose beauty had begun to repulse me. That idyllic setting contrasted way too much with the absurd plot that was about to unfurl beneath them. I wondered if I should go looking for him. No need. My growing panic turned to bafflement. There he was, emerging from behind the tree line on the road—on foot. Where was the Mercedes? As soon as I asked myself that, I answered it with the historical obvious; it had broken down. But why was he coming from the opposite direction from the shopping center? He crossed the road on to the far-off part of the ten-acre field. For about the length of a football field he zigzagged towards the house like a fully erect running back dodging oncoming defenders with a motion like one of those car dealership air people.

Unable or unwilling to answer my questions as they grew louder and louder, he came in the front door and staggered up the steps before making a beeline for the beat-up leather loveseat. He flopped down under the glare of Tiger Woods and friends who were rightfully outside on such a beautiful day. Then he was out. Panic set in. I got in the Subaru and tried to calm my nerves in fear of what I might find. Judging by the direction he staggered home, he must have taken the country way. A mile down our road, I took a left at the familiar, dilapidated country store. In no fewer than a hundred yards, I saw what I feared. The car was in the ditch in front of the 1790 farm's fence, part of which had been swiped off. Even worse, two sheriff cars and one Virginia state cruiser encircled the scene; the big country law enforcement dudes swarming around the stupid old Mercedes.

Great shifts in history often start with a moment of truth. I had avoided those, avoided conflict my whole life. But that was before this six-two, 220-pound crew-cutted state cop halted my car, commanded me to roll down my window, and scared the living shit out of me. Leaning into the window, he first asked for my license and registration, glared at it, and kept it. Then he asked if that car in the ditch belonged to us. He meanly told me to put my phone on the dash and not touch it, I guessed so I couldn't call home. He asked me a series of, I imagined, wildly illegal, invasive, and leading questions. "Does he suffer from depression?" "Has he had an alcohol problem for very long?" "Does he often drink and drive?" I almost expected him to ask me to assess his relationship with his mother. I was in a kind of shock. My brain scrambled to answer him, knowing that anything I said could be used as evidence in an inevitable court case. I was shaking from mini-PTSD and sheer, fibrous anger.

All the good will built up over our trip just a couple of weeks past vanished. The married "we" began to pull apart into the first-person singular that Fourth of July. Later, he wanted to apologize, but syllable-by-syllable his words had become lighter and lighter, having no grounding, no tether to the lived truth of the last few years.

Personally or collectively, we walk that fine line between senti-mental nostalgia on one side of our histories and bitter revision on the other. We are mightily tempted to cross into the one that makes us look better in retrospect. It is nearly impossible to maintain personal historicity, to remember the past as it actually was in that moment, not to mythologize old times for better or worse from the lens of the present. I will not erase my ex as a young father from the countless scenes of soccer, or basketball, or hockey games in the tiny grassless backyard or the ping-pong matches inside. Or the amazing homemade obstacle courses he made for birthday parties in that same backyard. Or the many teams he coached with one or the other sons and their friends. However, we must sometimes sacrifice the once great paradigm of the past when it shifts and threatens survival in the present and makes the future obsolete. Finding that exact moment, that pivot in time when change occurs is the hard part. The first day of notes (back when kids took notes) on the French Revolution included both its fundamental causes—ones built up over time, and the immediate cause, the triggering event—the storming of the Bastille. Likewise, a scene in the movie *Gandhi* reenacted the relocating of the Muslim and Hindu populations, and how they travelled in parallel, but opposite directions. This was a result of years of fundamental causes of tension, but the immediate cause of the oncoming civil war is simply a man throwing a rock at the opposing travelers. He threw a rock across a valley in India; I kicked over a glass of bourbon in a living room in Louisa.

It is true that we had been traveling in parallel but opposite directions, too. In actuality, I didn't have a direction at all anymore. My life had fully inflated with stress like a party balloon, and I had been pinching it shut for a very long time. Once I let go, it deflated with a huge farting sound and a caddywampus trajectory all over my rural Virginia county. That same trajectory became a metaphor for my personal history—not an upward spiral, more of the death variety. It took almost a year to bring up his case, and less than a half hour to issue the punishment. For about a month, I had the house completely to myself. No marathon driving. The constant tingling and tremors in my legs and fingers stopped. My breathing improved. I slept like a baby. I stayed after school and met up with some old friends. I think this was called having a life.

He returned a week early, perhaps expecting a welcome like a Union soldier home after the Civil War. It was not a good sign that my immediate reaction was disappointment. The mental reprieve from my intense anxiety during those three solo weeks ended abruptly with the anxiety of the upcoming holidays. Christmas of 2010 would not be just any old Christmas; a fiancé and a serious girlfriend were coming! Yet competing with the joy of preparation and a lifetime's anticipation of domestic, familial hospitality was an equally powerful fear of it all being ruined. Pulling into the parking lot at Lowe's to get some final festive doodad, it felt like my right cheek was about to hit my collarbone. I pulled down the visor mirror and was shocked at the sag, or extra sag, due to some weird palsy feeling. Miraculously, my doctor could see me in an hour. She reassured me nothing was wrong with my face. I was tempted to channel my father and make a joke at that grapefruit set up, but I didn't know her that well, and really wasn't in the mood. She then asked me three or four questions about what had been going on in my personal life recently. I was not used to a doctor going there. After a brief synopsis of the previous few weeks, and even briefer of the past few years, she spoke for my subconscious. "You're trying to decide to stay married or not." Shocked, I could not respond at first. But inside I was as relieved as if I had revealed that to a close friend. Somehow when she, a professional, stated it aloud, a sense of permission sparked.

A few days later, the long-awaited, long-imagined holiday scene came to life. The first morning at breakfast, my oldest asked if we wanted to see their gymnastics trick. Of course! He then promptly lifted his fiancé, stiff-armed, way over his head as she spread her arms like she was flying. So much fun! Later that night, we all stayed up, besides their father, in the living room by a roaring fire until nearly three in the morning playing Cards Against Humanity. For the first time ever, lovely young women sat around my dinner table talking girl stuff. We complimented each other's outfits. They helped cook. We giggled like girls. I just knew this would be the first of many Christmases, like in Downton Abbey, only in the Virginia country-side. We'd sing around the piano, play card games, have screaming matches between Father, Son, and Mother on a pressure-treated deck.

We had all gone to suburban civilization to see a *Star Wars* movie in two cars. The other carload arrived home first. We came in behind, laughing up the side steps before crossing the wraparound porch headed for the front door. Why do certain memories burn into us like movie scenes, complete with a soundtrack as we play them back in our minds? As I approached the living room window, the jaunty music stopped and the ominous theme began. There my angered son stood over his father, confronting him about drinking a homemade beer that he had told us was a gift for a friend. The three of us stepped outside as tempers flared. I left, still shaking, and joined the others watching football in the basement. The two of them soon appeared and everyone acted as if nothing had happened.

* * *

Four months later, I opened the back door of my son's Toyota and stared at my foot about to hit the sidewalk in downtown Portland, Oregon. I was there on a highly anticipated spring break to do fun wedding planning with my oldest and his fiancé. Just as I lifted my purse across my lap, my phone rang. It was my husband, in the middle of his school day. His last school day, as it turned out. Evidently, the real reason for his three-week absence came to light. His voice over the phone was calm, resigned, launching into a series of complaints about the place and how he had been thinking of moving on anyway. Again, shaking, ruination. I really didn't care about his reputation or that school or anything. Right or wrong, all I could think was, "How are we going to pay the mortgage?"

For the following year, I struggled. I did not struggle with commitment; that was still a given. I was in no way even subconsciously planning for a different future. I was struggling with keeping my heart warm. I could almost feel it trying to turn to ice, chamber by chamber in the cold wave of so many recent storms. As the new year of 2012 began, a tiny bit of hope emerged for salvaging my heart and a vision of some kind of future. He had his license back for one thing. Driving home from work that Valentine's Day, I even entertained possible romance. I arrived home to a homemade, heart-filled sign on the door—and him slightly staggering over a pan at the stove. He had made a steak. That was nice, even though it was only five o'clock. He decided to take some of it to his mother, a twenty-five-minute round trip. I pointlessly asked if he had been drinking, and he said no. Lying had become so second nature that challenging it had become exhausting, and seemingly the full extent of my intellectual life. While anxiously waiting for him to return, I strolled into the living room and for some reason walked around the far end of the blue loveseat. That's where I kicked over that glass of bourbon onto my Chapter Eleven rug.

It had been four decades since my mother had called me selfish, maybe only twice, but for a sensitive kid and later aspirational Christian its sting lasted. That night, though, a whole slew of other self- words conspired to turn me into some kind of freedom fighter: self-aware-ness, self-respect, and especially self-preservation. How far must I go to honor "those things we said in white dresses so long ago" as my friend Dianne once said? The long fuse that for many years I had warned him about somehow reached its end that night. Its ignition should have been something much more dramatic: like inviting a guy he'd met while he was away, a man who murdered his son-in-law, into our home; or abandoning some burning leaves that started to move toward the house before I raced down there with the hose; or several times finding bottles of bourbon out in the open in his car long after the fence swipe. No, it was just a little glass of hidden alcohol—and all the lying it represented—that kicked me over the edge. I slept in the other room. The next morning, he came to that door, repentant as usual. I told him he needed to find somewhere else to stay for a while. Telling of his true wishes about freedom and responsibility, he did not, and never would, argue or beg, or promise. He obliged. In some ways, I think he might have been relieved.

For my entire life, I had never been alone at night. But there are many types of fear. I would take the gamble of sleeping in this big house in the middle of the country all by myself over the other threats to my existence. Actually, I wasn't completely alone then. I had my sweet old hound dog Barley who could still jump up on my high bed to sleep with me. If she could have, she would have responded in what surely would have been her Scooby Doo voice with an irritated, "Ahhright, ahhready!!" after I told her out loud that night—at least three times—"I'm not going to be afraid in my own house."

I had never put much stock in therapy, more precisely therapists, since I had been one to my mother since around fourth grade. I had listened to and offered advice for decades about my husband's issues. However, I changed my assessment of the profession when I visited a local person named Bob. Bob the Therapist started seeing my husband in the spring, then saw us both separately and together into the summer. In my sessions with him, bells went off; knots unraveled; birds sang in my head. I recorded a summary of them in a floral journal:

> His first comment was "you want to _make_ meaning out
> of what has happened to you." Right away—good. MAKE
> meaning—integrate. Perhaps my self-image as analytical
> and perceptive can't reconcile subconsciously the fact that
> two people took advantage of me for so long . . .

> Why do I need to excuse my mother? Just like I spent
> forever excusing my husband—to my detriment, excusing
> his irresponsibility. My constant insecurity over $ and not
> being able to run my own life with a plan. That is huge to
> me and he always called that a lack of faith in Jesus. So
> manipulation—that is the word—my anger at myself for
> allowing them to manipulate me in the big ways.

I was to see Bob again on July 3, a Tuesday, at four o'clock. I arrived at the office, but it was deserted. Once back in my car, my phone rang. Bob was so apologetic and wondered if I could come in the next day—the Fourth of July. Another Fourth of July added to my personal history. Once there, Bob told me in no uncertain terms that my husband would only make progress in his life without me. Exactly three years to the day from the opening shots of some internal war begun on that country road with our car in the ditch, Bob, like my doctor hinted at two years earlier, gave me the final permission to surrender. Much later in my life, I would wonder why I needed anyone's permission to claim, or really reclaim, some internal freedom, to declare some psychic independence, to pursue a singular happiness.

A week later that same July, my husband wanted to meet. We had been separated since February 15th. By President's Day, I already felt a return to a blissful outer predictability and soothing inner calm. He asked to meet for lunch at a strip mall, a nice one with a Target, because he had the remnants of a Bonefish Grill gift card his brother had given his mother. I am not sure he knew that for me this was the end. I was nervous, thinking of how to time and frame the pronouncement with respect for our shared past but protection for my singular future. Right at the end of the meal, I said it would probably be best to make our arrangement official and permanent.

At that exact sad and rather monumental moment, from across the nearly now empty restaurant, our names were being called out with raucous enthusiasm and serendipitous joy. Well, well, well. What do you know? It's one of our very oldest couple friends from college and the old church in Williamsburg, some of the nicest, funniest people I've ever known. We cheerfully caught up on each other's kids and reminisced about people from the old church. Of course, they had no clue what we were doing there. Near the end of our talk, this thing started happening that often accompanies moments of serious awkwardness in my life. It's a kind of out-of-body, third person, breaking the fourth wall and seeing funny when what is happening is not funny; no doubt inherited from my father. This time I hovered over the booth watching myself fake it through this ridiculous plot twist. Eventually they got up to go, hugs all around, no clue whatsoever.

Like in all major shifts in history, the trauma and disorientation of leaving part of the past behind gives way over time to a new relationship paradigm, a new way to relate to that past drained of its immediate emotion. We ended that Bonefish conversation on an agreeable, almost inevitable note about our separate futures. As before, he seemed relieved. Of course, I would periodically fight some retrospective resentment for years. As more time passed though, my overwhelming, almost debilitating at times, emotions were disappointment and shame, until they gave way to a kind of uneasy acceptance. In that same elapsing time, much to his credit, there was no drama, no resistance to a new, better kind of relationship, and even open acceptance and welcoming of my new life. Back on that hot July afternoon after seeing those old friends, he went to the restroom. I stepped out on to the narrow sidewalk to wait to give him a ride. I looked over at Target and shook my head at what just happened. I had just ended my thirty-two-year marriage at a strip mall. Waiting there for him, a lyric from "It's Too Late, Baby," a song on the first record I ever bought, Carole King's *Tapestry* blared from Bonefish's outdoor speakers: "There'll be good times again for me and you / But we just can't stay together, don't you feel it too? / Still I'm glad for what we had, and how I once loved you . . ."

On Your Mark, Get Set, ...

In the last throes of marriage, my resident fear of financial ruin lost its key to the penthouse of my psyche. I knew that I would carry the full burden of paying for the house, but that stress did not compare to the kind that had threatened my health. Even with those post-2008 HARP adjustments, my mortgage would be about 70 percent of my teacher salary (frozen for several years then)—40 percent more (hilarious)—than is recommended. But going 100 percent against my practical, planning brain, I just threw my hands up in trust. The spiritual—not fund—type. Besides, I had been trying to predict the unpredictable for decades anyway. Only those predictions did not involve me. Others soon did. Five years before my marriage decision, my artwork merged from sidewalk shows onto the information superhighway. One night in 2008, I was possessed by some kind of technology ghost, most likely my late father's, in yet another nonverbal show of Daddy's love from his platform beyond. I made my own website. "Notification of payment received" in all caps soon followed in my Gmail one day. Hold on. What is this? A scam? Oh, wait. No. Someone in Altoona wants a Pronoun mug! More "notifications" trickled in here and there from grammar nerds all over America.

Only three months after I was completely on my own, a gift agent from California wanted to represent my grammar line at the New York and Atlanta gift shows. This stuff that I designed on my school computer's Publisher program, applied with my two hands on plates and mugs on my ping pong table, and then fired in my basement kiln was headed to New York City! GrammarRULES was going national! For the next few years, wholesale orders came in from all over the country. My profit per piece was a bit depressing but taken as a whole, that influx gained me entry into the edges of that unknown land of Discretionary Income. It came at a cost, a substantial physical toll on my mid-fifties body. So many nights after teaching all day, I smacked those labels on, or fired up the kiln, or sat on the guest bed watching *The Voice* and smashing each mug into an individual box for one picky Brooklyn store. Four times a year, I lugged those forty-pound boxes up from the basement to place in an even bigger box of Styrofoam peanuts in the guest room so I could walk them out that door on to the wraparound porch for the UPS driver to pick up while I was at school teaching the causes of World War One.

Mema loomed large in my mind during this time because I added another income source from this new concept called Airbnb. A dozen or so folks rented the downstairs guest room before I got the courage to rent out the whole house. I had many, many takers for a weekend in the country, which greatly helped me stay afloat on that frozen teacher's salary. Keeping the house up, as in painting, cleaning, refurbishing, repairing, cutting the grass (my fellow country-dweller friend Paige says, "nothing like a good mow"), tapped into some ancient trait of the Egerton women who never looked to anyone but themselves to do all of that. I can easily summon a mental picture of Mema in her seventies cutting the big grassy plot behind her house with a push mower. It makes me feel guilty that I had a riding mower, unreliable as it was at times. Most every Sunday afternoon, while stripping the dirty sheets or cleaning the bathrooms, thoughts of her came easily. When I got in a funk about my financial situation, then another funk about all the work required to keep a rooming house going on top of a teaching job and a tiny gift business, I gained literal strength from realizing her blood runs through my veins. This is the feminism I have known: a shit ton of work and a shortage of cash. Much like me, she must have also been acutely aware at all times of her bank balance. She had her Norlina Tourist Home. I call my place the Three Notch Tourist Home and International Conference Center.

On Valentine's Day, one year to the day since kicking over that fateful, bourbon glass, I got a call from my true loves. My oldest son and his darling wife were inviting me to join them in Paris for six days in the coming summer of 2013. I could hardly respond; I was so moved. And maybe a little nervous. This was a foreign proposition in all ways. When others in my cohort began to travel, I masked my jealousy with some faux disdain at its pretension and wondered how anyone could afford it, when my discretionary income was limited to the dimes and quarters I found in the washer. I was fifty-five and did not even possess a passport. I had only flown twice in my whole life. But when your son invites you to Paris, you go! To pay my way would require a drastic move: I would teach summer school. Six weeks of June and July in my classroom with twenty tenth graders would buy six days of August in the French capital with my kids.

Our history department was envied, we liked to think, for our sense of fun. Every day about ten of us, a couple more men than women, enjoyed lunch together. We heard that other departments ate in silence or talked about the latest administration email. Not us. It was an unspoken rule that no one could talk about school stuff for more than two minutes. Instead, we discussed history, and sometimes current events, but mostly we just cut loose. Some of the young guys quoted movie lines in character, or we tried to one-up each other with jokes laden with double entendre, or cracked on all of the dumb stuff the students said or did, or just used that twenty minutes to let out any pent up "Fucks!" that must be suppressed around the students who sometimes make you want to say "Fuck!" Having had three boys, I was right in there most days seeing and raising the pun or zinger ante. Although word got around about my split, this was not the time or place for any personal "sharing." But one day my excitement got the best of me. I revealed that I was teaching summer school, and why. My colleague Mark kind of lit up. He had just been to Paris over spring break and told me to come around to his classroom to see his photos.

Like the rest of my fellow teachers, I really did not know much about this person except, like everyone, his much younger wife fought breast cancer for over a decade and had passed a year ago. I also knew he enjoyed a countywide reputation as a stellar teacher and track coach, so much so that he was wooed over to Tucker from another school by the same department chair that hired me two years later. He was voted Most Favorite Teacher by the students almost every year of his career. His test scores, despite not caring about them, ranked at the top of the history department. Kids filled his classroom before school every day to joke around, and often some needy kids got a couple bucks on the sly for lunch, or a water for ten cents from his personal Kroger supply instead of having to spend a dollar in the vending machine. His teaching style belied all the claims of an ever-changing pedagogy handed down from on high. He was the sage, a hilarious and knowledgeable and unrepentant sage, on his Room 58 stage. Weirdly, as our mutual students pointed out, he could not teach without his own "stick of learning," just like the dowel rod that a kid wrapped with a masking tape handle for me. As loved as he was by the students, he had a love-hate relationship at times with authority. He could put back a few in the right setting, too. And yes, he is Irish. Although his lineage must have included a healthy portion of "black Irish" because he rocked a kind of Papa Hemingway vibe—salt and pepper November to May beard, broad shoulders, and dark, sharply arched eyebrows over some killer green eyes.

When I ventured around to the back of Building Five, Mark was excited to show me the Paris pictures he had framed and put on his wall. Not because of me; because of his animating love of travel, begun early on in college with his Dennis Weaver–Matthew McConaughey mashup, deeply twangified roommate Alvin. They first went to Paris in the 80s, back when people used a paper map and evidently asked a lady at a booth in the train station about a place to possibly stay. (I can only imagine her trying to decipher Alvin's English.) Mark also took his family to Italy and Prague, and he went to Egypt and Germany with prize money he won twice from a prestigious teaching award, nearly unheard of for this huge monetary prize given to only twelve teachers chosen from among three school jurisdictions. As he stood right behind me looking at the photos, there was a little moment, maybe as he described the Arc de Triomphe, that I felt something unusual. It was something akin to femininity. I stopped listening. Something about a deep voice coming from about eight inches over my shoulder, feeling smaller, enjoying listening to his sheer enthusiasm "oh you gotta' see this!" A tiny waft of weird desire arose; what would it be like to escape into one of those pictures with him? What? Where did that come from? Stop it. That was stupid. We were colleagues. We were old. We were old colleagues. He doesn't even know me. Snap out of it.

This same year, 2013, would be my mother's last. Even though she was on her way out, from January to October, she was also on the go. She lived in four different nursing homes after she was pretty much kicked out of her original one, and, ironic for her Christian woman persona, ended up in a fantastic Jewish-run facility. At the end, nothing was really wrong except she complained of a back problem that weakened her to the point she landed in the basement with more medical attention. There, when I told her about the Paris trip, she squeaked out, "What a wonderful opportunity," which I took as her blessing. But as the end of August and the actual trip approached, she was fading and could barely speak. I put my face very close to hers and told her where I was going, and that I would be back in a week. Always a mother, she repeated "what an opportunity" and then told me to be careful at least three or four times. That was permission enough for me.

I just watched a silly little TV show called *Emily in Paris*. My show would have asked the unlikely question, *Am I Lee, in Paris*?! I had to get there first. This meant conquering a new fear, an international flight—alone. My anxiety levels just getting to Dulles Airport and parking were through the roof. Once I boarded, two impossibly handsome French pilots looked at me and simultaneously greeted me with a soothing "Bonjour!" instantly calming my nerves. The blonde, French-twisted flight attendants made me wonder, "Who are these people? How can they look so perfect?" Once that Air France free wine started flowing, all was well. Then I had to negotiate Charles de Gaulle. Now the train. At home, I had spent about three hours on this miraculous website that allowed me to walk virtually through the airport's interior to find the trains. The kids had drilled it into me. Take CDGVAL to Terminal 2—look for a green door to buy your ticket. The ticket, I mean *billet*, guy was helpful enough, but just to be sure, like other old lady travelers you see, I poked my head in the waiting train and asked sheepishly—and stupidly, "Paris?" Immediately, a gay couple from San Francisco welcomed me in with big smiles and reassured me that I was indeed on the RER-B. Like a spy getting her orders, I had been told to depart at the Luxembourg Station; walk straight ahead to traffic roundabout with fountain; look for brown awning on Café Luxembourg.

My son had a work thing so Alexis would be waiting for me. And there she was, as planned. My contact. Sitting at a little table facing the road like I had seen in *An American in Paris,* she looked adorable as usual. Only there, my petite blonde San Francisco daughter-in-law looked adorably French, and she is fluent! As for me, I may have been in the best shape of my post-kid life, having lost fifteen pounds and two pants sizes by not cooking for anyone but me for eighteen months, unless you count opening cracker boxes and wine corks. I made sure to dress comfortably for the flight, but also according to my notion of fashionable—black jeans, a crisp white cotton blouse, and J. Crew blue-checked cotton blazer found at the Fan Thrift Shop for just this moment. This was my movie. *Am I Lee, in Paris?* "Ma mère!" Alexis greeted me as I rolled up with my suitcase. Indeed, I had arrived. I did it. The payoff was pure joy. Joy I sensed from the other Parisian patrons, too, who smiled broadly at our huge embrace. After some midday wine and lunch, we walked into the Luxembourg Gardens. What was this, a Disney cartoon? I fully expected someone at the side entry gate to hand Alexis and me glittery ball gowns so we could swirl our way around the fountain a few times before exiting behind the Senate building for our apartment at 25 Rue de Tournon.

The week was magical, of course, because it's Paris, but more because of who planned it for me. Paris is the city of romance, but what I was feeling went beyond the romantic; it was the subtle euphoria of a rite of passage mixed with maternal bliss. A kind of six-day still point in the turning world of motherhood. This first child who so unexpectedly burst into my life when I was twenty-four, along with his two brothers not much later, became my familiar world. He, who as a baby had determined the very schedule of my day—and so many days to come, now scheduled my daily activities in a completely unfamiliar world. He and his wife opened up this world to me, one so far beyond the one circumscribed by the Richmond Beltway. But our family circle was broken, or maybe a little askew now. I am tempted to say that it was weird being there alone. It wasn't. It had been a year and a half of independence already. I think, not sure, that the kids included me as some "it'd be good for her" role reversal.

When I left my marriage, I knew that it deeply pained my boys, even though they were all adults living across the country and only came home once or twice a year. I know from experience that little kids hate to hear their parents fight, and the same goes for big kids. It may have been the most difficult part of my decision, knowing that I was ruining their concept of our family's future. I do not presume to know all of their feelings and reactions, but when I was in the thick of the craziness, the alcohol, the unreliability, they listened and understood. To varying degrees, each had witnessed it firsthand. I was determined though, as difficult as it would be, to mark an endpoint to my sharing with them. I was not going to do as my mother had and make all our conversations about "the problem." Because then I would live out the rest of my days as nothing more than "the problem." What better way to change the conversation than by casting our eyes outward to the walls of the Musée d'Orsay, or the old Tony

Curtis movie in a tiny Parisian movie house sitting in giant, comfy, blue velvet seats, or looking at the eighteenth-century apartments on the Place des Vosges while sketching them from the grass.

My brother called me while I was in Paris. Of course, I feared the worst about my ailing mother. Opposite. He could not wait to tell me about the conversation he had with Mom the night before. In her semi-drugged stupor, she blurted out, "You know, I never cheated on your father." What?! My family never talked about these kinds of topics—namely sex. (The only curiously vague reference came once from Dizzy in Mema's kitchen; something about old bodies, "well the sensation is all the same in the dark." What sensation, I wondered as a ten-year-old? That phrase has come to comfort me of late, though.) Of the millions and millions of words exchanged between Mom and me over fifty-five years, perhaps a few hundred concerned people's bodies. She was more interested in their words, their secrets, their feelings, including occasional nuggets of praise for her. As I got older, I did get a sense that my mother might have been a little frisky in her earlier days; she did not marry until thirty-two, and she really enjoyed the company of men, and vice versa. She went on, "But if I was going to cheat, it would definitely have been with ___," a former neighbor who later as a widower often came to see her after my father died. (In her mid-seventies, she almost spilled something to me about what happened on one of those visits.) My brother egged her on, "Why him?" She answered, keeping in mind that in just six weeks she would be dead, "Why do you think? He's sexy!" I had never, ever heard that word uttered from her mouth, except possibly once under her breath, after she watched Tom Jones sing "It's Not Unusual" on Ed Sullivan. My brother and I enjoyed one huge, prolonged transcontinental laugh. After I hung up, I told the kids this improbable tale to more guffaws from just thinking about an old lady having any remaining mojo. Until it happened again, only with me.

Our apartment in Paris was divided by a spiral stairway. One door to the right led into the living room with its giant open windows and view of Saint-Sulpice. A small kitchen and the kids' bedroom were in the back. My room was across that stairwell to the left, a tiny space with a twin bed and my own lovely private bath. That tiny room would become my own little Arc de Triomphe, a memorialized space in my personal history to which so much in the future would refer back. Alexis had taken a head shot of me in the Tuileries on Friday. Sunday I would travel back to Virginia just in time for Teacher—or Bullshit—Week, as we affectionately called those five days of interminable, pointless meetings. For fun, and in a kind of follow up to the Paris pictures Mark had shown me in his classroom, I emailed the photo to him on Saturday. The subject line was "Lee/Paris!!" I wrote, "This is where I was yesterday! See you in Café 3 on Monday!" Then from five years of taking Spanish, not French, I added "Se la vi!" Later that afternoon, as I readied to go out to our last dinner, I checked my school email for any back-to-reality info. Among the ones from the four principals was an email from Mark. I opened it maybe more eagerly than I realized. His response gave me a little start in my heart. Responding to the photo, he wrote:

"I thought all the great works of art were inside the Louvre :)
I am ready for stories." (He actually added the emoticon.)

Whoa. I stared at this for a long while. First of all, very clever. Second of all, very sweet. Third of all, me not used to this. Fourth of all, I'm fifty-five. To this day I can see myself standing there in my little Parisian home, confounded and grinning. Right then, Alexis popped in to see if I was ready to head out. Never was I, mother of three boys, so glad to have a daughter-person in my life. I held the computer screen up to her. She stared at it, then at me, and with her beautiful, dimpled smile, quite matter-of-factly replied, "Hmmm. I think he likes you."

Planes are just plain weird. You cannot think about the fact that you have placed your properly land-loving body in a flying tin can that is being propelled through the sky at about eighty percent of the speed of sound. But you can think about how amazingly it transports you from one world to another. I had been in glamourous Paris, France, between the Luxembourg Gardens and Boulevard Saint-Germain. A few hours later I was in the Walmart parking lot in Louisa, Virginia, between two Ford pickup trucks. There I shopped inside amongst a panoply of—not elegant French-twisted ladies—but my large rural neighbors who were tossing—not baguettes and brie—but Doritos and Cheez Whiz—not into their bicycle baskets but their motorized shopping buggies. Even still, that mysterious beauty of travel lingered. It lingered on into the next morning as I made my unceremonious entry through the fading blue, heavy metal door into a dimly lit, dirty linoleumed school cafeteria. From Café Luxembourg to Café Three. I wanted to yell at the top of my lungs to everyone, "I just got back from PARIS! Yeah, the one in FRANCE!" Instead, the epic buzzkill of all buzzkills squeaked over the portable microphone: "OK. Welcome back everyone. Let's have a seat. We need to talk about some new lunch procedures."

After enduring torture by a thousand PowerPoint slides, I finally saw Mark in the mailroom later that morning. He came bopping in as I was at my box. I played it cool about the trip—and his email. Very casually, he said, "Hey. How was it?" Then a wee bit more haltingly, for him, he added, "We should go to lunch one day this week. You can tell me all about your trip." Of course, I just as casually agreed. Weirdly at that moment, I couldn't help but think that even though this wasn't actually a date date, it was one more than I had ever had when I was a student on this very campus. Later that afternoon, I saw him a little ahead of me on his way to his car at the end of the day. As we both were about to get into our respective driver's seats, he summed up the coming week, which he often said only served to destroy a teacher's natural enthusiasm for a new year. "Well, summer's over. The bullshit has begun." I have no idea what came over me; but without pre-analyzing his reaction, my lifelong tactic, I slyly replied, "Well, we'll always have Paris." He grinned. I slipped in my car and drove away, also grinning.

I headed, of course, straight to Beth Shalom, to see my mother. Her condition had been lodged in the back of my mind the whole time I was away, but I did my best to be selfish, uh, I mean, live in the moment. I'd had her blessing though, for that "wonderful opportunity." Venturing down to the hospital-smelling basement with trepidation, I peeked around the corner to see her lying there, surprisingly awake. It seemed as though she had aged many times more than just the one week I had been gone. Perhaps the contrast of being with two early thirty-somethings in that life-filled city, my *joie de vivre* crashed into the sadness of her looming death, making her look more like a corpse than I wanted to admit. Still the old superior conversationalist Sarah survived. She knew exactly where I had been and asked me her signature pertinent questions. Her head was tilted ever so slightly towards me on the pillow and her watery eyes gazed at me as I spoke. I chose carefully how to answer, not to overwhelm her with travel talk, a foreign topic to her. She mostly just wanted to hear about the kids, anyway. Then I took a chance. After all, she was still my mother for a few more weeks.

"So, there's this man at my school."

As soon as the word "man" crossed my lips, it was as though an electric current passed through her convalescent bed and she, like Dr. Frankenstein's monster, shot to life.

"Who is it?" she pressed, with a slight lilting tone that could have been mistaken for a teenaged girl eager for the latest gossip. This was not the gravelly, pained voice of most of that summer.

"Well, another history teacher, a little older than me. He lost his wife two years ago."

My mother had witnessed all of my marital see-sawing. At times she became bewildered and grew frustrated at my blind support of all the changing jobs and puzzling behavior in the early days. Every once in a while, she even challenged me to challenge him on his responsibility, but I always defended him. My epic conflict-aversion syndrome could not have borne the two of them ever going at it. Besides, most of the time my "problems" did not live up to her problems. After so many years passed, and I was reaching my wit's end, literally, at our new house in the country, she was reaching the end of her familiar life in her beloved home that used to be in the country, but now stood at the end point of massive suburban growth. She did not possess the mental space amidst such a colossal move to console me. That changed once she settled into her new apartment. Just like during middle school, when my insecurities and disappointments overwhelmed me, she would come in my room and lay beside me and drape her leg across mine and encourage me about my future. Now as I was easing out of middle age, she listened about my past. Up to and through my separation, she listened to his antics and my anxieties until she could listen no more. As time went on, I sensed her growing impatience. I forgave her for that, after struggling with the wildly disproportionate amount of my life I had listened to her. But

I am realizing now as life goes on and your story is ending, it is hard to pop back into the realm of the unresolved. Still, she completely supported me when I needed it the most. It was actually good. As with my sons, I purposed to change the subject and pivot forward.

Woven through the countless conversations we shared over the years was a tacit assumption that the mother-daughter relationship was *the* relationship about which all others revolved. This seemed to stem from a condition—maybe, I wouldn't know—particular to mothers of girls. I was her daughter, always and forever. That bond is paramount. As she often said to me, "No one will ever love you like your mother." That is true. That truism had a codicil, though; the other relationships the daughter may have become part of the mother's story, too, as they impact her protection and love of the daughter. So it was in this last intimate moment with her, a final little footnote in our life story. I continued:

"He just asked me to go to lunch with him this week."

Despite the fact that she had no idea who this guy was, she made a snap judgment, one I interpreted as stemming from her respect for mine. Her following two words would become some ultimate parental permission slip, a last will for my happiness, and final testament to her love for me. Perhaps it will even be my epitaph. She looked straight at me. Now tired, her words spilled out slowly. In a tonal delivery to rival the Wicked Witch of the West's "I'm Melting!" she said:

"Pur . . . sue . . . it."

A broad grin involuntarily spread across my face. Like her admission to my brother Brian about our old sexy neighbor, I could not get over this late-stage symptom of Mom getting jiggy with it. Partly amused and wanting to hear more of her enthusiasm for my potential romantic life, and partly literally wanting to know her ideas on what to do, I followed up with, "How should I do that, Mom?" Without hesitation and with the authority of Dear Abby, she wheezily declared, "Invite him to dinner." I almost expected her to end that declaration with the moniker "dummy," but that was just my insecurity. I humored her, as one would a dying wish, by agreeing. But the whole idea of Mark Condon driving to my house in Louisa for dinner was absurd.

I went to lunch with Mark on the Thursday of Bullshit Week. Before this, he had only registered in my life as the popular teacher from Room 58. Now I was alone with him in a car. Beyond ironic for a long pattern to come, he drove. This lunch also flew in the face of the decade-long protocol I had observed about teacher day lunches: men eat with men at Joey's Hot Dogs, women eat with women at Olive Garden. But here, he and I were, one of maybe three tables of patrons at a nearby pub at 11:45 in the morning for a quick meal. Some initial observations included: his car was very clean, therefore he's as organized in his person as he was known to be in his classes, making copies for units months in advance; he was very open, as in he told me how much he weighed for some reason—I did not reciprocate; he asked great questions about Paris, so my fear of the awkward silence never materialized. In fact, awkward and silent are nowhere near any adjectives for him. Something prompted a two-sentence answer about my marital status, but no elaboration. We laughed a decent amount, especially at how I could not stop my habit of saying "gracias" everywhere we went in Paris. Riding back to school, I had a flash of feeling like I was sixteen and on a date, or more accurately, what my friend Nancy told me it felt like to be on a date then. I also got a stronger feeling, like the one when he stood behind me in his classroom back in April, that feminine smaller feeling. Only this time it came from sitting across the front seat from his larger frame and his pretty shapely black Irish hairy leg on the accelerator.

I could not have known at the beginning of the 2013–14 school year that I was about to be history. At least some outdated textbook version of me. But this is how history works. Eras and epochs are ascribed after the fact. Each year of my junior Theory of Knowledge class, to get the kids thinking, I posed the question: "why do we need new history books; aren't the old ones sufficient? I mean it's the facts. They don't change." That led them exactly where I wanted to go—interpretation, culture, values, authority, pretty much all of the knowledge issues we would explore for the coming two years, always requiring a justification of all of them under some overarching ethic. I, too, had already entered a phase of reinterpretation, of a shift in my personal culture. That would prompt something altogether new as I entered the suburbs of old age. At the risk of resuming my teacherly lingo, I'd say the biggest revision in my historical methodology, a biggie in our knowledge class, involved a reordering of the legitimacy of the authorities governing my actions. In other words, *I* would now do me. My patternicity (yet another) of neutered hesitancy and presumed invisibility would come to an end. *Pursue it.*

At the end of September 2013, my mother took a turn for the worse. As the month progressed, she just faded into the morphine. The last week of visiting her meant merely holding her hand and looking at her. She couldn't even muster the gravelly, halting voice of the two weeks before. On Friday, October 4, 2013, as usual, I stopped in after school. I arrived around five and stood at the foot of the bed. She stared at me for a while, then suddenly she spoke after weeks of silence. "Where's Brian?" So typical. Asking after my brother. I couldn't help it. I sarcastically responded, "*I'm* here!" and then moved to sit beside her. After hardly any words for weeks, she looked straight at me and said very plainly, "I love you." The next morning, Brian texted that she had passed away in the night. My eulogy seemed to write itself the night before her service. I tried to sum up her life:

From her mother and aunt, Mom inherited a dignity and pride that did not rely on one's socio-economic background, but from some combination of knowing where you are from and what you can do, and from knowing that you are deeply loved. This is what she passed on to me, too . . . Mom hated to read. She may have read five books in her adult life; instead, the stories she knew were those of her friends and family. Indeed, she may not have been a big reader, but she knew how to read people. On the flip side, she reacted to anyone who crossed her or failed her with equal force and an unmatched sense of justice . . . She was a great listener, and a charming, compassionate conversationalist. Too many times to count, I, like many of you, sat on the back porch, she in Mema's old rounded rocker and I in granddaddy's old high backed one, chairs from her mother's front porch. Those chairs saw us through a lot of life, and some death in over thirty years. Then, it was the two aqua wing chairs at Spring Arbor until it became the hospital beds where until only about ten days ago, we carried on the conversation. When my youngest son was around five, he asked me, in that philosophical phase of his life, "Mommy, where do all the words go?" All the words that I shared with my mother have piled up over the years, layer upon layer, and will now begin to be compressed into memory. Like you, I will miss her voice, more familiar than my own, but as I told her Friday night, I will never forget her. I leaned into her ear, on what turned out to be the last night of her life, and hoping she could understand me, told her that she had been a good mother, a good friend, and that we had written a good story together.

In the short space of about twenty months, the two relationships that had forever circumscribed my identity no longer defined me.

Another big turning point—in retrospect—came the next month, November. Its first day was a Friday, a pep rally Friday, but I was decidedly un-peppy. The end of the school day at the end of the school week, in my book, was not the time to listen to 1200 screaming teenagers, a half-hearted pep band, and the overly boisterous art teacher try to whip up school spirit for our perennially bad football team by screaming into a squealing microphone. No, Friday afternoons at this stage in my career were for decompression. That particular Friday only four weeks after my mother had died, left me even more languid. My grief had been gradual due to her slow deterioration. It would be dishonest to say that I cried a lot over losing her. Mostly, I missed the touchstone to my own history, our family history. So many times in those first few months, and even once in a while now—nearly a decade later—I say to myself, "I need to ask Mom about ___." The primary sources of that personal historical era, three adorable floral softcover notebooks from Anthropologie Alexis gave me, reveal just how content I was. I do mention an occasional desire for male companionship or attention, but in a strange way, my life felt full though I was alone.

Tucker's sprawling 1960s campus made skipping out that Friday so tempting, and so easy. The gym stood a full acre across campus from the Café Three parking lot and my car. The temptation was even greater because I didn't have a class. Each grade was called down one by one until all eight academic buildings were empty. Who would miss me? I waited in my classroom. When I was sure the coast was clear, I slipped down the eerily deserted sidewalk the opposite way I was supposed to be going, darted through the cafeteria dumpsters, and quickly dropped my briefcase in the backseat of my car. Then the first glint of guilt hit. I should probably go down to the gym and show my face so I didn't get in trouble. Yeah, that's the real me; doing the right thing, obeying the rules. I retraced my escape route and noticed that the lights were on in my department chair's room next to mine. I didn't want her to see me in such a compromised situation. So just in case she hadn't left yet, I went around to the back of Building 5 to head to the gym. Mark's classroom was on the end of that side. Well, what do you know? He was still there and the door was wide open. He was standing in the middle of the class holding both ends of his pointer stick, throwing out ideas to two students who were there to get help on college essays.

Having a more tenuous relationship with the rules than I did, Mark seemed not to even be aware that there was a pep rally, much less that we teachers were required to attend. We talked for a second, he never even asking why I was on the sidewalk in front of his room. After the two kids left, he got his things and just nonchalantly headed towards the parking lot, with like twenty minutes of contractual time left on the clock. So what did I do? I followed him. We chatted on the way there, but again, as we were about to get in our respective cars, Mom's advice echoed in my head. Pursuing it, I hinted,

"Yeah. I hate to go straight home on a Friday afternoon."

He paused. I could almost see some ancient mojo reignite in him, the mojo that his buddy Alvin called "digging your ditch before you lay your pipe."

"Do you drink beer?"

I remembered the advice my son's standup comic friend once offered about improv, always say yes. And thank goodness my sons had introduced me to good IPAs. A "No, I'm more of a white wine girl" might have been a deal breaker.

"Sure."

"Come on. Follow me. Let's go to JJs. It's over on Staples Mill."

In what would become a pattern for the next six months, each Friday we hustled over to this nondescript bar in a strip mall that housed a Hallmark Card shop and big Kroger. The key was to beat the crowd of old(er) people and blue-collar regulars to get the corner seats at the bar so "we don't have to turn our necks too far to talk," thereby minimizing any risk of injury. I cannot recall the actual questions I asked, but there were a lot of them, mostly about his youth and the adventures he had. Mark went through the 70s the "right" way, in experimentation and the sowing of the wild oats. I was evidently the weirdo. He spent his time at concerts and in bars; I spent mine in class and Bible studies. He traveled every chance he got in his bachelor 1980s; I had had three kids by then. I also made note of the number of friends he mentioned that were still friends many decades on, a rather notable fact for older men it seems. After a couple hours and beers and appetizers, we headed out towards our respective homes. As would also become a pattern, we both honked our horns as he slid on to the first beltway exit north and I kept going to the cloverleaf to go west. I did think how easy and fun it was to talk, but how he did most of it. That was fine with me, even though I had the glancing judgment of "typical male" run through my mind heading down the highway.

That proved to be very unfair. Back at school that Monday, as he was heading to his side of the building and I to mine, he casually remarked, "Hey that was fun. Next time, I'll ask *you* some questions." Hmmm. First of all, observant and self-reflective. Secondly, "next time." Thirdly, me felt some little wrinkle in my chest. I responded with a big laugh and "yeah, that was fun." A couple days later, he roamed around to my side of the building during our mutual third period planning block. The purpose was to see if this coming Friday would work. Sure. On that second evening at JJs, he did ask me questions, then he got a little serious. He opened up about something in his past, which is his story to tell, that he was not too proud of. The definite sense I got was that he was giving me an out even before either of us could have, or needed to, define our relationship. Some strange voice that was not exactly mine came through my head as he laid himself a little bare there before me. "I am not going to judge this person and his life." In light of my own past story and a new becoming, it seemed he deserved a do-over, too. His honesty, one of the initial manifestations of his what-you-see-is-what-you-get personality, actually endeared him to me. He trusted me with this information, and he did not want me to get involved if it bothered me. In that amazing process of how we become close to a former stranger, or colleague, this was one of the first of many cornerstones. In my former life, I would have judged someone like him, a lapsed Catholic, as needing that something more, that intimate relationship with Jesus, as a prerequisite for our own. My old born-again mindset had perhaps actually set me apart from others who did not strive for perfection, had no spiritual ambition, who did not use the same vocabulary. And yet, here he was confessing in all honesty and humility his humanness. No sanctimony. Besides, a couple days later at lunch, on his sixtieth birthday actually, he wore that butternut yellow Kohl's sweater and had exchanged his 90s-style, old-man, gold aviator eyeglasses for some pretty hipster black, square-edged ones. I might have noticed how they both looked pretty sexy on him, a newly minted sexagenarian.

The next Monday my feelings about his feelings (he was fond of bragging about his lifelong Irish absence of feelings until I asked, "you get angry, don't you?" to his big guffaw and "Touche!") might have clarified. During his duty period, he came into my world history class where I was wont to teach sitting at a student desk in the back with the projector. He just blurted out, "Hey, where's your teacher?" The kids were dumbfounded wondering who this old guy was. I shook my head in disbelief before getting up and joining him at the threshold, laughing. With those advanced tenth-graders staring at us, he laid out his logic for our next JJs visit. "So, since we get out Wednesday for Thanksgiving, technically tomorrow is a Friday. You up for it?" I quickly agreed, especially since that year I had no cooking to do, a Thanksgiving spent by myself. Then he poked his head back into the room and said, "OK. You guys can go back to sleep now." A few girls grinned at each other. My middle-aged woman invisibility syndrome, a mutated strain of the old neuter complex, probably blinded me to the fact that other people might have begun to notice this new collegial connection.

Indeed, as the year went on, evidently other teachers and some students speculated about us. This was such foreign territory for me. Nobody ever speculated about me. It would have been very disappointing to those speculators, though, to know that we never touched each other, and would not, that whole school year. This, despite what Vicki Rodriguez, a mutual student who, like a few other kids, called Mark and me her Tucker parents, proclaimed to me the next year when I told her Mr. Condon and I were dating, "Well, duh, Miznap. Julie and I saw you guys hustling to your cars every Friday. I mean, really, you could have cut the sexual tension with a knife!" I wanted to say that at our ages it only would have required a butter knife. Or that the hustle was to get a beer and those corner seats at the bar to save our neck muscles. In fact, as the Nora Ephron, obligatory romcom montage of the autumn leaves, snow, then spring buds on the one tree in the mall's parking lot outside of JJs would have shown, each successive Friday brought a successively more awkward parting. Not even a hug. He did help me on with my raincoat once.

Forward to Reverse

A dventurous would never have been a word used to describe me. I was not prone to pursue it. But while sometimes a risk doesn't pan out, other times it's a sure bet. On spring break at fifty-six-and-a-half—and every half-year counts at that point—I took a trip to San Francisco with a man who wasn't my husband. It may go down as the first time in my nearly six decades of life that I could have been described as doing anything that approached interesting. Forget that I had been divorced for two years by then. Also, forget that he and I had never touched each other, which remained the case during that trip. Those facts didn't matter. My entire neutered puritanical persona was on the line.

While in Carmel, my old friend Phyllis, who grew up there, called me after I sent her a picture of the entry to the gorgeous beach with the cypress tree in the foreground.

"Are we in love?"

I recoiled at even the suggestion. "No. But this is good for me."

"Good answer," she replied.

I have no idea why I answered her in that way. *Was* it good for me? Or was it wrong of me? I'd so carefully protected a personal narrative that never took me out of character, a character of the highest moral standards and fear of others' judgment. Stepping on to some new path of memory-making may be unwise. What if I cannot find my way back? Nearly three-fifths of my life and at least half of my identity involved the family I married into—a big, upstanding, loving, wonderful family of five sons and adorable nieces and nephews. This is what I always craved after my own more tumultuous childhood. For so long, I had my place in that family photo, right next to the oldest brother, and right in front of my three sons. I—Mom, Aunt Lee, Hon—didn't belong in a kitschy room in the Mayflower Hotel in San Francisco in my late fifties while Mark, a colleague, a kind of friend, lay across the room in his athletic shorts and Virginia Tech T-shirt on a separate double bed. I guess my unstudied answer to Phyllis about this trip being "good for me" may have implied the same kind of benefit as a colonoscopy. I knew it was going to be awkward, but in the end, it would benefit my health.

The whole idea began in January of Mark's final year of teaching. Like any teacher worth their salt, he was already planning spring break. As I stood in his classroom doorway, he was looking through a time-share catalog that his brother had given him.

"What are you doing over spring break?" he asked.

"I was thinking about going to Oregon to see my son and daughter-in-law."

"I've never been to Portland. That'd be cool."

"Who said *you* were invited?!"

"Jeez. What about my feelings? Then, how about Key West?"

I was bemused. This was completely beyond the scope of our friendship at that point.

"Hey, San Francisco is available."

Hmmm. Something inside of me shifted, seismically, when he said San Francisco. I could almost picture it. Maybe I even needed it. San Francisco may have been my Saratoga, my Midway, my Stalingrad, the turning point from living in a defensive posture, to actually advancing. I couldn't believe what I was about to say.

"San Francisco could be fun. But we need the right set up. You're not going to hear me tinkle or anything."

He was a little embarrassed, I think, when I went straight to the nitty-gritty of mutual travel, especially when we had never done more than sit at a bar and talk for a couple hours at a time, and one of us might, being our ages, say, "Be right back. Gotta pee-pee." It was a pretty deliberate decision, though, despite my fears of the inevitable dreaded awkwardness and social anxiety that would no doubt accompany this trip: the grasping for questions to ask; the heightened table manner awareness; the fear of silence; maintaining a pleasant attitude; no bodily noises. A week away with a member of the opposite sex, whose best stories you'd already heard, a few times, could bounce me so far out of my comfort zone that I feared my hair turning gray on the spot and my speech being reduced to incoherent mumbling drool.

During our mutual planning period, the only planning that got done was for spring break. He would show up at my classroom door once in a while, pull up a plastic chair and sit next to me at my desk while we carefully mapped out our day trips and must-sees and booked things with his memorized credit card number. A small, flirty feeling came over me once in a while, especially when he smiled at me for just a little bit longer than was comfortable. Despite my professed ambivalence to him as anything more than a friend, those looks made me squirm and smile and tug down on my skirt a little.

The day finally came. I was still slightly regretting the whole thing, but it only took until we got to an airport bar to know that everything was going to be alright. After I had only taken one sip of pre-flight beer, he did some bit imitating a gynecologist in the midst of a spread-eagle examination. He cupped his hands to his mouth, and channeling the old lozenge commercial set in the Alps which involved blowing a huge alphorn, he echoed something like "RICOLA!" Beer actually came out of my nose from laughing so hard. What was I, six? I could not stop laughing, which lowered the self-consciousness factor right away, as only beer spewing out of one's nose in a public place will.

Appropriate for two old American history teachers, we stayed at a quaint old hotel called The Mayflower. The room had a perfect oversized closet where I dressed so all decorum was maintained. I bought a highly concealing black "tent" nightgown as he called it. During our first breakfast, I got that slight sweaty feeling around my forehead while thinking of something to say, but each meal became more natural as we talked about what we had experienced the day before and what was up next. We hiked a good couple of miles in the Muir Woods; we had a fabulous time at a cool museum in Napa Valley called di Rosa; and visited three vineyards. In one singular day we walked all over from Alamo Square to the Grateful Dead house, ending up at the Legion of Honor for an Impressionism exhibit where I first saw his absolute ecstasy over art, calling me over to look closely at an incredibly detailed painting of a young girl. He used my name, "Lee," a rare sound to me who had for so long been "Mom" or "Hon." We stopped at the Cliff House for happy hour and the view. That very same evening, on the advice of the seasoned hotel clerk about a good local dive, we experienced the oldest bar in San Francisco called The Saloon. It was the tiniest, seediest, coolest place, complete with a gray pony-tailed, old hippie bartender and full jazz band. We found two stools at the bar before the place started filling up. He sat with his back to me when the music started. A couple of times, I was a little distracted from the band for looking at his shoulders. I almost reached out to lay my hand on one of them as a tacit recognition of such a fun day, but held back.

I also held back when I stood behind him on the beach in Carmel as the sun was setting. It sure would have been nice to hug someone, but I wasn't going to start something that I wasn't sure I wanted to finish, especially knowing we had to share a king-size bed this one night of the trip. Of course, the tension that Vicki Rodriguez noticed was there, at least on my part. But some ancient, Southern woman dignity unclouded my notions that night. It was good to nurture the old neuter complex; I didn't want to risk looking ridiculous, like the woman teacher he told me about, a fellow chaperone on a student trip to Europe, who came late one night to his hotel room door in a red negligee. He declined the invitation, being married and all. I felt for the woman, but then wondered why I, compared to her, was so uptight or had to add that pesky idea of "meaning" onto anything approaching a physical relationship. If I had been worried about awkward silences and strained conversation just over breakfast, imagine breakfast after sex. But we were having fun without all of that complication. Instead, we stood on that gorgeous beach about ten feet apart with our hands firmly in our jacket pockets and watched the sun go down.

I didn't realize it then, but this is how it would happen, how a relationship would form—a slow revealing of our separate pasts, pasts that once may have seemed inescapable until the light of the shared present began to break through. He told me more about his youth, about how he and his still good friend Alvin would introduce themselves to impress the ladies. Coming from my jean jumper, turtleneck background, I was oblivious to the tomcatting proclivities of young men. Upon meeting new women, the lifelong friends would take turns with the phrasing. In a slow lilt, they'd declare to their prospects, "I'm Mark. I'm Alvin. We're young . . . we're good lookin' . . . and we know how to act." Being in San Francisco that spring break also summoned the memory of the epic trip he took cross-country in 1974 with "four girls and a German shepherd puppy," part of his personal folktale that I've heard many times by now. That trip included a stop in Los Angeles where they visited an old high school friend who was making headway in the music business. They met him at a fancy LA party where a film producer approached Mark and asked if he'd ever considered being in the movies. Did he want to take a screen test? (Maybe he'd heard the young, good-looking, acting quote?) His long-ago answer endeared him more to me as someone, even in his twenties, who already knew himself and his true values. He told the guy that although he was flattered, he loved being a teacher and, no thanks. (Any teacher worth their salt is an actor/comedian/ entertainer, anyway. We learn our lines, we practice our delivery, perform five times a day, and we actually know our audience, and they know—and sometimes—really love us.) Thousands of kids, now grown adults, are thankful that Mark answered that way. Over that week, we also shared our family histories, especially the common paternal connection to World War Two, and our mutual enjoyment of talking with those older relatives when we were young. We never spoke of our own pasts. It was as though the only experiences that mattered that week were the ones we were having in the moment.

Although this trip had been more fun than I probably wanted to admit, I was ready to part ways. We had become a lot more familiar, but I was still very aware of our unfamiliarity. He wasn't my family, my boyfriend, my husband; he was just a friend that I'd gotten to know over the past five months at a bar on Friday evenings. He was going home, and I was going to Portland for the final three days of break. At the San Francisco airport, Mark seemed a little uncharacteristically nervous, although I may have been transferring my own anxiety on to him for how to say goodbye. It ended up as, "OK. Gimme' a hug," followed by a one-arm-around-the-shoulder-that-you-give-your-sister variety. I may have said, "Thanks a lot. That was fun," and headed to my gate in the opposite direction. Once I reached Portland, I waited on the arrivals curb at PDX under the dreary April sky, like I had done at the same time three years earlier when my wedding-planning visit was marred by my ex-husband being found out and fired, seemingly a lifetime ago. Now I was coming off a week with some guy from my school. When my oldest drove up in his vintage 1982 Mercedes, I was never so glad to see him. He made sense to me. I knew my role with him. I knew his whole history. He knew mine. I belonged. He opened my door from his side and with that very familiar, as in *family*, very ebullient tone of voice he has, yelled out, "Hi, Mom!" Yeah. Mom. That's right. I'm Mom. I threw my suitcase into the back seat, hopped in, and burst into tears.

* * *

A longtime artist friend from Ecuador once posited that it is a mistake to think of our lives according to our linear age. Life is more episodic than chronological. Some days we feel eleven even if we are sixty; some days of our teen years, we feel ancient. He also wondered if our inner lives are lived in a kind of reverse, while our outer bodies, shall we say, advance. My spirit during this epic year had been gradually lightening during my middle age, a time that the culture often portrays oppositely, as a time of heaviness and loss. I clearly remember being ten, thinking of Dizzy when she married for the first time at fifty-five, how I could never imagine reaching her age, how scary it would be. Yet something not at all scary was afoot in my mid-fifties; some post-menopausal, pre-menstrual convergence of feminine freedoms. Being around Mark, despite him not being family, of not knowing my full history, had revived some ancient ease with myself, an unself-consciousness that balanced out my long-held idea that going "deep" with a person was only achieved in serious conversation and some religio-spiritual connection. My girlhood rekindled. I craved a Lorna Doone. My Daddy silliness resurfaced, and more importantly, was appreciated and encouraged, and often outdone. Yeah, I was having fun again. And, again, we still hadn't touched each other.

On the penultimate day of Mark's storied thirty-eight-year teaching career (and our chair's forty-third!), our department took them out to lunch on our last Thursday. I made him a gift, one of my relief sculptures of his beloved Virginia Tech. I think it may have had an unnoticed hairline crack. I opened my email that Friday morning and saw:

Lee,

I am so sorry, but I was not able to get your gift into the house in one piece. I feel terrible. I know you spent a lot of time, and I really appreciate your efforts, but more importantly your friendship. I don't want to feel bad on the eve of my last day of work, so I'm spilling my guts to you in hope of alleviating my Catholic guilt. I am looking forward to spending some good time together this weekend. I feel we haven't talked in a while.
Sorry,
Mark

First of all, honest. Second of all, "looking forward," and third of all—hmmm—"I feel." I immediately went around to his classroom where he had rooked some kids into packing up thirty-eight years' worth of stuff to tell him that it was no problem. I'd make him another one. After about nine months of friendship, he gave me a little hug. Slightly more contact than the sidearm one at the airport, this hug was barely two seconds long and shoulder, not belly, forward, but—ohmigod—it felt so good.

The next day, Mark gave his retirement speech. I saw him walking up to the modest Lakeside Country Club and asked if he wanted me to look it over. "No. I'm good." I admired his confidence, before my admiration turned to something akin to passion. His opening line of what I now simply refer to as "The Speech" laid it out there, "I could have made a lot of money." He went on to tell of an epiphany he had while coaching at a summer camp during college that made him realize a degree in accounting wouldn't provide an outlet for his love of American history, an educational version of standup comedy, coaching sports, not to mention a devotion to the well-being and utter amusement of teenagers. Another line given that thirteenth day of June also perfectly echoed my longstanding advocacy of teachers' professionalism, and the bureaucratic threat to it. Hopefully, it emboldened the young bucks there to maintain a necessary defiance, especially coming from a guy who was known to question questionable authority himself a time or two. He said, "I ignored all the 'noise from outside,' and when I shut my classroom door, inside it was *my* world and you were welcome to it," even making a sly comment directed right at our administrators. He ended The Speech with an emotional *raison d'être* that started to chip away at a wall inside of me. His integrity and professionalism and years of dedication commanded the respect of everyone there. Our colleague who became kind of Mark's unofficial mentee in both pedagogy and snark, a sensitive guy not known for sentiment, leaned into me as everyone was avidly applauding and said, "I'm going to really miss Mark!" Me too. The whole scene made me want to run up to the podium, end the platonic, and start the romantic. I felt like attacking him in front of the entire faculty.

That weekend would mark the end of some personal Paleozoic period. The night of The Speech, Mark and I were both invited to our department chair's retirement party. The next day he had agreed to accompany me to the wedding of a friend's daughter. I counted on staying at my brother's that Friday night, but he informed me when I called on my way to the party that his in-laws were visiting. I could sleep on his couch though. No thanks. Nor did I really want to drive the forty-five minutes back home in the opposite direction of the wedding, in the dark, either. I already had my wedding clothes in the car. What to do? The solution would be to stay at Mark's house, for practicality. Which was my proposal to him as soon as I saw him at the party. He agreed and immediately informed our friend who had driven him there that he would not be needing a ride home. After all those months, I finally was going to see his house. It was nice; a little in need of a woman's touch but clean, for the most part, and comfortable. We sat outside on his deck for a couple more hours before he ushered me to his empty college-aged daughter's room. He went to his room. It was Friday the 13th; nobody was going to get lucky.

It was weird to wake up at his house. Fortunately, he had just gotten an iPad to replace the school computer he soon had to return. Because of his epic ineptitude with technology, setting it up took up a lot of the morning and a lot of frustration on his part even though I was doing all of the work. In the afternoon, we headed to the wedding at an old farmhouse venue on the river; we missed the exit we were talking so much. All of my friends from the old suburban church were there, people who once had known me as a kind of mononym with my former husband's first name blended in with mine. And here I was with someone new. While I was glad to see everyone after so long, I stayed close to Mark. He was completely at ease. This June night would be the second time we actually touched in as many days, this time on the dance floor in a slow dance to "I Only Have Eyes for You" played by the band under a big tent. After only a little wine for me, he grabbed one more scotch for the road, sneakily handing the bartender a twenty. (I would witness this type of generosity to strangers—like one very crusty, nearly toothless, and thankful cab driver in Russia—many times in our future.) When I turned on the headlights, two miniature donkeys were staring right at us. They appeared out of nowhere. They looked like two donkey policemen who were about to ask me for my license and registration. I looked at Mark in the passenger seat and asked, "Wait, do you see two donkeys?" He took a sip of his cocktail-to-go and nonchalantly replied, "No. What donkeys?" That set the tone for a raucous ride home and an extended evening on his back deck.

After changing into jeans, I sat in the porch swing as Mark alternately sat in a chair or performed a scotch-induced dance around the deck to the classic rock playing quietly from his porch speakers. More scotch and a bottle of red wine facilitated a wide range of topics, from earthly travel to the time he traveled out of his body after an accident and saw his late father and grandfather. More wine led to his spiritual ideas about life, how we are all energy and we'll return to the source of it. More dancing, which by this time had devolved into purposely hilarious random, uncoordinated movements of his arms and legs. Energy. He exuded it. That had been sorely missing at the end of my earlier life. Finally, around 1:30, we tapped out. Despite the wine, I felt surprisingly sober. I headed up to his daughter's room as he turned off the lights downstairs. As I lay there still in my clothes, Mark appeared at the door with the hall light behind him. "Do you need anything? Some water?" he asked so sweetly. After all these months and a shared trip with this guy, my hesitance lifted. My answer to his offer came in the form of the same motion you use while standing on the sidewalk to tell your friend who is parallel parking to keep backing up. I beckoned him to come to me. "Yes. A hug. That's what I need."

He sat on the side of the bed. I sat up a little. He leaned over and warmly embraced me. Just a hug. After a couple of wonderful seconds, he said, "Let's go to my bed." I complied, still in my jeans and tank top, still holding back from the new and holding on to the old. Before we both drifted off, he made a quiet, half-conscious request, "Leg." I giggled, and draped my jeans-clad right one over his gym-shorted one and laid my head on his shoulder. We just fell asleep. It felt weirdly familiar and altogether new. The next morning, I woke up an hour before he did, feeling a little weird, another milestone on the journey from awkwardness to familiarity. Instead of waiting to have some morning exchange in bed, I went downstairs. He came down about an hour later, and got right at the issue at hand: how does he get all of his music from his school computer on to the new iPad? No "about last night." It really wasn't anything to review, anyway: we just fell asleep, fully clothed, together. After some hemming and hawing about breakfast, he said, "Let's go to Bamboo for brunch."

It just happened to be Father's Day. Well, well, well. The booths at Boo (as this iconic Richmond bar is affectionately called by regulars) was full of couples about our age there with their adult kids and a few grandkids to celebrate something called family and fatherhood. I had just spent the night in the bed of some other kids' father. And I was still in the same clothes. After hitting the potty there and looking in the mirror, it appeared that I had not even brushed my hair from the night before. Even though Bamboo is known for its absolute rundown, slightly gross, magnificent atmosphere, I felt a little scruffy compared to the other patrons there with their pastel outfits and combed hair. When I returned to the table and started to sip my mimosa, Mark looked serious. He swirled his Bloody Mary then looked straight at me with those nice green eyes. "Thank you," he said. "Last night was nice. I have really been missing the element of touch in my life, and you gave me that."

I was delightfully taken aback. I couldn't help but think that I was supposed to be the more emotionally mature one, the one with all the feelings. Shouldn't I have brought it up? If I had, I may have ruined the moment, because of my propensity for analytical killjoy-ism. Instead, I sat across from him feeling a little scuzzy and unkempt, but both deeply appreciated and appreciative. All I could muster was a "me too." That little bit of physical contact, not even approaching affection, lifted some of my long held, quasi-puritanical/quasi-cultural notions about my actual body that would later result in modeling that grass skirt, if only for a few seconds. My body had forever had a number attached to it: a number at any given time ten to fifteen (or twenty after a stupidly planned visit to the doctor two days after New Year's) units more than I wanted. That number created some false equivalency as to the purpose and power of my very self. Maybe this was the beginning of an overdue revelation that the sense of touch is as important as the sense of sight when it comes to assessing one's desirability. Especially at my age. And his. Whatever it was, a light bulb came on. My self-acceptance factors underwent a major reordering. The physical slid way up the scale to complement the other areas that had always done okay, the ones no one can see. Or put in a bathing suit. I even began to wonder about the softness and comfort of those other bodies that I had—for half a century—admired, the low-fat/no-fat long lean ones. Sean Penn's line to Samantha Morton's mute, plump character in the movie *Sweet and Lowdown* never ceases to amuse and reassure: "I like a woman with a little meat on her bones. Makes a man feel like he's been somewhere."

Mark could have quoted that line to me the following weekend. Yes, after that switch flipped in my head, the lights came on, or actually off; my newfound body image had its limits. Our relationship did not change; we just added another expression of our companionship to those nights talking on his deck or my balcony. Or to our future travels. Or to the countless live music events we attended, from Richmond's wonderful folk festival to a Mahler symphony matinee to an Irish trio at a local dive. Or to every thirsty Thursday after school with many new friends at Bamboo. On the first of many trips to the river house of one of them, it sure was nice to now feel free to give him a hug on the beach. Our host and soon-to-be good buddy, an old, liberal country boy with a big heart who had done very well in life, noticed. We often imitate his initial appreciation of our connection that mirrored his own rediscovered love later in life. He observed in his charming drawl, "You know, Mahk, that's what it's all about. Companionship."

I really was living in reverse; doing things in my late fifties that are usually reserved for the twenties, like going to a club. Until it closed, Emilio's was a happenin', but tiny, jazz club that had a white Louis Armstrong sound-alike on vocals and guitar, a hipster drummer in a three-piece suit and pork pie hat, a hefty VCU student on bass, and the incredible keyboardist Debo Dabney, a lean Black man about our age who wore Dr. Huxtable sweaters and a few gold chains. He lit it up, too. Like Boo, the place welcomed all backgrounds of Richmonders: Black and white, young and old, gay and straight, and a regular table of three quite elderly Jewish couples. Once the music really got going, I could not help myself. Even after a full day of teaching, I had to get up and dance. I was not alone, but it was not with Mark, who remained more of a private deck dancer. One Thursday, when the band took a break, a young Black woman who had been dancing right beside me sidled up and just blessed me in her sweet Southern accent, "Hi. My name is Vanessa. What's your name?" Like that long ago party I attended with my boss from Sears, the spirit of the dance welcomed everyone. Despite the pot and alcohol that came along with some folks at Emilio's and Bamboo, at times those places seemed like a different form of communion, of fellowship normally reserved for Sunday mornings, not Thursday nights. Those evenings became a ritual of sorts, one that offered a less burnished tradition and some new revelation of humanity for me.

My actual Sunday mornings also morphed into something new, a kind of consecration of our relationship as it became at once more traditional and more unique. He started a new pattern of coming to see me on the weekends. We rarely watched television in the first year or even two of our romance; instead, our evenings were spent on my balcony looking at the mountains and the horses, eating, drinking, and just talking and laughing. We still do. Sometimes I would wear the Betty Draper, the name I gave my mother's white tulle peignoir from the fifties out there for fun. Then we started Poetry Sunday. It was completely Mark's idea, a glimpse into the kind of creativity he honed over decades of teaching. In the morning, we had coffee on the front porch. Then we headed upstairs and both climbed into the twin bed in the room that also shared that great view. He had purchased a book of poems by Billy Collins for this new ritual. We took turns choosing two poems each. It was required that we read it twice to each other. Then we made our astute observations about its imagery and what it said about life. As a kind of relic, the table of contents is marked up in pencil—and on his insistence, we had to use the same white pencil with blue snowflakes—to note the dates that each poem was read. The poetry set a romantic tone for part two of the morning, which led to part three: an appetite for bacon, biscuits, and eggs—over easy for him, hard fried for me.

Since that last penciled-in date of Poetry Sunday, I guess it could be said that the rest is history. It was certainly not the history that I saw being written in my home in the country. That volume was supposed to be filled with countless anecdotes of family, a place where my primary role was still wife, mother, and grandmother. And while I do play those latter two roles a few times a year, the house has become the setting for a business, but also a little playground for me and my newfound, old playmate. One evening early on, sitting at my dining room table in candlelight, I touched on that theme. In a rare moment of actually expressing the feelings he does not possess, Mark asseverated the sentiment. He admitted that from childhood he had lived mostly a charmed life until his beloved father died suddenly when he was only twenty-five. When his much younger wife got cancer and fought it for a decade and finally succumbed when his children were still teenagers, he confessed that he felt this "couldn't be happening to me, of all people." Then he poignantly, and maybe a little haltingly, added, "I am looking at the reflection of the candles and my face in these windows, and I think, 'how did I end up in your dining room in rural Louisa?'" Belonging is a fast and loose concept. Where *do* I belong? To whom do I belong? Just how far can the concept of family go if it does not involve shared DNA or a preponderance of shared memories, especially from one's youth? And in both personal and cultural histories, just how much history is required before it is no longer a new history?

Long, long ago in a Bible study at my suburban church, the one divorced woman any of us knew made a comment that stuck with me.

She said, "The hardest part of divorce is that you lose your history." Shared history had been paramount to my notion of relationships, of any kind. Yet after so much turmoil, I guess I gradually stopped living in the shadow of some unreconstructed, idealized past, and just surrendered to the messy freedom of the real present and the unknown future. My identity had been nearly totally circumscribed by that past, though. Yet here this person came along, and after only a fraction of my adult years being with him, many times I feel like he knows me better than almost anyone. I have not wanted to admit that. It could be his quasi-clairvoyance and natural intuition, but he often completes my thoughts or correctly predicts what I am thinking. He offers helpful, simple, and pointed advice when I need it. He also listens thoroughly, sometimes referencing something I told him years back, another trait of being a master teacher. And I would love to know who told him that sometimes a hug is all a person needs to calm them down so I could thank them. And, so unusual from my past experience, he apologizes immediately if he even slightly steps over my sentence and begs me to go on. This kind of connection would not seem very likely, especially at our age and our divergent pasts. Mark and I did not share anything close to the standard roles of marriage: raising kids together, a long social life, financial partners, extended family. Those roles are supposed to naturally create a shared intimacy, a totemic history. But sometimes, some deep essence of a person gets lost in those roles, and a craving gurgles up, a craving to be known for that essence—whatever that is.

Our first trip after "the tent came off" as he says, we traveled through Canada and the Pacific Northwest. (We serendipitously hit Calgary during the big Stampede weekend, which provided one of his best jokes ever. Imitating the winning bucking bronco rider's answer to what he was going to do with the ten grand he just won, Mark whispered in my ear, "Well, I'm off to be a microbiologist because it's time to stop horsing around." My father could have just as easily made that one.) On one of the many gorgeous drives around Olympic National Park, this idea came up of the utilitarian role that I, and most mothers, feel they play sometimes, all wrapped up in that "w" word, wife. In a moment of deep honesty, and as a kind of turning point in not only my relationship with him, but also with myself, he simply said, "You've been fulfilling someone's needs your whole life. I don't need you. I want you." I didn't, but I could have cried. He's not prone to too many of those kinds of remarks, but that one was deeply moving to me. As they say, I felt known. Soon after that comment, we turned into the parking lot of Hurricane Hill where we embarked on an epic climb on a perfect day, reaching the summit to just soak in that unparalleled 360-degree view. I did not want to come back down off that mountain.

As in the entire concept of America in which an absurd amalgamation of disparate pasts weaves itself into some kind of tenuous meaning, the notion at one point in time of having an intimate relationship with Mr. Condon from Room 58 was equally as absurd. All of my meaning was wrapped around who I formerly had been. Yet as time went on between us, our beneficial friendship was not at all new; it was *re*newal. And the primary process of that renewal—no question—was a major release of a pent-up childhood silliness long tamped down by adult expectations and struggle. From winter nights around my fireplace to summer nights on his deck, we often engaged in a kind of one-upmanship of wit or word games or invented preposterous situations until I crack up at his, or he lets out one of his signature high-pitched "ah-ha, very good, Lee," to acknowledge my slam down. These goofiness outbreaks were not confined to domestic shores, either.

Bath, England. July 2018. Risking a "had-to-be-there" story, this goes down as one of the top three hardest, can't-laugh-in-church moments of my life, only it wasn't a church. It was the lovely, staid Holburne Museum at the foot of the famous Poulteney Bridge. (Recently made popular by Bridgerton, a costume drama reimagining eigthteenth-century England.) One gallery there is dedicated to portraits of important Brits in a thoroughly un-reimagined past. As we entered, only one young woman was in there very properly appreciating the art in this extremely quiet, regal space. After looking at a few bust portraits, Mark zeroed in on a life-size one. He leaned in to identify this magnificent painting of the very well-to-do Earl seated by a window with one leg propped across the other knee, painted by Thomas Gainsborough. Misreading the subject's name in a fake British accent, Mark whispered to me that here before us was none other than Robert Craggs Nougat, later Earl Nougat. "Nougat?" I asked quietly and quizzically in an equally fake British accent. No, this was actually Earl Nu*gent*. To cover his mistake, Mark began what became a pun Jenga, a little game of Outwit, still in the accent.

Him: "Well, I hear Earl Nougat had quite the *Pay Day*."
Me: "Uh, yes. Nearly *100 Grand*."
Him: "That's nothing to *Snickers* at!"

He won this round. His gut was moving up and down at record speed and his shoulders were convulsing. Mine were, too. As to not bother the appropriately behaved young woman, we were maintaining our whisper, but each comment became more of a repressed wheeze as we tried to keep from busting into full guffaw. I was sixty and he was sixty-four. To the nice ladies who sold us tickets, we looked like normal American grandparents, but we were acting like children. It was a soul-cleansing laugh better than any drug trip. Not that I would know.

Mark is fond of saying "I want to live!" by which he means travel. Seeing how animated he got over the whole idea, I needed to go against type and embrace his sense of adventure if we were to go forward. And forward we went. Every spring break and every summer from April 2016 until the summer of 2019 before the pandemic hit, we went to Europe, eight times altogether. This was truly foreign to everything about my history or goals in life, evidenced early on by that disdain for travel talk borne of jealousy, no doubt. Any awkwardness from our first platonic trip to San Francisco transformed into a new familiarity. We didn't share kids or money or a house, but we have shared so many experiences that formed a different kind of foundation. And only he and I were there. Those trips were not just fun as sightseeing excursions, but like in Bath, his personality made all those sights much more fun.

The first night in Florence we discovered the rooftop door at the Hotel Lucchesi was open. Nobody was up there. That started our secretive nighttime, rooftop rendezvous drinking wine under a blanket on the chaise lounges until midnight, gazing at Santa Croce right below and the Duomo (which we climbed) down the way. The last night we were shocked to find the hotel's bartender slinging $12 cocktails on *our* rooftop. That summer in Amsterdam was like a fairy tale, really, to this provincial Southern girl. All the museums, the canals, the walks, and a wonderfully free, sensual evening with the sheer curtains blowing in the excellent breeze from our open windows in the Max Brown Hotel overlooking the lit canal and the old Dutch East India Company in the background. And when in Rome kind of thing, we sat on a stoop and he smoked a joint, giving me a few hits just as a Dutch cop drove by and looked right at us. Mark remarked, "I feel so safe."

Or the entire trip to Russia, starting with Passport Control in St. Petersburg where the airport guy looked right out of a Wes Anderson movie with his slicked back black hair and fake epaulettes, sitting way above me and staring a hole into me. A wee bit worried, I look over to my safely through companion for reassurance. He's dancing a ridiculous jig to make me laugh. Then the big, bald, mean-looking Russian driver greeting us at the St. Petersburg airport holding a handwritten sign "Lee Knapp." That may have been the height of my personal absurdity.

And on and on: Norway! Vigeland Park as a reminder to this Richmonder of what public art can be; Barcelona! Gaudi, Montserrat, observing the traditional Catalan dance from our hotel balcony on Palm Sunday; Vienna! Mozart concert, Loos American bar, Vienna Boys Choir singing the Hallelujah Chorus on Easter Sunday, the incredible walk down from the Vienna Woods to the charming Schubel-Auer heuriger; England! Me driving the tiny roads in Cornwall, walking the Southwest Coastal Pathway from Lizard Point to Kynance Point and back, Canterbury Cathedral; Lisbon! a sweet Fado performance, Beleem's famous pastry, Nunu our darling guide to overwhelming Sintra.

Our last trip before the Germ Invasion was to meet up with my oldest son, Alexis, and my three-year-old grandson in Lyon, France, where she had a sweet three-month teaching gig. I'll never forget turning into the little lane and watching Alexis and the baby coming down the open stairwell, chatting up a storm. I called out his name from a story below. Despite all of my cool memories to that point, the one of my three-year-old grandson spotting me and breaking into a huge grin is tops. We all moved on to Avignon before Mark and I split off for Copenhagen and Stockholm, only to return to my fireplace and front porch for the next three years.

For the first couple of years after taking a teaching job at my old high school, I did struggle with how lame it all felt. Those same laments of an Act One, unreconstructed George Bailey indeed tortured me with how provincial my life had become. Not that I ever had any dreams of seeing the world like many couples I knew had been doing. I may not have been jealous so much of their travel, but of their accumulated stability, how they were beginning to sit back and enjoy a little of the fruits of their labors over the first three decades, how they could have possibly already paid off their mortgages. I had been struggling for years just to survive my present, and any former vision of a brighter, stable future had slowly faded into a daily scramble to pay bills. Then, this same high school, this very acreage where I spent my youth honing a love of both history and humor, offered up a person with whom I could share both. Indeed, the narrow campus opened up a wide new world to me.

PART FOUR
Massive Resistance to My Solid South

How Can You Live in the Northeast,
How Can You Live in the South?
Paul Simon

Culture Clash

I f I happened to be standing on the wide front porch of my new in-laws' rented house on Martha's Vineyard some July afternoon in 1981, I might see him enter my view of Vineyard Sound from the right. Actually, William Styron's golden retriever crossed the plane first. Although at times it was hard to tell them apart. Both rocked long manes parted by the breeze. Both stood tall and proud. They shared a look of self-conscious detachment as they strolled slowly past the ambling, rustic homes of white clapboard or cedar shake. Both man and beast appeared a bit weathered, which made them all the more attractive. Even from my hilltop perch of the white house with the steeple-like tower, down the long narrow yard to the low stone walls lining the street, it was easy to see that Styron had the bearing of the intelligentsia mixed with a little movie star. And even if I hadn't shared a weekend with him when I was twenty, or didn't recognize him as one of the twentieth century's most accomplished and controversial authors, I would have taken note of his regal air and wondered, "Who's that?"

Along with other notables of the time like Mike Wallace and Art Buchwald, Mr. Styron lived just down the road from this tiny tony summer community known as West Chop. Its residents occupied high-powered jobs in New York and Boston, as well as the huge, stately, cedar-shake mansions around a spit of rocky shoreline facing Cape Cod. Most families came for the entire summer, which required paid help to entertain their kids. That's where I crossed the plane. My then-husband and I were hired the year before—when I was right out of college and newly married—to be leaders of this imaginatively named Group, the assemblage of five- to twelve-year old children of these elites. From nine until noon each weekday, I entertained the little ones. He led Wiffle ball games and manhunts while parents played golf or sailed or mostly played tennis.

West Chop maintained nine meticulously manicured clay courts, which were mingled in between the fancy inn, the quaint, old-timey post office, and the barn-like, high arch-windowed pavilion called The Casino where dances, kids' activities, and God-less Sunday services were held. A sparkling view of Vineyard Sound signaled the entry to this loop of rustic paradise, a living painting of the sea. Countless gleaming white sailboats and seagulls glistened against the deep blue water. Huge black and white ferry boats crisscrossed the water with the same predictability as the freight trains that shook my North Carolina grandmother's house, forty feet out of her back door, about twelve times a day; their arrival first signaled by the tinkling, then clanging, of the crystals on the candelabras in her huge dining room. This kind of members-only access to exceptionally beautiful geography was beyond my one-week-each-summer, aqua-colored stucco, cheap hotel room shared with my parents and two brothers, umbrella-crowded Virginia Beach experience. "Up here" one had to request a club key to gain access to West Chop's gorgeous private beach on the south shore of the island, next to Jackie Onassis's place. And, in my mind at least, one had to refer to oneself in the first-person plural while doing so.

I may as well have gotten a summer job on the moon. If the moon required being a big cheese at some investment bank or television network to make a landing there. I had just finished college where I learned from many big books many big things about America. Two of them, two defining American notions as old as America itself, congealed in a big *duh* of real life that summer. They had been simmering all through my courtship and engagement to a Northerner from decidedly more means than I: there are class and regional differences in our great country. That is to say, these people are rich, and they don't act or talk like me or my people. I was a tuber of the barely middle class, fed by a few white trash root hairs on my father's side and proud poor whites on my mother's.

At first, I worried about this, as if my public school underpants were showing. (Decades later, my youngest son was asked by a kid who went to the elite private school in Richmond, "Don't you go to one of those public school churches?") I was tempted to expunge any *heys* or *y'alls* from my speech, like an Eliza Doolittle from Dixie. But it didn't take long before something flipped inside, as if Eliza had told Professor Higgins to go to hell. I contrapuntally reveled in my barely middle class Southern-ness. I wondered, even hoped, my intelligence and sophistication were being judged as inferior so I could judge—and envy—their money from a place of purity. When one of the West Chop matriarchs, who had grown up in a prominent Richmond family, found out where I was from, she was eager to make a connection with me. It turned out to be more of a disconnection.

"You're from Richmond, dear?" she asked in her lingering drawl.

"Yes, ma'am. Born and bred."

She responded with a nearly incoherent, mumbling diatribe about how Richmond had changed, something about those ghastly car dealership owners being let into the club, excuse me, Club. Then she got personal:

"Now, what was your mutha's maiden name, dear?"

No one had ever asked me my mother's maiden name before, since a password then was only required to enter a fourth grader's secret fort in the woods. I may have seemed a naïve plebeian suburbanite, but I recognized her patrician intent instantly. I opened my eyes wide in a look of feigned innocence, stared at her wattled neck, crazy permed hair, and that mustard stain on her misshapen white Izod cotton sweater, and answered her using the same neck motion of an insulted turkey.

"Hicks. And for regional pride, again, "Sarah Hee-icks."

Silence. I would have gotten the same reaction if I had said Sarah Yokel. Or Hayseed. Or Hee Haw. Yeah, that's right. My mother was born Sarah Elizabeth Hee Haw. This well-meaning holdover from the days of an uncomplicated Monument Avenue was innocently trying to place me in what she knew of the city, a quadrant of streets anchored by the country club and a decidedly private school church. Even though this area of her provenance stood probably five miles from my childhood house, she couldn't have found my neighborhood if her life depended on it. Needless to say, we had nothing left to say.

It actually became a little exciting to feel like a stranger in a strange land, up in that faraway country called Massachusetts. It solidified my allegiance to and identification with my homeland. I wasn't going to forsake my origins or give in to any temptation to pretension amidst this very nice, but wholly unfamiliar, tax bracket. My great aunt Dizzy had a finely tuned ear for haughtiness, perhaps also borne of her own envy for a life she could only dream of, but I still hear her voice running through my head whenever I tell someone that I lived on The Vineyard for a couple of summers. I fear it sounds like I'm dropping a Larchmont lockjaw "Tha Vinyahd." After Mema's and Dizzy's cousins, George and Eleanor Davis in Lickskillet, North Carolina—so named, *obviously*, because, "The Yankees came through here, stole all our food, and even licked the skillet!"—put a plaque on their brick driveway pillars naming their 1860s house "Lake-of-the-Woods," Dizzy often derisively commented, "That's the damndest thing I ever heard of—naming a house."

Until marrying a Long Islander whose parents hailed from Philadelphia and ended up in an upscale part of Connecticut, this untraveled Southern girl could count her trips to the North on one hand. They seemed to fall in five-year intervals, as though my psyche needed that much time to get firmly reoriented back in my Southern reality: 1964, New York World's Fair during which we had three flat tires that seemed to be a warning about what happens when Southerners ventured up yonder; 1969, a visit to my mother's cousin and her nine kids, Bobby Jean, in guaranteed un-Bobby Jeaned New Jersey; 1974, Swarthmore College to see the sister with unshaven legs and armpits of the one boyfriend I had in high school; 1979, traveling to inner city Philadelphia to meet the first of my new Yankee family, his adorable maternal grandparents who still lived in a row house near Ogontz Avenue where by then they stuck out like white, white-haired thumbs. On the way into the city after dark, with a big atlas across my lap in the passenger seat of his rusted out Datsun 510 wagon, we got off 295 way too soon and landed in South Philly on Broad Street. Approaching a long yellow light that had just turned red, he resisted the self-preserving urge to run it and ended up lurched into the crosswalk. A big dude in a long, banana-colored leather coat and matching wide-brimmed hat with a feather pointing northward from its band stopped his syncopated stroll in front of the quarter-panel of my side of the car. He looked at me, then at him. We got the message. We backed up real fast and the man went on about his business for the evening.

A few months later, I would defy all of my father's dire warnings about filth and crime and violence and head to New York City where my fiancé would pick me up and drive us to meet my future in-laws in that cesspool known as New Canaan, Connecticut. I arrived at Penn Station around noon, where I first learned of my future husband's ménage à trois relationships with cars, illegal parking spots, and a lack of cash. As I walked out into the caverns of skyscrapers looking upward like a slack-jawed yokel just begging to be pickpocketed, he was having a hard time finding the same rusted out Datsun that he had left—"JUST FOR A COUPLE OF MINUTES!"—in a No Parking Zone in midtown Manhattan. This led to a long walk to a garage wanting $65 cash in 1979 dollars to spring the car, which wasn't happening with his nearly empty wallet. That was followed by a harrowing cab ride downtown with a charming Caribbean cab driver ("least you have agleeable girl; most girls get out train, see no cah, go back home"), to an elevator at 2 Wall Street that opened onto the impressive offices of Bacon & Whipple (later my silly, not-Wall Street father would ask my father-in-law, "So, Fred, how are things at Sausage and Sniffle?").

Mr. Knapp emerged from behind a wall, in a cloud of mist with angels singing as I recall, smiling broadly to meet me, surely thinking we had surprised him at work instead of meeting later at home. We surprised him all right. I stood to the side as he opened his wallet and the $65, plus the return cab fare, changed hands. So, the first time I met my future father-in-law was to ask him for money. That mise-en-scène would repeat itself in various settings for the rest of my married life: the honeymoon, including covering a shortfall discovered at checkout that required an expensive long distance call and somehow money traveling over wires, overwhelming Christmas gifts, mortgage help, and renting a big house for his other four sons and extended family the second summer we worked on The Vineyard.

The very first time I saw this new world was a little over a week after my wedding night and honeymoon to Bermuda, both of which involved firsts. The second one required flying in an airplane, around a famous Triangle, for the first time at twenty-two years old. I'll never forget Daddy returning from the one and only plane trip of his entire life, having traveled by troop ship to Europe in his teens. When he returned, my two brothers and I, all under the age of ten, backed him up against the front door inside the living room and just stared at him in amazement. Daddy had been up in the atmosphere, and here he was back at home. Still in his London Fog and fedora with briefcase in hand, he looked (if possible) with his barrel belly and skinny legs, almost Don Draper glamorous. He had only flown to Rhode Island and back for something to do with his Masonic Lodge, but he may just as well have been Buzz Aldrin freshly retrieved from his Apollo capsule that had parachuted gently into the Pacific. Another first, for me at that time, would be to live, *actually inhabit*, a region of my own country that somehow did not feel that way. Landing in West Chop on Martha's Vineyard where people were required to wear something called "tennis whites" and never raised their voices or shelled a butterbean, had the same sense of the exotic as if I'd found myself in Casablanca or Mumbai or Pittsburgh.

It seemed Styron's daily routine during these years on the Vineyard consisted of waking at noon after late-night discussions with the local illuminati, eating lunch, and then, before settling down to write, taking a stroll to pick up his mail at the West Chop post office. This was also my summer address—not just the zip code—the *actual* post office. This white A-framed building with dark green trim was no bigger than a single car garage, but it housed the community's post office, a tiny space cordoned off in one corner complete with iron bars at the window. There was an old-timey chest freezer full of popsicles, also wooden candy racks, expensive tennis gear, and, if you traveled up the two-foot-wide spiral staircase tucked behind the postmaster's cage, you'd enter my two-room home for the first two summers of my adult life.

Even then, I was still nurturing an intellectual life that fully bloomed in college, one singularly focused on the cultural traits of the South—an obsession with the past, memory, a heightened sense of place. Those unarticulated notions were seeded even farther back in early high school when my ninth-grade history teacher, Mr. Whitten, now my good friend Steve, made a comparison of the study of history to the strange, ghostly feeling one gets in a grandmother's house.

The room went quiet all around me and became a bit fuzzy, as happens in a moment of deep resonance. I knew that feeling. I had been getting it every six to eight weeks of my early life when my family would drive the two hours south to visit Mema and Granddaddy, also known as Tom and Mattie Lee Hicks, my mother's parents. My older brother Dalton's predated, so undiagnosed and untreated, ADHD made the family's capacity for road travel, even after trading in the green '58 Chevy BelAir wagon for the exciting '67 Oldsmobile VistaCruiser with its partial glass roof, about an hour. We could only make it forty-five minutes to Petersburg before Dalton's fidgeting and hitting of me and my younger brother Brian's thighs and arms required us to stop at King's Barbeque for lunch. We'd finally reach the first exit from Interstate 85 into North Carolina, marked by the familiar square NORLINA highway sign. After turning left on to Number One South, we were in serious tobacco country. Row upon row of the golden weed sped by the window. My excitement grew when we started to see more stucco or cinderblock one-story houses closer together because Mema's house, the de facto center of Norlina, couldn't be far. My brothers and I would play a game to see who could first spot the back of her big white house that appeared to arise from a section of low-lying, patchy asphalt like the Taj Mahal from its reflecting pool. Her house, and all that it represented, would also loom large in my psyche for decades to come.

As would an encounter I had with William Styron. As I stood in front of the big window of my Yankee post office home in the summer of 1981, he casually entered its creaky screen door. I turned from the postmaster's window and came face to face with the famous author. A soft, angled light fell on him, which made him appear very kind, not intimidating like I would have expected. (I remember a nurse friend telling how at the hospital one day she turned suddenly away from her patient to see his visitor, Roger Mudd, the next best thing to Walter Cronkite, standing right in front of her, appearing to glow. She joked that for a moment it was like staring into the face of Jesus. Same.) I was only twenty-three, but Mr. Styron and I had shared a weekend three years earlier, when I was a sophomore at the College of William and Mary. J. J. Thompson, a young, brilliant professor of Southern history who was as cool as his name suggested, asked a few history majors to join him at a Southern writer's conference in April 1978. Dr. Thompson knew about my preoccupation with Norlina, how it could have been the setting of one of those Southern novels that would be discussed at Hampden–Sydney College that spring weekend. There we listened to the somewhat coherent, mostly sober ramblings about writing, alcohol, and notions of a New South—or the very existence of a "South" at all by James Dickey, Willie Morris, and Mr. Styron, heavyweights all in the fading sub-cultural genre of Southern lit. So when I saw him in the West Chop post office, a universe away from Farmville, I was eager to remind him of our connection. Again, like with the old matriarch, it would be another disconnection. I would eventually credit him for exploding my mythology around Norlina, but not before blaming him for fracturing it. After all, I had worked long and hard to create a story that would give me some kind of illusory, fuzzy-filtered, unique alternative identity. That is, before the myth gave way to reality, and the fuzziness to clarity.

A Norlina Historiette

N orlina got on the map when the Raleigh–Gaston Railroad merged with the Seaboard Coast Line. Sometime between 1898 and 1900, track was laid in Norlina that would make it a connecting town on the more direct all-Seaboard route from Atlanta to Richmond. Today, on a simple Town of Norlina website, which includes photos of the bus station, train station, and "Mattie Hicks' house," there is a short history of the town's highlights. Its beginning was marked by the entry: "Friday, November 29, 1912—Fifty lots were sold roughly for $95.00 to $300.00, with a large crowd present. A brass band and much Norlina enthusiasm were present. A letter from one of the 'high-up' railroad officials states that Norlina would be made a local freight terminal, which was quite an addition to its population." Mema was ten; Dizzy was just four months old. I am fairly certain that my great-grandparents were amidst that brass band and much enthusiasm, and very likely bought the lot that Mema's house stood on.

Built in 1916 by unlicensed family members and townspeople for my great grandparents and their six children, the house was a big white wooden square with one gable in the front. An obligatory front porch stretched across it facing south. The back had a one-story elongated addition that held the kitchen on one side of a narrow hall. On the other side was the huge dining room that, according to a few photos I found, used to have eight or so four-top tables like a restaurant. This was part of the enterprise that became the Norlina Tourist Home, a common, pre-highway, pre-motel trend across rural America, not at all unlike Airbnb, only without reviews and corporate fees. My mother's job as a little child was to bound up the steps and flip a little switch in of all places the upstairs bathroom to light up a square, black and white "Norlina Tourist Home" sign by the highway. Their competition, the big fancy Norlina Hotel, stood across the street a few hundred yards south. On the guest register, besides the name of Amelia Earhart (who I guess decided to drive that day), were the unbelievable, like "Martians visiting Earth" unbelievable, names Paul McCartney and John Lennon! Two Beatles in Norlina?! Talk about your long and winding road. Also, ironically for his signing of the 1956 Interstate Highway Act that would cripple or kill such places as Norlina, President Dwight Eisenhower stayed there a few times. These were Norlina's heydays.

By the mid-fifties, the house was no longer a tourist home. It had been sorely neglected by Mema's mother during the years my grandparents lived in Richmond (the third R of success taught in North Carolina schools: Readin', Ritin', and the Road to Richmond). When she died, it fell on Mema to leave her fun life in the city and return to the town of a thousand. Mema poured all of her creativity into that house. By the time I came along, Norlina was just another forgotten town in Warren County, the poorest county in America's second poorest state, but her house was known across its land as a beautiful, tasteful showplace.

The house stood in a wedge of land that separated Number One Highway, a mere fifteen feet—fifteen feet!—from the west side of the house. Only forty feet from the back door lay the railroad tracks. Immediately across the road from the front steps was the bus station. Mema's house might as well have been the Port Authority of Norlina. My grandparents squeezed out a livelihood with long-term rentals of four of the five upstairs bedrooms and boarding some of the locals. Fascinating me to no end were the little black iron numbers nailed to each bedroom door upstairs, like it was a life-sized play hotel. Living for years in Number 1, the bedroom to the right of the bathroom, was Mr. Bob Price, a mash-up of Cesar Romero and Gary Cooper—and legendary in little Norlina for his anomalistic, suave good looks. On the other side of the bathroom in Number 2 was Miss Ezzard, a second-grade teacher with tightly wound brown hair kept under a net à la Ruth Buzzi and a weirdly strong grip she used to squeeze the crap out of our cheeks. Next, around the upstairs parlor was Number 3, the room of Mr. Matthews, a lanky, late-middle-aged math teacher. For a good portion of my early days, an old railroad worker, Mr. Elliot, lived in Room 4 with the simple iron bed with brass poster caps, which now stands in my upstairs guest bedroom. Mr. Elliot lacked two fingers on his left hand and would pull his coat sleeve down to hide it as he ate. I found myself sometimes staring up his sleeve during dessert.

Before I learned as a young adult that being Southern was fraught with contradiction and violence, I latched on to Norlina to connect me to a culture, some kind of unique, almost strange, culture that bore little resemblance to my own only a hundred miles away. My house was 1100 square feet of 1950s suburbia on a grid of streets where the houses essentially looked alike and were inhabited by tidy nuclear families. Mema's house towered over everything in town, and a random assortment of old people lived in their single bedrooms and shared a bath down a hall. Some ate meals with her. I ate with my parents and two brothers every night. The bulk of my suburban Richmond culture was transmitted over three channels in thirty-minute, scripted bundles of *Gilligan* and *Gidget*, which I watched often alone in my den. It was a secondhand culture.

In Norlina, they made their own. The old people, every single night after dinner, weather permitting, rocked the fourteen porch rockers and talked, usually all at once. Since I always sat on the side between the front door and the highway, the alley side of the porch seemed as remote as if it were behind the Iron Curtain. That is where the roomers sat, mostly the old men like Mr. Elliot and his eight fingers. The wicker rockers that were designated for Mema and Granddaddy mimicked their bodies: his was narrow with a tall back, hers was ample and round. Even when the many tractor-trailers would pass by on Number One, those fifteen feet away, Mema didn't stop talking. It was almost cartoonish, as though someone used the remote to mute her. She had most likely become oblivious to the booming truck noise. Her lips would still move, but you couldn't hear anything coming out until the giant truck passed and her story became audible again.

On my solo summer visits, I slept in The Blue Room, the nicest bedroom normally reserved for my parents. At night it became a fun house as the deafening sound of the tractor-trailers' engines struggled to find the next gear after going through the speed trap. Their headlights shone through the white sheer curtains onto the front porch and shook the wavy glass panes. A distorted silhouette of the four rectangles then swirled around me before angling through the highway side window and repeating the light show. Then, at least twice during my transition from wakefulness to sleep, trains barreled through town, shaking the bed and the whole house with it. It was as though that four-poster bed was in the middle of a darkened subway platform. Wide-eyed, I would lie perfectly still with my arms at my sides in the very middle of the bed, feeling both a little frightened by the sheer decibels of Norlina's infrastructure and comforted by its predictability. I felt like I was in the center of the universe. I also felt so deeply loved.

As I did when Mema made my favorite dessert, coconut cake. From the downstairs bathroom window on those mornings, I would see her in the middle of the alley with a hammer and an ice pick, her go-to cooking utensil, and wonder why she was trying to bust open a hairy brown ball. Seconds later it registered that it was a real coconut. She drained its milk, then banged it into pieces, somehow managing to grate its meat from the concave shell. No bagged, store-bought coconut would ever match it. My mother was a recipe cook, but Mema was a true Southern cook, and like all of them worth their excessive salt, she cooked everything from memory. She was known all over town for her cooking, especially her famous fried chicken ("don't get big breasts or fatty thighs"), unparalleled blackberry cobbler with a butter and sugar glop on top called "hard sauce," wine jelly and syllabub, both of which required her to make her own wine! She was most renowned though for her highly addictive White House rolls, ("add enough flour until the dough feels *velvety*"), and be sure to dip them in a beat-up metal saucepan of melted Crisco before folding them over not quite in the middle. Bake until golden brown. Eat at least four. Greens never appeared in a salad. I am not sure anyone in Norlina even knew what a salad was. No, green things were to be boiled until their natural color disappeared into the oil slick of bacon grease floating on top of the saucepan. Bacon grease is a mainstay of Southern cooking, of course. My friend Steve tells of calling his Lynchburg grandmother from college to say the fried apples he made in his hotpot didn't taste quite right. "Well did you add the bacon grease?" He sheepishly replied no, to which she wheezily stated the obvious, "Well, that's your problem."

Since television formed so much of my young psyche, much to my disappointment Mema only got ABC out of Raleigh. And that required a lot of fiddling with some kind of bunny ear cum circular steel metal rods that were attached to a box with a dial that when turned made a sound like a metallic fart, which must have turned the space station looking roof antennae. There were, though, a few television musts: Mema's uncharacteristic addiction to her "story," *As the World Turns,* which she played on a portable black-and-white TV in the kitchen as she worked. She liked the soap opera but hated a soap commercial (perhaps borne out of jealousy, but I like to think it was a reaction to laziness and self-indulgence). In a derisive, judgmental voice, she always imitated the one in which a woman is taking a bubble bath and says, "Calgon, take me away!" There was also Granddaddy's enjoyment of Saturday afternoon baseball, which didn't require him to hear because he couldn't; and only the most unredeemable hicks would stay on the porch from seven to eight on a Saturday night and miss Lawrence Welk.

Just before seven, someone usually yelled out the time. So as not to miss the maestro lifting his baton and his "and a wonna, and a tooah," the old people rose from their rockers and in Rockettes unison shuffled through the front screen door, taking extra care on that little step and the edge of the rug. The sexa-, septua-, and octogenarians then bum-rushed, in slow motion, Mema's long narrow living room to get a good seat in one of the sofas or wing chairs lining the walls. Since the television console was about twenty feet away, they all craned their turkey necks hard to the right to bob their heads and their multiple chins to the musical stylings of the Lennon Sisters or Norma Zimmer. This was the one weekly glimpse they got of the wider culture, a world outside Norlina, never mind how corny and wholesome and sexless that world appeared. Lawrence Welk's lingering German accent was their European vacation.

The older people that I knew in my suburban world—teachers, friends' parents, church folks—were on a sliding scale of predictability. In Norlina, the old people were off that chart. Mema and I occasionally visited Mary Norris, a gentle, mumbling older woman right out of Faulkner or Dickens. I have a memory of a creaky plank door opening on to a scene of her sitting on an old horsehair Victorian couch. Her long gray hair lay around her shoulders, as sunlight stole through the old blinds in horizontal lines, backlighting her scary, although smiling, figure. The room seemed to be in constant motion from the stalking and tail swishing, pawing and purring, of cats, dozens and dozens of central casting cats. I was scared and mesmerized at the same time. Then there was The Sheriff, a Jimmy Durante lookalike, if Jimmy Durante wore oversized, threadbare khaki pants held up over his sizable belly with suspenders, a plaid shirt, and a red baseball cap. The Sheriff stood most nights at the curve in the dead middle of Hyco Street, directing traffic. And sometimes there was actually traffic. Then there were the preachers at the Norlina Methodist Church. The most memorable was the lanky minister who preached on the Golden Rule. Stretching one syllable into three, and three sentences into a twenty-minute sermon, he drove home the metaphor he clearly thought was brilliant. "A good rule . . . is a good friend. I said, A gooood roooool . . . is a gud frend."

I also would have been hard-pressed to find the suburban equivalent of my great uncle Happy, the fourth of the six Egertons. Born

Frances Macon (a name he hated), Happy lived not far from Mema and across the railroad tracks; he seemed to take an interest in looking after his big sister Mattie Lee and her much-older husband, Tom. You would hear Happy coming before he appeared in the kitchen, slamming his way into that back hallway, yelling out, "MaddaLee!" He would emerge into the kitchen with a brown paper bag, or sack as they called it, filled with tomatoes or okra or cucumbers he had grown. Happy was a know-it-all with a sixth-grade education who had been a railroad conductor for forty years. He talked a lot with those "well, yep, yep, yep, datz right, whaddayaknow" fill-inisms. I remember one ridiculous "conversation" he had with my brother about how pigs do not possess veins. As a younger man, his full nickname was Wild Happy. He was the brother of the four Egerton boys to frequent a drinking and gambling establishment in Norlina's heyday years, playing cards with his gun by his side.

In my youth, I made no connection between my mother's people and any history other than my own. Wrestling with these relatives' complicity in the larger story of the South would come later, much later. I did feel, every time we arrived at Mema's, and I bounded up the concrete stoop beside her carport, opened the metal screen door with the intriguing italic "H" in its center, and walked into the very narrow, green and silver keyhole-motif wallpapered back hallway, as though I had entered a very different world. This was a world inhabited by people born from the 1880s to barely into the twentieth century. And yet, I felt strangely comfortable around them, and preferred their company to Robin, a second cousin my age who lived across the highway. Even though I have fond memories of my weeklong, solitary visits there in the summer, I also remember the utter silence, the heat radiating off the pavement, the sound of each tick of the living room clock waiting for its eight-note chime every fifteen minutes.

Despite the absence of anything young in Norlina, these old people were all so full of life. Yet the whole scene would later contribute to my adolescent sense of looming death. It *was* a ghostly feeling, how the past felt present in that hallway, how the fleeting future felt so present in me. Even then, this world, this permanent presence in my young life, spoke of its own impermanence. The smell spoke of it: the same mixed message, musty, sweet odor that escapes on special occasions from Mema's china closet now standing in my pantry, holding her prized Bavarian dishes with the delicate pastel flowers.

It is hard to say when, or why, I stopped just being a natural part of this world, grinning shyly at some old person at the drug store when they would say, "Well, well. You're Mattie Lee's granddaughter!" and became an observer of myself between these two worlds. Norlina would become a ten-part Hallmark Channel miniseries; Richmond, my own bad soap opera. Its first episode may have been when I was around eleven. My mother and I pulled into the concrete driveway of our house. The headlights of the VistaCruiser shone on the windows of the small den, what some would call a "family" room, and she said something like, "This house is a battlefield. It feels like a war zone every time I go in." This was because of the three-way screaming matches already begun between her, my older brother, and my father about my brother's increasing delinquency; my mother always defending him. By the time I was about twelve, the police started showing up at our front door to question him about a missing motorcycle or a report of trespassing on some construction site. The neighbors warned their kids to stay away from "that house"—mine. I rarely had friends over at that time for fear of some conflagration. The screaming and constant contention most assuredly factored into my later romanticizing—and sanitizing—Norlina's history. My immediate world was chaotic. It appeared to have no escape from so much violent emotion. Our postwar ranch house was the intractable, raging, uncertain present; Mema's early twentieth-century Queen Anne the dispassionate past. Its history had long ago resolved, reduced to simple, lighthearted, oft-repeated, word-for-word stories uttered night after night on the porch, despite moments of tractor-trailer muteness.

When we all visited Norlina, my mother would saunter into the kitchen in the morning, all sleepyheaded, well after we'd all had breakfast, and snottily grouse at her mother who was offering to make her food, "Wait 'til I have my coffee, will you." Even as a child, I thought she was babyish. Here she was a woman in her middle- to late- forties, assuming her mother, twenty years older, would wait on her. She was aware of her attitude, too. She used to say how my brother treated her was payback for how she had treated her mother. I was into my thirties before Mema and I crossed the line into openly talking bad about my mother's temper. In a rare show of emotional self-expression, Mema apologized to me for not doing more to control that temper when Mom was young. She realized how I had taken the brunt of it later in life. This was amazing; someone else noticed. To be fair, when all was peaceful in my mother's world, I got lots of attention. She listened to my middle school issues, hugged me, and often told me that all I had to be was a girl; all that I did was just extra. Still, when her world was stormy, it was I who had to calm the seas. Beginning even in elementary school, the dynamic between us was set. I was trying to help her by analyzing my father and my brother. I learned early that caring about my mother meant being her marriage counselor, her sounding board, her mother.

Unlike my mother, though, Mema was not physically affectionate. But I didn't need hugs; I needed quiet. On my solo visits, I could be a child there, left alone to my own play while Mema went about her daily work routine, which in the end inspired me more than anything else about her. When Mattie Lee was twelve and just starting the sixth grade, her mother needed her to work in the kitchen of their tourist home so she had to give up school. Dizzy made it to the seventh grade. In our later talks, I could still sense the resentment for being taken for granted and forced to grow up so soon. Then she ran away and got married. At seventeen, she met Tom Hicks, a thirty-four-year-old man. (How many times did she repeat their math; "He was twice my age but never again!"?) Her mother did the 1919 equivalent of flipping out. It took no time though for her mother to accept Granddaddy since she needed Mattie Lee back at the house to work. And work she did from then on until she gave up the house at ninety years old. For those eight decades, Mema put on her gathered-skirt work dress, laced up her black, low-heeled shoes every day at seven a.m., only stopping for fifteen minutes to down a six-and-a-half-ounce Coke straight from the thick, green bottle at precisely 10:30 a.m.

Maybe this pedestal-placing, this heroicizing of Mema lingered on into my adulthood in part because of some kind of generational Oedipus complex. I noticed by my mother's reactions that the more I purposefully admired my grandmother's more phlegmatic demeanor and physical energy, the angrier she became. Or it could have been some residual teenage urge to distinguish myself from my peers, to latch on to something seemingly more authentic than suburbia. In my classroom, some of the more precocious kids chose to emphasize one part of their heritage over another, almost always the non-European part. Some turned to their grandparents' ethnicity to tout an identity they considered more real, less American. I was the opposite. In my adolescence, I ignored the glamorous story of my paternal grandmother: the story of an orphaned, Ukrainian-born, Chinese-educated nurse who fought the other nurses to tend to the visiting American tobacco salesman who had fallen ill in Shanghai, whom she later married. No, I focused my historical imagination on a small North Carolina town a hundred miles away.

To me, southern was not a noun, not a geography. It was an ill-defined adjective describing a subculture so unique that it even created a literary genre, one that Norlina perfectly epitomized. I may have crossed a line from idealizing it to exploiting it. Its story would be my destiny, a way to combine my fourth-grade teacher's report card comment that "Lee has a talent for writing," with being voted in twelfth grade "Most Likely to Succeed," a cruel test to place on a life. A month before attending the college conference at Hampden–Sydney, I turned in a paper to Dr. Thompson, the professor for my History of the South class. He allowed me to write it on Norlina instead of a traditional research topic. This required that I visit Mema in my '66 VW Bug on a few weekends in the spring of 1978 to interview her. We would sit on the porch on a sunny morning performing some snapping or shucking maneuver on a vegetable, and I would ask her all kinds of questions about the town's history. She was baffled by my interest. I clung to my desire to keep writing about it, to write something Faulknerian, something great and profound about my grandmother and her people. Listening to Morris, Dickey, and Mr. Styron at that conference at Hampden–Sydney during my sophomore year of college had a marginal effect on that urge, except for a substantiation that being Southern was complicated and, if analyzed too closely, may lead to excessive drinking.

Outside the Box

When I saw William Styron in the West Chop, Massachusetts post office a couple of years later, my sense of being a stranger in a strange land, an immigrant from the Southland, proud of her real heritage, was still at its height. Much of my identity was still tied up in my grandmother. I was eager to make an earnest Southern connection with him, imagining from this fellow Virginian a warm response and engaging conversation. Maybe he would become so engrossed in my pithy and sincere and entertaining anecdotes that he would offer to mentor me or get me a book deal. Or best of all, invite me to one of his smart dinner parties. I summoned my courage and casually approached him. I don't remember exactly what I said about meeting him at Hampden–Sydney, but I'll never forget the subsequent interchange.

"And where are you from?"

With that question, unlike the similar one from the old matriarch, I felt he exhibited the manners and gentility of his Tidewater upbringing by taking an interest in this young worker at the club where he got his mail each day. I wondered if he had assumed that I was actually a Northerner who had just ventured down South for my college years. I wanted to clearly establish my true pedigree with him, and maybe even share a laugh over that oft-needle pointed epigram that reminds those like us that "to be a Virginian, whether by birth, marriage, adoption, or even on one's mother side is an introduction to any state in the union, a passport to any foreign country, and a benediction from Above." That's not exactly what happened.

"I've lived in Virginia—Richmond, in fact—my whole life," I answered with an expectation of the verbal equivalent of a secret handshake with a fraternity brother. There was a short silence and a slight grin appeared. With a small side-to-side shake of his head, he asked: "How can you stand to live in the South?"

I stood silent and wide-eyed in front of him. I was completely dumbfounded. I couldn't speak. I guess there wasn't going to be any dinner invitation. *How could I stand to live in the South?* At that time with my Southern chauvinism at its peak among these uptight Northerners, I may have wanted to ask him how anyone could live anywhere else. But I was just too stunned. And I was still too Christian and too young and too intimidated to have answered him with the genteel benediction, "Fuck you." I may have meekly squeaked out something brilliant like, "I like it," as he took his mail and left me reeling for the next forty years. *How could I stand to live in the South?* His phrasing presumed that living in the South was some kind of torture. His remark reminded me of when my cousin Linwood, Bobby Jean's oldest of nine, once brought a girlfriend to Norlina. She was from the upper Midwest somewhere, one of those M states. We all ate dinner at Harry and Dizzy's house across the highway from Mema's. The girlfriend was very quiet as the fried chicken and bacon-greased collards were passed around amid the loud, unsophisticated, drawl-heavy, wildly entertaining conversation. Dizzy told me later that in clearing the table after everyone had left, she took up the napkin where the poor girl had been sitting. It had writing on it. Where she got a pencil, who knows. With great laughter Dizzy repeated her plea, "Get me out of this crazy place!"

I suppose like anyone with a strong connection to a culture, a connection that has crossed some psychological line to disproportionately define her personality, it is disconcerting to say the least when confronted with the possibility of another way to live. All along you saw other people's ways of doing life as not quite real. It is like being inside a glass cube, carrying on inside the cube in the only way that you know is correct. From your protected space, if you look out at all, the people you see are acting like freaks. In actuality, the bigger world is staring at your cube like you are some midway attraction. You're the freak. Which is how I felt after my post office encounter with the self-exiled famous writer. His comment challenged the innocent notions of how I had seen myself with how outsiders saw me. Yeah, how *could* I stand to live in the South? What *was* wrong with me?

I was left to wonder which prong of superiority his comment plunged into my heart first: was he channeling H. L. Mencken's famously outrageous 1917 essay about the South, especially Virginia, as the "Sahara of the Bozart," a desert of culture and sophistication? "Virginia has no art, no literature, no philosophy, no mind or aspiration of her own. Her education has sunk to the Baptist seminary level; not a single contribution to human knowledge has come out of her colleges in twenty-five years . . ." That part is tame and just the beginning of his merciless shredding, but it ends with throwing a bone to the South. "The Southerner, at his worst, is never quite the surly cad that the Yankee is. His sensitiveness may betray him into occasional bad manners, but in the main he is a pleasant fellow-hospitable, polite, good-humored, even jovial . . . But a bit absurd . . . A bit pathetic."

Jovial, absurd, pathetic? Are these the words that came across the rest of the country's mind as it judged me in my box? Was Styron humming those words in his head as that little grin appeared on his face? Was there a hint of pity and condescension in how he shook his head side to side? Or almost worse: did he intend his remark as a compliment, as in how could a young person who lives on Martha's Vineyard in the summer live in Virginia the rest of the year? More to the point, were my earnest goals of literary greatness doomed? In a fit of *treppenwitz,* that great German word for clever comebacks that come too late, I wanted to ask him, "What gives you the right to judge an entire region, especially when you left it long ago for New England?" This encounter left me to later question the intellectual honesty and accuracy of an expatriate's view of their homeland. Didn't this perspective only substantiate myths that may live in his mind, but no longer in reality? Was the South he knew just a concept, a set of reductionist stereotypes from a bygone era that may have borne little resemblance to the region as it existed in 1981?

I lived in the South. In real time. I never left, except for this summertime gig that I was beginning to regret after the interchange in a post office in Massachusetts in some pretentious place, some "Lake-of-the-Woods," called Martha's Vineyard. However, despite my indignation at Styron's rather rude question, hadn't I also had a similar mindset to his, only mine was from the opposite perspective, from within the region? I had also used some kind of reductionist stereotype of my own. Norlina, Mema, all of it became material for a cool story that was supposed to provide me with an escape and a purpose. I had removed my people from their skin and turned them into fictional types. Mema as Mrs. Tiggy Winkle; Happy, a Dixiefied Falstaff; Mary Norris, Miss Havisham.

In the excarnation of my people, I had also given them a pass, a morally anodyne place in the deeply flawed society they inhabited, that no coconut cake could make up for. Yet, I needed to belong, to hone an identity, but I was using history for my own purposes, which always means it is not real history. My tendentious reading of Mema's past was too clouded by a misguided nostalgia. I had built part of my identity on the myth of Southern womanhood through heroicizing my grandmother. Of course, nobody wants to admit that their heroes have flaws. Isn't it better just to keep compounding the mythology so as to ward off any vertiginous cognitive dissonance that would render your life unlivable? Of course, the day inevitably arrives when the naïveté of our younger selves is shaken and shattered by a Molotov cocktail of truth lobbed in a 6½ ounce Coke bottle on to the front porch of your grandmother's house at precisely 10:30 a.m.

It would take me a long while, into my forties, and a short distance back to my old white, now wildly diverse high school, to put the flesh back on to those people, and actually see them with all of their faults. Yet so early in my life experience, and in a culture that had then still not confronted the brutality and immorality of our full history, Mr. Styron plunged the second prong into the heart of my carefully curated identity. Perhaps my measure of white guilt made me interpret his question as an indictment on the South, coming from his perceived moral high ground that the North held in America's racial geography. This, despite the real estate agent strongly advising against our uncle, a Philadelphia banker who had the looks and patrician bearing of William F. Buckley but a countervailing Everyman disposition, inviting his Black friend, a judge, to play tennis in West Chop.

Many years later, I came upon an *American Masters* PBS special when Styron's book *Tidewater Morning* came out in 1993. I watched with intense curiosity as the show followed him back to his hometown of Newport News, Virginia. In one scene the famous author is attending a Black Pentecostal church in a rural area nearby. Styron had that familiar look of a well-heeled man used to the finer things of life. (Something about the skin tone, not unlike the skin of the old white men in the Virginia House of Delegates, or the businessmen in Midtown Manhattan, or all the men in Europe, a comment that Dizzy might have disowned me for.) He sat in a folding chair looking just a tad out of place among a group of Black parishioners who clapped their hands and held them high while singing praise songs, while the famous author joined in. Although I had read that he was agnostic at best, he seemed to be seeking some kind of peace or belonging or expiation for the sins of the people who had raised him. Evidently, his inherited guilt would have lain most directly on his paternal grandmother's father, Caleb Clark, who not only owned a cotton plantation in Hyde County, North Carolina, but also thirty-three Black people. As a child, Styron was able to know his grandmother and hear the stories of the plantation before and after the Civil War, to have a direct connection to the Old South. She told of Lucinda and Drusilla, her playmates, how they would braid each other's hair, play games, knit socks, and find all kinds of nineteenth century ways to amuse themselves in rural, coastal North Carolina. They shared a relationship like most little girls, like ones I see at school between white and Black girls, only Lucinda and Drusilla were Marianna Clark's slaves, legally deeded to her as a gift from her father.

This was his grandmother who died when he was twelve, old enough for her to have had an influence not only on his boyhood but on his whole aesthetic and eventual writing career. His ancestral home stands probably a little over a hundred miles from Norlina to the east. I wonder if the older Mrs. Styron had a front porch, and I wonder if that is where she shared memories of her enslaved girls, and later of her continual starvation after General Burnside's men ransacked the farm, sending her family, along with the Black people who remained, literally into the woods to scrounge, side by side, for food. By Styron's account, she was a lively, chipper old woman who even into the 1920s and 30s harbored bitterness toward anything from the North, including his Pennsylvanian mother, just for its geography. I wondered if the famous author also sat with his grandmother in rocking chairs while she recounted these stories. Did they snap green beans or shuck corn together while she did? He had obviously loved her, but on that television program he posed an unanswerable question that I am paraphrasing from deep personal resonance: *How can we so dearly love and respect our ancestors who so dearly loved us, knowing that they did not question, and even advanced, the fundamental injustice and immorality of their society?*

My mother used to say about raising children that "more is caught than taught." This is a complementary adage to "Do what I say, not what I do!" It supposes a morally discerning child with an inherent hypocrisy meter. The abiding mystery to me as a student of history and teacher of young people is why some kids maintain those intuitions of justice despite what they may have heard at home, making them more agents of change, and why other kids do not. During my bath on the night after my very first day of school in September 1964, my mother tried to elicit my reaction to having Janet, the one newly allowed Black student at my suburban elementary school. My mother's questioning, to her credit, was not from any kind of judgment or worry; it was more curiosity. "Did you notice that you have a little, uh, a little colored girl in your class?" I must have instinctively caught a whiff of something fishy, as in why would she single out this one little girl in Mrs. Nichols' class over the others. Evidently, as she told me later, I stopped playing in the Mr. Bubbles, turned my little banged forehead her way in a quick and decided fashion, and retorted, "Yeah. So what?"

I did not hesitate to challenge, in my six-year-old way, my mother's softly implied distinctions among my classmates in the bathtub that day, nor later in my teenage years in response to my father's overt racist language. Maybe that says more about the lack of fear I had of them, because I sensed they respected me. They listened, and perhaps, in my father's case, subconsciously questioned old assumptions. However, I would find it almost impossible, indeed unspeakable, to take issue with the senior generation in Norlina for fear of the wrath I had seen spill out of them over other issues: the lazy, rich cousin Bobbie (Roberta) with her five-carat diamond ring who visited regularly and allowed Mema to wait on her hand and foot; how the state of North Carolina stole her land for the highway; how the spinster sisters Nell and Sue who occupied the two mauve bedrooms downstairs left all their money to a Baltimore nephew after Mema took care of them for decades; and anything to do with something called food stamps. During one summer visit when I was about six, I remember Mema complaining about "the nigras." We had gone to the Quality Foods five miles away in Warrenton. At the checkout, there was a Black woman in front of us who placed two big steaks and a six-pack of beer on the belt and pulled out food stamps to pay. Once back in the car, using a higher pitched voice that kind of scared me, Mema railed against the woman and argued vehemently, kind of to me and kind of to the air, that she couldn't afford steak. She had to work for her living. And something about "they just keep having babies to keep getting more food stamps."

I suppose there comes a time in a child's life, too, when the kid finally sees the adult in relationship with the world at large, lacking the innocent or loving tone that they have intimately shared. At some point, too, adults make the calculation, consciously or not, that they don't need to watch what they say around kids anymore. Sometime before the bathtub inquest, maybe 1962 or '63, I remember sitting at the kitchen table in Norlina. Happy had stopped over on one of his unexpected visits. We were sitting around the kitchen table. He was spitting mad. "That Martin Luther King, why cain't he just keep his mouth shut? He ain't nothing but an outside agitator. Getting them n****rs all riled up." Happy went on and on with a look of intense anger, which made his already huge frame look even bigger for its animation. I had not even started school yet, but this display was jarring. I could not reconcile the intense anger I witnessed in that kitchen with the love and humor and kindness these same people displayed towards me. Not yet aware of the great sin, the great hypocrisy of American history, the initial image that they planted in me as a very young girl was that this King person was disturbing the peace in North Carolina, stirring up unnecessary trouble. He should go back to his home. As though the Black people I saw around the edges of Norlina, walking on the railroad tracks, standing around the bus station directly across from the front porch, or occasionally getting a prescription at Walker Drug were completely content and didn't need, or appreciate, some minister from Atlanta upsetting their world.

This outrage at the civil rights movement up to this point would pale in comparison to when, in 1969, economic welfare issues and racism literally intersected three miles due south of Mema's front porch in a place called Soul City. The brainchild of lawyer and civil rights leader Floyd McKissick, Soul City was to be a large planned community of homes and industry meant to stem the tide of thousands of Blacks fleeing to the North by luring business to the South. The plan gained national attention and, in the minds of my relatives, threatened to attract all kinds of Black people, possibly of the militant variety so close to Norlina. Norlina! Needless to say, this plan did not go over well with the already 40 percent *minority* residents in Warren County, who happened to be white. With such an influx, they would be even more outnumbered. The subset of that white minority, the rocking chair crowd on Mattie Lee's front porch, responded to this invasion of both Blacks and "Yankees" in a way that may have rivaled the way the whole South reacted to the election of Lincoln. The porch volume was at a full ten whenever this topic came up. "Who knows what kind of drinking and carrying on will go on up there?" "Let 'em all go to Chicago and New York!" "This ain't no place for some n****r city." No surprise, Soul City failed at the hands of the notoriously conservative, racist senator from North Carolina, Jesse Helms. The Norlina crowd was exultant and sang the praises of Senator Helms as if he were some kind of messiah who saved their Canaan from the heathen Hittites.

My political naïveté diminished, naturally, as my intellectual prowess, such as it was in high school, grew. By around junior year, the analytical training I had honed by examining intractable family problems, but more so from observing my mother's preternatural ability to lay blame and nail hypocrisy ("You bought a new shirt? I thought you said you didn't have any money") started to pay off on my report card. In my US history class, notably in *Richmond, Virginia*, it didn't take long, perhaps the end of October, for me to question Mr. Whitten, "What? So Thomas Jefferson owned slaves? I thought he said 'all men are created equal??'" My righteous indignation grew at the unfair treatment of Black Americans that I witnessed on television. This is about when, as a "sanctimonious" (my mother's description of me) teenager, I began to regularly reprimand my father for using the n-word. Yet I never once exercised that same indignation with the elders in Norlina as I came of age.

I guess I had honed a certain role to play around the people of my past, one that became difficult or impossible to step out of as my education and exposure to new ideas—critical ideas—about American history and the Black experience increased. While it was that very Norlina provenance that prompted my intellectual awakening, particularly in the American experience, I couldn't find the courage, or social morality that would have superseded my deep filial respect. I could never bring myself to challenge the older people in my life with the newer version of me, one that I felt they might reject.

My lack of a moral inventory of the story of Norlina that I wrote in college reflects this timidity and deference. Despite my high school awakening to white guilt and white supremacy, my investment in my grandmother's story did not allow for any dissonance. The borderline mawkish tone characterizes the paper I turned into Dr. Thompson a few weeks before meeting Mr. Styron for the first time in the spring of 1978. It begins:

```
It would be easier to say that there was much
of her within me, but in actuality there was
much of me trying to be within her. Discovering
the past through her eyes requires me to fill in
the gaps with my imagination, to subconsciously
visualize and hopelessly romanticize the
incidents of her life and town.
```

That tone did not end when I submitted the paper. For decades afterwards, those stories flowed through my mind in a gauzy, cinematic haze of nostalgic scenes. Mema and her "shadow," as she called her friend Earlene, along with a Black midwife named Aunt Bertha aiding a beautiful, pregnant "gypsy" girl who lived in a camp a few miles from the house to have her baby in a nearby field. My beloved, knock-kneed, gray-haired old Walter Matthau of an Aunt Dizzy as a chubby eleven-year-old on summer nights of 1923, dragging her sister's Victrola on to an unfinished Number One Highway at night, lowering its needle and dancing to some scratchy big band as the sun went down. I can almost hear the familiar whimsy in her voice as she remembered it. "I wore out three pairs of shoes that summer." Her future druggist husband, Harry Walker, bragging to me about organizing something called a scrip dance, how he even got "Saxy Dowell and his Quintet to come down from Richmond" to play in Taylor's Hardware Store. "Harmless" veterans of World War I who rode the rails during the Depression, hobos, coming up the railroad embankment to the back door of the Norlina Tourist Home, getting a free meal. A young man at the top of a telegraph pole, ear to its wires, yelling down World Series scores to the men below in the train yard. Barely averting a race riot after an early iteration of the Norlina KKK took two Black men into the woods and shot them in the back.

History Hitting Home

T his is where the gauzy haze should have lifted. When I wrote the paper, this story served as an example—historical evidence—of "race relations" in the South. An actual place that I was very familiar with intersected with History from history books. How cool. And one of the worst chapters ran through my mind as fiction, and yet its characters were actual people I knew, my people. And I wasn't too interested in indicting them. Rather, as I wrote then at twenty-one: *I wanted to relive those times with her . . . but my connection to those events come through thought, not participation.* My only conclusion was that *realistic meaning emerged from these stories she told me when I realized that they are history. History is the study of such stories in the aggregate.* The problem was that in my adoration of my grandmother, I had failed to adequately feel the injustice and pain that those murders inflicted on other participants in the Norlina story. I failed to make a moral judgment.

This is the failure of much of our collective history, too. From the first time I wrote about it in that college paper, I used the killing of two men, who at the time I would have called "two anonymous Black men," as some kind of perverted personal credential of my amateur historiographical skills. I may have trotted out the Norlina Race Riot story, told with all the regret and horror I could muster across the six or seven decades, and two generations that I was removed from it, at a dinner party or a Bible study, adding the almost amusing anecdote about how her brother Happy once asked Mema to make him a robe out of Black satin. "*I didn't think anything of it. It was just like the ones I made for the church choir.*" Did that brother ever wear it? Did he join that mob that lynched two Black men? I can hear Mema's familiar front porch voice recounting in testimonial form—no emotion, no compunction—the story of that night when I read it from the lone remaining Xeroxed copy of my old college paper:

Around midnight on January 22, 1921, like
every other night in those years in Norlina, a
southbound train was headed into the station.
Just as it rounded the bend, shots were fired
in the dark of the train yard. The two Taylor
brothers, whose family owned the hardware
store, fell to the ground. Two young Black boys
fled back across the railroad tracks into the
night. The train pulled in to the station, and
the passengers were told what had happened.
A man headed for Texas got off and started
yelling and encouraging violence and revenge.
He took a room at the Rosewood Hotel by the
tracks and stayed for several days. The Taylors
were taken by train to the nearest hospital.

The sheriff deputized some men in the town
to help him search for the culprits. In the
Black community the children were crouched
under beds and the adults hid under the
porches or anywhere they could find. Many were
handcuffed and taken to the school auditorium.
Fifty or sixty Blacks lined the room and
occupied the stage. Whites paced the aisles
echoing each other, "Kill 'em, kill 'em."
Emotions were running high with the thought
of the two boys laying [sic] up there in the
hospital near death. Finally, seven or eight of
the Blacks who were suspected most were taken
to the jail in Warrenton. By that time the
governor had sent troops to guard the jail.

There used to be an all-night restaurant here
in town, called Jack the Greek's. We were out one
night soon after with another couple who we did
our courtin' with, and your granddaddy stopped
there to get some cigarettes. He came back to the
car and said that the place was packed full of
men, every table full, and he sensed something
stirring. The men had hoods now, but they weren't
the Ku Klux Klan. That didn't organize until
later. Well, we drove back by there in a few
minutes and the place was deserted."

The hooded men had gone over to the jail in
Warrenton. Part of them went up the street past
it and shot several bullets in the air. The
state troopers ran up the street to investigate.

```
Meanwhile, the other men ran in, rushed the
jailor, and took two of the suspected Blacks.
They only took the two that were the known
instigators since they had to work so quickly.
The men threw them in the car, drove them out
of town, let them loose, and shot them.
```

In the early days of internet research, possibly fifteen years ago, I was astounded once to see a tiny square-inch reference to these killings on a New York Times archive page. Norlina in The New York Times! How was this possible? This was my carefully curated town, insulated, beyond geography, beyond time, out of sight from outsiders in some other real-time America. Yet there it was, a pinprick of reality in my inflated mythology. But now, countless newspaper archives exist online. During a seven-day free trial on Newspapers. com, I cross-referenced "Norlina" with January 24, 1921. That search yielded no fewer than 171 results. The Topeka State Journal, The Sioux Falls Argus-Leader, The Buffalo Commercial, Tampa Tribune, Santa Ana Register, The Las Vegas Optic, all with similar headlines: Two Negroes Lynched at Norlina. The 171 sepia-toned squares of old-timey typeset, all with the word Norlina highlighted in yellow right in the middle of each result, over and over again, city after city, created a visual ladder of shame.

This little town that meant so much to me in the closed society of the imagined past, had been given its fifteen minutes of infamy across America. From each newspaper square, I could decipher the same fragmentary snippets of facts—Bullock, apples, mob, riddled, jail, Williams—in each. The one exception in the 171 was the last one, a train schedule in the Richmond Times-Dispatch announcing a 9:00 departure on the Seaboard Airline from Main Street Station on the morning after the crime. It was as if to say that life would go on, the eighteen to twenty trains would keep running, taking passengers, who may have had no idea what had happened there, through Norlina. The railroad is what put Norlina on the map joining it to new commerce and promise, and yet it was in the train yard in the first hours of January 23 in 1921 that it joined other cities and towns in that time which would be known for brutal, racist, murderous, unpunished vigilantism.

The most thorough recounting came in the *Charlotte News*, found on The Red Record, a site dedicated to cataloging lynching in North Carolina by decade. The headline says more than was intended. "Warrenton Gets Back to Normal After Lynching." That sums up no less than the entire process of historical change. Normal. For whom? The incident that prompted both Black and white Norlina men to meet that night with guns in the railyard was supposedly an argument over the price of some apples between a Black teenager, Plummer Bullock and perhaps his defender, Alfred Williams, a Black man in his forties, with the white grocer earlier. In the hail of bullets, the very popular Taylor Brothers who owned the hardware store were shot and taken to the hospital. Then a mob of over a hundred white men forced the Black jailor in Warrenton, just a few miles from Norlina, to open the cells of two of the prisoners. Plummer Bullock and Alfred Williams were sent to run barefoot into the cold night and then shot in the back. Their bodies were mutilated. The article describes how the brother of the teen, Matthew Bullock, was the true instigator, but somehow escaped imprisonment by running home. It goes on to say how the Warrenton Blacks grew agitated and threatened an uprising before the police and deputized "home guards" restored order.

Matthew Bullock, Plummer's older brother and alleged ringleader of the Black rioters, was the center of four months of *New York Times* headlines. Amazingly, after reaching home in Norlina that night, he escaped to Canada in his father's car. In her book, *North of the Color Line*, Sarah-Jane Mathieu used Bullock's story to highlight the birth of the Klan there. According to Mathieu, he may have either made his way on foot over the ice or folded himself into a group of Black worshippers to gain entry near Hamilton, Ontario. He changed his name, worked construction, joined a church, and stayed out of trouble for nearly a year. It seems he was then betrayed by someone who sent his picture and true identity to Camman Morrison, the governor of North Carolina, who demanded that Bullock be extradited to stand trial for attempted murder in Norlina. A standoff between the governor and a Judge Snider in Ontario followed. In those *New York Times* articles, Morrison reassured the world that Bullock would get a fair trial and revealed his twisted, unconstitutional justification of vigilantism. He stated that "people in some sections of the country do not seem to understand that so-called lynchings in the South are nothing more than the killing of a criminal by the friends and frequently outraged relatives of the victim of the prisoner's crime . . ." He used the phrase "so-called lynchings" several times.

During the days when the Canadian judge was deciding whether to extradite Bullock, The New York Times interviewed his elderly, minister father who had come to Hamilton, Ontario, from Norlina for the decision: "Asked as to what percentage of the white population of Norlina harbored extreme hatred against the Black population, Mr. Bullock replied that they nearly all did. 'Oh there are a few good people there, just as there are everywhere, but there's a whole host of bad ones,' he said. Feelings still ran pretty high between the two races in Norlina, Mr. Bullock said. Mr. Bullock continued, that for a Black, there could be no justice in Norlina." When I read this, I could not help but wonder if the elder Mr. Bullock would have ever come across any of my people, and to which category they would have fallen in his mind. I didn't have to wonder very long.

In response to another of my questions as we sat on the porch one beautiful spring day of my junior year in college, Mema recounted a memory of the day following the murders:

```
The next day we walked up to the house from the
apartment we were living in at the time. The
Texan was out front yelling to everyone, "Wanna
go see two dead n****rs, wanna ride and see the
two dead n****s?!" Sure, I went! There were two
boys laying up in the hospital almost dead, and
people were angry. I heard that the coroner was
out of town, so the nigras stayed up there on
the side of the road for a couple of days for
everyone to see.
```

The horror of this scene is matched only by her reaction to what must have been my naïve question, "Did you go, too, Mema?" I really want to erase her unanticipated, enthusiastic response, "*Sure I went!*" from my beloved grandmother's story of the killings. I don't like to think of her as a nineteen-year-old girl, married two years by then, who could muster that much anger and revenge. I think of the famous Little Rock Nine photograph of Hazel Bryan screaming in hatred at Elizabeth Eckford and wonder if Mema could have looked similarly in conversation with other Norlinians during the crisis. Sure she did. I had seen that face a few times, like in discussions of Soul City or at the Quality Foods in Warrenton. "*Sure, I went!*" Why would she ever want to go see two dead bodies, a man and a teenager, that were most likely beyond just being riddled with bullets, perhaps also castrated and charred from the common practice of burning lynching victims afterward? As though this was her civic duty. How could viewing dead, mutilated Black bodies on the side of the road satisfy some kind of sick revenge for her two friends being in the hospital? "*Sure, I went!*" Instead, I wanted her to say that she was sick for years over the whole event, to profess to her own racial guilt, to assure me that even though she had only finished seventh grade, she somehow understood the American idea of equal justice under the law. I wanted to hear how she agonized over the tragedy. Especially once I learned about her very personal connection to one of the victims:

> The nigras had been meeting in their churches for I reggin' a month after that, and we got wind that they were to come into town on a specific night in March. I went up to the house since your granddaddy had to work that night. He had given me a pistol, but I wasn't going to stay down there by myself. My mother was afraid they would come up the bank in the back and set the house on fire or something. I remember there were two men rooming there that night who sold patented medicine, and we sat up by a wood-burning stove all night. Later we heard that the nigras knew the whites were ready for them in town so I reggin' disbanded. There was never any more said or done about it. No animosity is there now.
>
> Course you know that the chief of police here now is a black man? And you should remember Indy, the colored woman that did washing and ironing for me? Why we love Indy

```
better than anything. In fact, Elizabeth and
I took her a cake for her birthday last week.
Well, Indy's brother was one of them that was
lynched.
```

This defied belief. Not only in the glib, self-centered estimation that no animosity remained, but in her equally oblivious assumption about Indy. It made me wonder if it were really true. Fortunately, The Red Record website also contains death certificates for lynching victims. As just one of thousands in this shameful history, Alfred Williams's record in its municipal matter-of-factness, so unemotional and businesslike, tells a lot about that night.

Name: Alfred Williams. Date of Birth: about 1876. Age: 45.
Married: Tempie Perry Williams. Occupation: farming.
Name of Father: J.B. Williams.
Cause of death: Pistol wounds around chest, back, thigh; *lynched by mob.* [italics mine]
Informant: J. B. Williams. Mother's Maiden Name: Indinia Alston.

Indinia. Like the newspaper accounts of the killings, reading this name written in someone's loose cursive across a line on an old form in a North Carolina office so long ago, startled me a little, made me take an extra chest-raising breath. It really was true, then. Indy, Mema's helper and friend whom I had met several times, must have been named for her mother, Indinia, and called by a nickname, Indy.

As much as I loved Mema for all she gave me internally, I wish I had an alternate memory of her in this story. I wish I could remember sitting on her front porch hearing her voice soar in moral triumph at how she cussed out her wild brother when he asked her to sew him a stupid, ignominious hood so he could be just like all the other cowards in town. I would like to summon in my mind's eye her beating on Happy's chest and warning him not to even think of joining that mob, using that same high-pitched food stamp tone. And I really wish Mema had had a more emotional side, that during one of my college trips she would have tearfully recounted how she apologized to Indy at some point in their long friendship, if that term even applied to their relationship. But none of that was ever going to happen. Instead, her answer to the thicket of racial guilt can be found in the most telling statement Mema made to me in all of my interviews of her about Norlina. It is not original to her, nor does it lie in the dead past. I must have asked her about how she felt about "race relations," the popular euphemism of the day for a one-sided relationship, one of white supremacy. In a kind of honest ignorance and employing the same unquestioned moral authority to speak for both races that a mother uses to speak for her kindergartener, she answered me. *"It's simple. We always got along with the nigras, as long as they knew their place."*

Her tone was one of complete obviousness. The white supremacy was matter-of-fact, as matter-of-fact as Alfred Williams's death certificate. Whites, especially poor whites like my people, had an ingrained notion that they were not just better, it was worse than that. They convinced themselves that "getting along," according to their preconditions, was the moral equivalent of social and political equality. Privately, personally they knew and loved certain Black people; but that would never extend to any broader public, societal equality. This unspoken code of racial etiquette gave whites a moral pass, a weak substitute for actually abiding by the real law. Taking Indy a birthday cake made up for murdering her brother. No apology, no penance, need be made for lynching since that boy and man failed to stay in their place that day at the grocer's. They got what they deserved. This was just citizens avenging a friend's murder, as Governor Morrison explained. Perhaps as a kind of deep compensation for the violence, the injustice, and the lack of any guilt on their consciences, these people, my people, were very kind to Blacks, deferent Blacks, that is. But it would have been impossible for that generation of Norlina white people to imagine and then dignify any Norlina Black people as equals.

Harry Walker, the druggist husband of my beloved Dizzy, would occasionally get a knock on his back screen door on a Sunday afternoon. There would be an older Black man asking in a very humble demeanor for an emergency prescription refill or some over the counter medicine for himself or his wife. Harry, and sometimes Dizzy, would kindly walk the man across the highway to the back of the drug store and go inside to get him what he needed while he waited in the alley. As yet more evidence of the ahistorical, youthful righteousness that knows how to shame its elders, one of Bobby Jean's nine kids, probably in the 1960s, witnessed this. He started crying. He overlooked the good deed Harry did and instead saw the bigger picture. "Why did he have to come to the back door?"

Her son may have come by this naturally. Bobby Jean once told me that around the age of twelve, when her own sense of justice was blooming (which would have been in the late 1940s), she was riding in the back seat of the car when she said something to her father Street along the lines of how Black people should be treated equally, that prejudice just wasn't fair. Street, who is my grandmother's next brother, abruptly pulled the car to the side of the road and slammed on the brakes. He looked at her sternly from the front seat, and told her in no uncertain terms, "You are white. You are better. Remember your last name."

Less obvious, but to me somehow more telling of the American Black experience than *their place,* is the other part of Mema's statement, *as long as.* That phrase sums up our contradictions from the start. *As long as* runs deep in our schizophrenic national psyche. America is a land of opportunity, *as long as* you work hard, which, if completely true, would flip the tax tables on a lot of people today. All men are equal, *as long as.* And who gets to decide which of us needs an *as long as?* Of course, worst of all, *as long as* implies a physical threat, one that was made good on in Norlina for young Plummer Bullock and Alfred Williams and thousands of other people, in other places, where extralegal justice and mob violence cast America in the same lot as any other totalitarian regime.

As long as still plagues our nation. *As long as* you keep your hands on the wheel, *as long as* you don't play your music too loud, *as long as* you don't wear a hoodie, *as long as* you don't play with a water gun while being Black you have a better chance of surviving an everyday encounter with an authority. A stellar junior girl did a Theory of Knowledge presentation on one of these police stops, namely the murder of Philando Castile, an event that upset her so much she could not enjoy her much-anticipated sixteenth birthday. This all-too-real life and death situation led her to the question, "What are the limits and conditions for empathy in a multi-ethnic culture?" In preparation, she told me how her father, a successful lawyer often seen on local television ads, had forgotten to renew his car registration in time. The new sticker would arrive one day after the old one expired. One day. I was thinking how a couple of years back, I too forgot to renew, but mine was eight months overdue. I finally got pulled over and given a $75 ticket. But her dad is Black. She told me how her sister bawled and begged her father not to go to work that day, the first day of that new month. She was afraid he wouldn't come home, that he would be pulled over and not survive the encounter. I was dumbfounded. I feared the annoyance of a ticket; they feared the worst.

After she passionately presented her PowerPoint about this deadly police encounter, one boy got up and asked me privately if he could go to school counseling. I later emailed the counselor to see if everything was all right. She replied that he was upset by the presentation. This student is also African American, the brother of a former student and Yale graduate. After a few class periods passed, he looked me straight in the eye, and with a little grin said, "Ms. Knapp, I never told you why I wanted to leave class the other day." I grinned back and said, "Let's go into my office." We stepped outside on to the sidewalk. The two of us stood there alone in the chilly February morning. He told me how he had been pulled over no fewer than three times in the seven months since he had gotten his driver's license. This was in his upscale neighborhood, driving his parents' Volvo. He was a very mild-mannered student. I had no problem believing his claim that he had not been doing anything wrong. He did have a small Afro whose silhouette may have made a policeman tailing him suspicious. It had really upset him, especially with all the police shootings.

Later I thought about my three boys. His mother has three boys. I never once had to worry about any of those scenarios. Nor did my kids ever get pulled over, except once when the older two were driving a rental car on the way to the Jersey Shore, a free upgrade of a low-slung Dodge Magnum station wagon with heavily tinted windows. There was no reason for the stop. The cop was evidently very surprised when my blue-eyed, sandy-haired, Ancestry.com-verified son of Western European descent rolled down the darkened driver's side window, and his blue-eyed blonde brother in the passenger seat leaned in and asked, "Is there anything wrong, officer?" All they had to suffer was trying not to laugh as he gave them a little face-saving shit before sending them on their way.

Workarounds

A lthough it is still an incomplete and fraught process, *the lack of an as long as* is what I have always thought it meant to be an American. The old European ideas of peerage no longer applied to political, and eventually cultural, power. But in reality, it's more like the comment made by the young man of a couple who stayed in my Airbnb room, a New York City councilman from Brooklyn. He replied in his best sing-songy, Woody Allen voice after I asked if they'd enjoyed their visit to Monticello, "Eh. It's complicated." On the first day of school one year, I asked my US History class to entitle a short paper "I am America." They answered a few questions about themselves and their origins, followed by what they were interested in learning about during the year. One young Black woman wrote that her grandmother always warned her to be cautious around white people, not to trust them, and taught her some kind of "white people workaround skills." So that caused her to want to learn more about racism in American history and the origin of her grandmother's fear.

Her grandmother was passing on a very different approach to life than I received from mine. In the public or social realm, I never considered that I would be at least discounted, or at worst in danger, for speaking my mind. I haven't lived my life worried about stepping beyond any limits on my psyche or the expression of my personality to the wider world. Indeed, the greatest gift my female forebears, Mema, Dizzy, and my mother, bestowed on me, especially as I entered adulthood, was an inner confidence borne not from money or pedigree, but from a degree of creative mastery over my environment. Mema said more than a few times, "We were poor, but we had pride." I am confident that this rings true more so for Black Americans, like this student's grandma, who were given the same example. Only I was never told to proceed with caution around anyone

And yet. While the big outside world imposed no *as long as* restrictions on my psyche, my small inside world did. I could possibly find a way, a sideways, internal, emotional, empathic entry into my former student's grandmother's advice about proceeding with caution around white people since I had to proceed with caution around my mother. It is no way to live. Inside a culture or inside a house. To feel like you have to be twice as perfect than your disrespectful, lawbreaking brother, and you will still get shit from those you have to love, incites a lot of anger over time. It perverts personality. It crushes souls. Since childhood, I subconsciously developed my own internal workaround strategies to avoid that sinking, shaky feeling in the wake of her temper. Saying I was sorry did not easily quell it, either. So my black belt, my Oscar, my Nobel Peace prize came for superior achievement in the art of what I would call maintaining a posture of defensive perfectionism. The theory goes a little like this: If you never do anything wrong, until you do, no one can tell you to go to hell and slam the phone in your face when you are a junior in college because you forgot the date of her small medical procedure.

When my oldest had just graduated from college, we had a nice lunch outside on the Downtown Mall in Charlottesville, a decade before it became the site of the infamous riot. It was a sunny June day. We both drank gin and tonics. I had been fretting over some family thing to him and he nailed me: "Mom, you think if someone criticizes you, they don't love you anymore. That's not how it works." Having raised three sons, this was as close as I'd ever gotten to a mother-daughter conversation. Did this long-cultivated aversion to conflict through accommodation show? Was it not time to deal with my deep-seated fear of the fear that comes with honesty, both incoming and outgoing? He was right, but I was still paralyzed by an inordinate need for a kind of permanent détente, complete domestic tranquility that was missing in my childhood.

But conflict is inevitable, unless one party just surrenders to others' conditions. *As long as* I did what was expected of me, mostly in the form of commiseration, with my mother and later my husband, our relationships were good. And for so long, I did it freely; it was my way of showing love. But this is not unconditional love; it's *as long as* love. Having been called selfish a few times growing up, which for an ultra-sensitive kid seemed like a thousand times, I determined to prove that wrong. Along with a faith that demanded putting others above one's self, I practiced my own workarounds. I would meet their emotional needs first, then pursue my own more solitary, creative passions. I found out much, much later that these are stereotypical passions. As it turned out, I wasn't just little old selfish Lee: I was a type! A selfish *type*! I belonged to a time-honored set of selfish types throughout history, artists who liked to make things and think about stuff.

This was perhaps my personal Booker T. Washington approach, writ small and white. Do what the powerful say and then gain respect. Before you know it, you're finally an equal person with a different agenda. The trick is: this never happens without some kind of ultimatum of a reasonable demand. I thought of this when we discussed these two turn-of-the-century Black thinkers in class. Of course, W. E. B. Du Bois was right. He straight up rejected *as long as*, not to mention some specious notion of staying in one's place determined by that same unjustified power. I sometimes wish earlier on that I had been less Booker T. and more W. E. B. in my personal life. Du Bois knew that this accommodationist tact was as demeaning to Black personhood as slavery had been. Resentment builds in the face of a real or perceived power imbalance. Indeed, what is it like to assume power, to be unapologetically, and most often undeservedly, demanding? What if I told someone—someone I loved—to go to hell, knowing full well they would still answer the phone the next day, pretending it never happened? I sometimes wondered why I had not mastered that art of being more feared than loved as Signor Machiavelli reminded me each September we learned about the Renaissance. Oh, to be feared. Maybe it is better to walk around with the no-holds-barred demands of "Yeah, you HAVE to love me!" Do people who presume supremacy in any form also presume endless forgiveness for their overpowering wills? There is a boiling point in those who have lived under the often unspoken *as long as* demands of a home—or a homeland. Mine was a long time coming.

All my life, my brother Dalton broke the law any chance he got. He had nineteen criminal counts against him before he was eighteen years old, mostly grand larceny and trespassing. As even my mother used to say, "He just thumbs his nose at the law." He never served a day in juvenile detention, or later jail. This was her life's goal. "Punishment is never going to change him." This was the great unchallenged and unproven contradiction in her mind. She constantly made excuses for his behavior. He was her Lost Cause, reinterpreting his illegal actions through the guise of ADHD. She was the extralegal, vigilante justice, with some kind of perverted code that justified his actual actions with the imagined reasons she ascribed to them. She never faced the fact that what he did was wrong. She never considered his victims. She had one, singular interpretation of the story—his survival. The law existed, but not for Dalton. And of course, he began to believe that he was immune from punishment, so he kept breaking the law and kept getting away with it. Not that my mother was rewarded for her life's work. He eventually turned on her at the age of fifty, when, angry over my mother's sympathy for his estranged wife and daughter, he drove his dually truck at full speed toward her dining room with his .45 on the front seat. He stopped a foot away, a skill he learned drag racing, I guess. He turned in his daughter for trespassing and stealing when she went into her old house, *his house*, to get her coin collection, an offense for which she spent a few days in the county's juvenile jail, the very same one my mother managed to keep him from his whole childhood. This is what happens when someone believes they are truly above the law, statutory and moral.

During this time when Dalton's family stayed with my mother, she lived in a sustained whirlpool of hysteria and drama that tried to suck in everyone who got close. Not a good memory, but one night she was cowering in her bedroom like a cornered hyena (if a cornered hyena wore a short-sleeved pink nylon/polyester nightgown trimmed in fading white lace), screaming and crying over something he had done to his daughter. I know I was supposed to feel empathy for this woman who was easily in her mid-seventies, but all I could feel was pity and disdain. Her world was so small it didn't take much for it to appear to be coming to an end. During those years, she hung up the phone on me regularly, or gave me the silent treatment, or cussed me out. I was dealing with my own pretty worrisome marital and financial issues, which she used to say she never worried about because "we knew the Lord," and he would take care of us. (I kept waiting for the mailman to ring my doorbell and have me sign for a certified letter with a check inside signed "Jesus Christ. Esquire.") A breaking point came.

As unlikely as this sounds at first glance, Martin Luther King's famous "Letter from a Birmingham Jail" not only offers instruction for social activism, it is also a guide for any individual living in an unequal relationship built on fear. There is no comparison to the kind of fear and pain he describes that the people of Birmingham, and all Blacks, lived under, fear for their very lives just because they began to demand equality and respect. He talks about real love, and how it actually requires confrontation, not acquiescence or passivity. Why? Because real love—of country or family—requires honesty to rectify any harm. He was literally in jail, many times, for acting on this rationale in his love for America, so again there is no comparison. First of all, King argues for a healthy provocation, what he calls a "constructive nonviolent tension that is necessary for growth." Most importantly, this provocation is an act of love. It is an act of love, as he says, by "nonviolent gadflies," people who create "the kind of tension in society that . . . allows people to escape the bondage of myths and half-truths." This is a worthy goal, to be a nonviolent gadfly. Perhaps they are like prophets who shine a light on those places of the heart that, collectively and individually, keep us bound and un-free. Pointing out such obvious contradictions in our own lives, or in a society, or sometimes in loved ones is the only way to bring about change. However, we must stay humble. These provocations should not be used to give us any advantage, but as King wrote, they are judged against a higher law, one that "uplifts human personality."

Just as Dr. King's emphasis was on our collective history, there had to be a moment of truth in my singular history. It took me long enough—I was around forty-five years old. My mother was nearly eighty, only ten years left of her life. Even after I had my own kids, she, an only child, seemed to expect me to have a mother's love for my brother. "What if one of *your* boys were in this situation?" She loved that guilt by grammar tactic of laying on the second person when it was clearly a singular first person issue: *You* don't really care what happens to *your* brother, do *you*?" It was past time to have my human personality uplifted. One afternoon, like so many before on her back porch, I just plainly told her that if she wanted to have a relationship with me in the future, we could not make Dalton the center of it anymore. To her credit, she listened and agreed. From then on, our conversations avoided my older brother. The only problem was that I have two brothers.

* * *

Just like my relationship with my grandmother, in America's relationship to its past, why are we held in bondage to "myths and half-truths," as King also wrote in his famous epistle? Why didn't we confront the hypocrisy and horror of slavery with wide-eyed honesty? Why not go on to fully realize not only the purpose of the Civil War, but of America itself? Why create a Lost Cause instead of facing reality? Why do we think that if someone criticizes America they don't love their country? Why is protest so often seen as a lack of patriotism, rather than the height of it? Is it not a good thing to course-correct when your children or your country is veering away from your ideals? "America is the greatest country in the world." "America, love it or leave it." "Our country, right or wrong." Just like my own strategy with my mother, this national defensive perfectionism wears thin over time. Is it not freeing to just let go and admit the faults in order to improve?

So why did I have to couch my love of my grandmother in these absolutist terms, to pretend she was perfect? I do wish she had not been so much a product of her time and place, that she could have had a moral imagination that made Indy a full person, a grieving sister, who could have sparked Mema's own sense of justice. She did recognize change, though, and change for the better. *Course you know that the chief of police here now is a Black man?* This was my sophomore year in college, 1978. In Norlina. The town fathers must have hired him. He was the law, and he carried a gun. She called him Ronnie on his insistence. She talked about him often, about what a "fine young man" he was. We were thankful that he would often come up to the house to check on her.

So, when do we get to judge people? Maybe the real question is not in the judging, but in the prejudging. How do we justify prejudice towards other people, whole groups, entire geographical regions like Styron did to me? Just how intellectually lazy is this? Where is the proof? Teaching among so much diversity has only stoked my 70s ideals of buying the world a Coke. Maybe it's quaint, or that overly sentimental tendency of old people to back-in-my-day you, but on that very campus back in 1976, there was hope among us young people that we would completely eliminate prejudice. If that happened, then racism, which we distinguished at that time as the unjust, institutional, powerful outgrowth of interpersonal prejudice all over society, would also fade away.

Why does it feel like all of that backfired? What does it say when just a few years back when I was still in my fifties, a thirty-two-year-old male colleague "accused" me of being *ridiculously idealistic?* *"Wow. You really think the best of people."* This came in one of a few very enlightening and collegial conversations with this young white male the age of my sons about his feeling that the rest of America is out to get him, that he is the evil one. This is a person who is very popular with all of the kids regardless of race or background, and he taught all ninth graders then so he deserves lots of saint points. I told him to use those feelings of being prejudged negatively to tap into the minority experience. Then I told him that when those zero-sum thoughts come into his head, "Reject them!" Such a young person to be so jaded and cynical. It was actually sad.

And yet. He could have found some evidence for his thesis in one of my classes of advanced students. A few had gotten their rush to judgment down to Olympic speeds and considered that the foundation of their intellectual prowess. Theirs seemed to be a new permutation of *as long as.* With dramatic eye-rolling and a "you just don't get it" condescension, these class leaders were quick to lay labels, pronounce, judge, or excuse entire groups without any nuance of thought or pretense of humility. They based their judgment exclusively on any evidence of racial or sexual transgressions. I confess that on one Monday morning after an evening of too much acquaintance-enhancing red wine with my new, retired companion, I couldn't hold in my reaction to one very insulting pronouncement about the beliefs that some of the other students held dear. After a very slow-motion deliberation in my head, my irritation escaped in an "oops, that was out loud" blurt. I called the student's name and said, "Wow. You are being so judgmental." The class uttered a collective, "Oooo," like I had just scored points in a rap battle. There was the most awkward of silences, followed by a thought that this might be the end of my teaching career. To this student's credit, our relationship was quickly normalized. I know some of the other students in the class were thankful to me for saying what they had wanted to many times. They had often been victims of these narrow moral litmus tests and suffered the judgment of being unredeemable "horrible people."

I wished I had rediscovered King's letter earlier so I could have required that class to read and discuss it as I did the following year. Perhaps the same question would have come to me then to goad them into a deeper analysis. "So what is the difference, if any, between righteousness and self-righteousness, and where does Dr. King's letter fit in this dichotomy?" The letter implies that righteousness presumes a higher law, uplifts human personality, and confirms the I-thou relationship among people. Actual laws must be agreeable to the majority if they are to be applied to them, too. One of many reasons that the letter is so powerful is that while he is critical of the white moral leaders of Birmingham for their complacency, he is not attacking their personhood. He is appealing to their humanity and to their patriotism, ultimately.

Among the following year's group, the discussion of King's letter became a call for empathy. One Black student recognized the recent tendency to go quickly to the label of racist when perhaps evidence does not exist for it. Another young Black woman spoke of a desire to listen more to the hearts of peers rather than presuming a position of knowingness and superiority because of her different experiences. King's ideas gave context to a conversation I had with that same student who had come to me earlier in the month during my planning period to apologize for changing the tenor of an earlier class discussion about sexual harassment. She confessed to jumping down the throat of a classmate and accusing him of certain attitudes after a somewhat innocuous comment he had made. It was right at the end of class. I definitely noticed and was a little nervous that a full-fledged argument might break out. Then the bell rang. The boy under suspicion made a beeline to the upset girl. I saw them going out the door, making up. She told me how she and the boy hugged it out and understood how each other felt. In terms of their outer appearances, they were quite different. By looks, he is white, a somewhat preppy type, more into science than social issues, but aware and open-minded. She is African American, a future lawyer, kind-hearted, and wise beyond her years.

The free usage of those labels "horrible person" and "good person" became so frequent among those classes that I finally asked them, "So what makes someone a good person?" They couldn't answer. I couldn't either even when applied to my closest relationships. Just as Styron pondered, I struggled with how we can love those who morally failed and fell on the wrong side of big history. Yet is one's response to social issues the only criterion by which to assess a person? My grandmother had a strong personal character, unselfish and diligent, but she was a Southerner of her time when it came to racial equality. My mother did not spew prejudice to us, but she also did not concern herself with societal justice. The biggest political conflict she cared about was against whom she may have to run to be the next president of not just Tuckahoe Park Garden Club, but the whole Richmond Federation of Garden Soviets.

Mom became a little more socially aware through attending a somewhat self-conscious Bible study effort to connect inner-city church women, that is Black, with suburban white ones. She really clicked with one new friend, telling me, "Nadine is so articulate, and so bright." Resisting a response to that charged racial canard and a diatribe about the smart young Black women I had taught during that time, I went personal. "Of course she is, Mom. She has a master's degree. You only made it through high school." This Bible study may have had an influence on Mom's late move to the left. Although never that political, she always voted Republican. She voted for George W. Bush after careful analysis and research, resulting in the conclusion, "He's kind of cute." Then the outrage of the Iraq War engulfed her, too. (Sometime during Bush's second term, she fell in love with Rachel Maddow. "That girl is so smart." I admit a kind of sibling-rivalry jealous feeling when she said that and wanted to yell back, "I'm smart, too!") She voted for the last time in November 2008. I stood in line for ninety minutes then escorted the nice young Black woman registrar to Mom's red Malibu for her to vote on a mobile device from the comfort of the driver's seat. She kept scanning her head up and down the screen looking for her man.

"Ok. Where is it? Uh. Bahama? Bahama? Orock Bahama?"

"You mean BARACK OBAMA, Mom?" I laughingly yelled at her. She laughed, too, and I could tell the registrar woman was trying to maintain her professionalism in front of this silly old lady.

So, yes, for all of these more progressive leanings in her old age, and for her way of charming anyone she chose to with her unparalleled skills of conversation, I suppose my mother would have been labeled by my smart students as a really good person. The small social world of her Methodist Church women certainly would have agreed. They might as well have been a medieval Viking village as far as my identity went. How many times did I hear the equivalent of their matronymic naming pattern? "Lee, daughter of Sarah, from clan of Pearson" become a slow Southern drawl of "Why, you're Sarah Pearson's daughter!? How wonderful. We love Sarah." These nice church ladies would have had no way of knowing the kind of turmoil the private Sarah created for Daughter Lee at times.

So what to do? An answer, or possibly a guide, for loving through the contradictions in our families—and our nation—can perhaps be gleaned from another phrase in King's letter. "Too long has our beloved Southland . . ." Beloved Southland. *Beloved*? Indeed, he always referred to himself as a proud Southerner. But how could King love a place that failed him over and over again? How could he, and all Black people, love a place that enslaved, abused, and killed their people? I wonder how many times Martin Luther King was asked, "How can you stand to live in the South?" It seems his answer would have involved a deep notion of unconditional love, one that he implies "will help men rise from the dark depths of prejudice and racism to the majestic heights of understanding and brotherhood." This is the kind of superior love Black Americans have given their country, this country. At one of Richmond's fabulous Folk Festivals, the twenty or so members of the US Marine Corps Jazz Band of all races rocked one of the tents with fantastic big band jazz, looking super cool in their deep blue, brass buttoned uniforms while blowing trumpets, playing the drums, working the saxophone. A Black female member came out to do vocals on a few songs. She ended the whole set by singing "God Bless America." I teared up a little at her introduction to it. In a sweet speaking voice, contrasted with her powerful singing voice, she talked about how much she loved the band and how much she loved America.

Laying it to Rest

J ames Baldwin came to live in William Styron's Connecticut
guesthouse in the fall of 1960 when both men were thirty-five.
They had already enjoyed literary success, Styron more broadly, in
their twenties, yet their experience of America was entirely antipodal.
In a remembrance of Baldwin on December 20, 1987, Styron wrote:
"James Baldwin was the grandson of a slave. I was the grandson of
a slave owner." He goes on to honestly reveal how his house guest
Baldwin, over many nights of dialogue, whisky, and cigarettes
exploded the "myths and half-truths" Styron's culture taught him
about Black people, those Black people who so fascinated him from
afar in Newport News in his childhood:

> Struggling still to loosen myself from the prejudices and suspi-
> cions that a Southern upbringing engenders, I still possessed a
> residual skepticism: could a Negro really own a mind as subtle,
> as richly informed, as broadly inquiring and embracing as

that of a white man? My God, what appalling arrogance and vanity. He was spellbinding, and he told me more about the frustrations and anguish of being a Black man in America than I had known until then, or perhaps wanted to know. He told me exactly what it was like to be denied service, to be spat at, to be called "n****r" and "boy." What he explained gained immediacy because it was all so new to me.

This honest confession proves that an elite education, one not in the realm of possibility for my grandmother, does not always guarantee enlightenment. It shows that a formidable artistic imagination does not always indicate a moral imagination. It reveals in a singular place, Styron's guest cottage, like a modern high school, how just interacting with those unlike you can be so powerful. Yet this quote also reveals the slow process of change in the phrase "or perhaps wanted to know." It is such a truth about any history, big or personal: people see what they want to see, whom they want to see, how they want to see them. Otherwise, a threat looms, a threat to how we have always known our people, our country, our very selves. It was twenty years after Baldwin's visit to Connecticut that Styron asked me how I could stand to live in the South. At the time, 1981, before so much demographic and cultural change, the South was still a manageable concept; so was I. But I had gone too far, developing a persona around that concept, around Mema, and myself. But of course, a persona is not a person. It is not an acceptable identity. It may have been nearly impossible in 1981 to imagine what would become of Norlina, Virginia, my school, my life. It would become equally as impossible to manage it.

In *The Fire Next Time*, Baldwin nails the impediment to one's particular moral imagination and to societal change in general: the near impossibility of shifting one's identity. He explains to his teenaged nephew that white people knew that they were not actually superior to Blacks, but "as you will discover, people find it very difficult to act on what they know. To act is to be committed, and to be committed is to be in danger. In this case, the danger, in the minds of most white Americans is the loss of identity."

C. Vann Woodward, the preeminent Southern historian, famously wrote in *The Burden of Southern History* about this problem of a changing identity. While the South was called a "peculiar region," he proposed that it was actually the rest of America that was the outlier in the grand sweep of history. First, the American narrative of uninterrupted abundance eluded the South, as it had all other nations in history. Second, the South did not participate in the larger American story of unbridled success and invincibility. Also, it alone experienced military defeat and occupation within a larger country where *that* narrative was unthinkable. Finally, in Woodward's telling, the South could not participate in the most prevailing of all American myths: a claim of national innocence:

How much room was there in the tortured conscience of the South for this national self-image of innocence and moral complacency? . . . Much of the South's intellectual energy went into a desperate effort to convince the world that its peculiar evil was actually a "positive good," but it failed even to convince itself. It writhed in the torments of its own conscience until it plunged into catastrophe to escape. The South's preoccupation was with guilt, not with innocence, with the reality of evil, not with the dream of perfection. Its experience in this respect, as in several others, was on the whole a thoroughly un-American one.

Because of the failure of Reconstruction, the South bypassed a ruthless reckoning with its collective conscience. The Lost Cause created a workaround identity, with no acknowledgement of its shameful past, or commitment, as Baldwin says, to act on what it knew had been wrong. I do wish part of my college paper on Mema included her apology to Indy. It didn't. And in a kind of microcosm of the entire region, I had to recognize my own immature need to overlook that, to make Mema's entire life story into a "positive good." In my youth, something was obviously lacking in my real time, present tense personality that made me draw so much on her past. But once this past is dismissed, and this old identity has been ransacked by skillet-licking Yankees, what replaces it—in a person, or a nation?

Emotional maturity, maybe? Perhaps a more truly integrated identity? An end to delusions of grandeur, of unexamined blame-lessness? Part of Bob the Therapist's advice to me so long ago was an assignment to locate where I may have gotten "frozen" in my past, times that I felt stuck, paralyzed. He offered that those earlier panic attacks and facial palsy were a result of being severely stymied in the process he labeled as "becoming integrated." I recounted his observations in the black and white floral journal this way:

He explained that the subconscious is running alongside the conscious mind with triggers from one to the other. The mind is pulling together all the various experiences in life and trying to create meaning and form an identity from them. Yet there are parts of life that resist integration. Bob stood up and first pointed one way as to the future, our evolving image, then pivoted to point to the past. He said behind us are frozen moments that don't fit with our

constantly emerging self. They are unresolved hurts or
assaults on our ego. My job is to see if there are any in my
life and then DO something about them.

If only American History could go to Bob the Therapist. Just a couple of sessions. It wouldn't take long to locate frozen moments in its past, unresolved hurts and assaults on its ego. And then, like me, America needed to thaw those moments, resolve the hurts, rectify the assaults in its ongoing efforts at literal integration. Baldwin wrote that "to accept one's past—one's history—is not the same thing as drowning in it; it is learning how to use it. An invented past can never be used; it cracks and crumbles under the pressures of life like clay in a season of drought." The South invented a past after Reconstruction that became useless to spark future change. It deluded itself because its psyche could not integrate such wholesale failure into its mythology. In my youth, I created a one-sided view of my family's past to invent an identity. Now, it was important for me to look back on my beloved grandmother with brutal honesty about her lack of moral vision when real history, a vigilante murder, a lynching, invaded my myth of her. I had to accept Mema as a product of her time without taking the equally judgmental and naïve attitude of total dismissal of her as a "horrible" human being. I had to forgive her. I suppose I had to also forgive myself for not challenging her or the other old people in Norlina.

Committing to a renewed and enlarged national identity, one more truly *e pluribus unum*, requires that we allow the *pluribus* to emerge from anonymity. Otherwise, reckoning with and finding forgiveness in our collective past is impossible, and meaningless. We cannot say, as I inadvertently did in past retellings of the Norlina lynchings, "two anonymous Black men" were lynched. This is why history teachers use video clips, even though they are still two-dimensional renderings, and, often, like the one I used to reinforce the causes of World War One, in black-and-white silence. Even so, during what was perhaps the fortieth time I showed Archduke Franz Ferdinand standing among all the other Habsburgs in their velvet pumpkin hats, with vertical feathers blowing in the Viennese breeze looking like lampshades in a brothel, I noticed something shocking. Franz made a goofy face at someone among the group. Was he trying to get a laugh? To mug for the newfangled camera? In that split second of grainy, stilted film, he became a real person in a real moment. It scared me, especially knowing what fate awaited him. This kind of shudder has come over me when I imagined one of *my* students in a deadly encounter with authority. When I think of my favorite students Michael or Damon being forced to run into the woods and get shot in the back, the Norlina story comes out of the grainy, black and white, irrelevant past. It is much easier on the heart just to leave history to the old newsreel, or old photos, or last week's dash cam recording.

But change is hard. How do we adapt? Who adapts? Dianne and I decided, perhaps in our Boomer chauvinism, that we have been a kind of "bridge" generation. We have not only been forced to keep up with technology, but adapt to an entirely new moral and cultural landscape than bears very little resemblance to the one we experienced as kids. However, it would appear that not every Boomer may have crossed our self-described bridge. Another person we have known forever once expressed her alarm to Dianne about how Richmond had changed so much in the last few years. "These outsiders are moving in and destroying our conservative values."

I could say that I have met this same change not with alarm, but with bafflement. Indeed, just how parochial can a person be? This parochial: sometimes when I reach my gate for a connecting flight back home from visiting my son in Portland, I get a little startled when I look over the counter at the blue screen and the white letters that spell out "RICHMOND." Like other people know about it? This is my old city. *My* old city. I look around at all of the seats filled with people waiting and think, "What are y'all doing here?" Plus, they're all strangers. I find myself actually looking for familiar faces. Again it's not some reactionary fear; it's more of a head-scratcher. Why would they have any reason—or desire—to come to a city so recently, so overwhelmingly defined by the Civil War? But they are coming. From all over the world. Just like my high school, the city is not the same place of my youth. And that is a good thing.

William Styron wrote in that Sewanee essay about some of his grandmother's last words to him: "Billy, always remember you are a southerner." He feared that she would have been greatly disappointed at his future choice to live in the North. Styron consoled himself by imagining telling her that the South was now overrun with malls and highways, cookie cutter neighborhoods just like the rest of the country. Just like Richmond. Historian C. Vann Woodward paraphrases an essay by Thornton Wilder to point out another way the Southerner differed from the rest of America, and thereby similar to all other cultures in recorded history. He observes that the majority American is abstract, disconnected. He belongs nowhere; place is unimportant, "he is related to everywhere, everybody, to always." He is indifferent, and even superior, to place. However, Wilder tells how Robert Penn Warren says that in the South there is a fear of this abstraction, that the massiveness of life had to be contained in the real. There was a more "European feeling—place, environment, relations, repetitions are the breath of being." I felt this without knowing it as a kid. Norlina was security, a bulwark against the pointlessness that accompanies the massiveness of life. That little town gave me, or maybe I gave it, that comforting feeling of the past in the present, of tradition, of belonging. Later in life, the American abstraction became personal. It was if someone snarkily asked each of my sons when they graduated from college how they could stand to live in the South. As though they threw darts blindfolded at a map of the United States, they moved to Portland, Oregon, New York City, and Washington, D.C. They added to their identities in ways I had not expected. But as in all unforeseen changes over time, there is an adjustment period before the new traditions and paradigms become the norm.

* * *

Mema finally had to "break up housekeeping" at ninety. One of the last times I saw her at the house, she was emerging from the pantry into the kitchen as I rounded the corner from the little back hallway. She was struggling to walk on her badly arthritic knees. She moved so slowly, so unlike how Dizzy described her getting a meal on the table, "I swear Mattie Lee has springs on that rear end." Now, she was holding on to the metal edging of the red Formica counter to keep herself steady. It had only been a couple of months since I'd seen her, but she had changed drastically. Gone was that little gleam in her intensely aware eyes. It was now impossible to imagine her lugging the hefty, steel Electrolux up the stairs, or ripping chickens apart with her hands, or even standing long enough to dip her rolls in the melted Crisco.

The process of breaking up the house happened when I was in the throes of raising my young children. Antique dealers from as far away as Raleigh and dozens of townspeople lined up on the day of the sale like tourists at the Biltmore, eager to grab one of so many treasures from that ten-bedroom house. I didn't attend, preferring to leave my memory of her house intact. All of this was precipitated by a slight stroke Mema suffered, which forced her into an old but nice affordable nursing home on the edge of Richmond's Fan District. The first time I visited her with my three young boys, we sat in the wood-paneled parlor room with many other residents gathered there. In all seriousness, because Mema was not a joke person, she leaned in and said quietly to the boys, "You know . . . there are a lot of old people here." They thought that was hilarious. She settled into her little room with a hospital bed, a night table, one wing chair, and an arched étagère with just a few figurines and three decorative plates culled from her old life displayed on it. When I was about to leave after a solo visit, she asked me to wheel her up into the hallway where a dozen or so ladies were lined up in their wheelchairs waiting for dinner. Before I pushed open the main door to go back home and make my fake stroganoff for four men, I glanced back at her. In that sea of white hair, pale skin, stooped shoulders, maybe a thousand years of life between them all, it was fairly obvious. Mema was the prettiest one of all. I would eventually say goodbye to her in this place on a November day in 1996. I sat by her bed and watched her labor to breathe, and once call Granddaddy's name.

* * *

A few years ago, my oldest son had an urge to go to Norlina, especially to photograph some of the Egerton gravestones. I don't think I had been there since Mema's funeral twenty years earlier. On the few visits we made in their youth, my boys always seemed grossly out of place, even though they were my children. Despite growing up in Richmond, they were more suburban than Southern. Perhaps I was being prepared on those visits for their eventual American abstraction. But on a visit to my house from Portland in his early thirties, I guess he wanted to satisfy his curiosity about this part of our family story. I was also curious. Why this interest in the past, this relatively minor part of his past that had greatly defined mine? He was only fourteen when Mema died. She was eighty when he was born. It was a sunny May afternoon when I came home from the hospital to our rental house with him, my first son. Mema was there waiting. I was all of twenty-four.

Sometimes we are aware, painfully, that we are in a moment of time that will not last, but celebrate it all the more because of its transience. There was no reason for that hint of death after I had just given birth. Mema was radiant at eighty, now a great-grandmother. My mother was not yet sixty. We were four generations there. My mother sat on the edge of the bed and lovingly pondered while staring at me, "How can you have a baby when you are still a baby yourself?" Seeing Mema in that dingy, outdated kitchen that didn't even belong to me reproducing her fried chicken and corn pudding was altogether strange. But how wonderful it all was. To have them there. To be the center of attention for a while. I remember Mema wearing her typical work dress with its sleeveless, square-necked bodice and big, gathered skirt, and her black orthopedic shoes. She sat in a straight back chair near my bed with her legs spread out like a baseball catcher, the fabric of her skirt forming a pool between her knees, her ample arms crossed on her thighs and her face extended, glowing, grinning with love and awe as I nursed him.

That Christmas when he was about six months old, we took him to Norlina. I can see it like it was last week instead of 1982. We put him on the bed in the yellow room where I always stayed as a kid, the one with the voluminous yellow tulle-edged dressing table and the faded Degas ballet prints. The old people, Dizzy, Harry, Miss

Ezzard, Mema, Nell, and Sue, lined up around the bed to form a kind of geriatric playpen. We all watched him flip himself over and over and back again, with that impish, darling grin I still see sometimes, especially aimed at his own son. So many howls of laughter, so many "Oh, Lordy, he's cute!" in a place of such clock-ticking silence, of ages measured in decades, not months. A baby in Norlina. As strange as fast food or rock music, dirty jokes, or wine before dinner.

My son meandered through the small-town cemetery quietly taking photographs with a few of his retro-looking film cameras. He paid no attention to where his feet trod. I tried not to yell at him the way I was yelled at in this place. I heard the echoes of Mema's and Dizzy's voices pealing out across the graveyard to my brothers and me. "Do not step on those graves! Walk around!" To me as, say, a nine-year-old child, their admonitions first sparked unparalleled fear then a holy shame. Why? Would we fall through? Would it be like a kind of horrific Jack in the Box that if you stepped on just the right spot, or wrong spot in this case, Aunt Lorena would come springing up from the ground? No, they were teaching us to respect the dead, the people they knew and remembered. So we would walk through the cemetery like the Queen's Guard, following the form of a grid, turning at right angles every six feet or so to be sure not to be disrespectful. But watching my son, this person who had lived by then about thirty percent of his life in a place that required driving west to get to the "coast" and not east to get to the beach, and the other part of his lifetime close to here in miles but in a very different time, disoriented my own inner compass. Even though my sons were raised in Richmond so close to my older parents, the twice-yearly gatherings of the big, many-cousins, fun-uncles Knapp family made the bigger impact on their ancestral identity. So seeing him mingling with the familiar Norlina names—Houser, as in Richard Houser, the railroad engineer who let me drive the train once when I was six, Taylor, Haywood, Allbridge—made him look so thoroughly Knapp, and even more unlike me.

Since my son was taking pictures, I pulled my iPhone out of my purse and half-heartedly took a few digital photographs of these impersonal, lifeless headstone etchings. Using that thing seemed only to accentuate the unexpected distance I was feeling from this world, like using store-bought coconut for a cake. Shouldn't I be queuing up for an onslaught of emotion and nostalgia, the tears and fuzzy memories montage of my movie. Instead, I was a little impatient to leave. What had long rooted me seemed to be rotting there right in front of me. I should have felt a pride and a tenderness reading Dizzy's name for all the fear she struck in me as a girl to "stand up straight, cross your legs!" Or for the fun we had in her beautiful apartment at 2222 Grove Avenue in Richmond where she lived before succumbing at fifty-five to Harry Walker's proposal. There she often made us oyster stew and taught me how to properly eat it, tapping the spoon on the far edge so any drops fall back into the bowl before reaching the mouth. This was also where sharing her double bed as a little girl required me to dodge her hefty, snoring frame by rolling in tandem with her all through the night, giggling to myself all the while. Or remembering her in the hospital with two giant black eyes after thugs beat her up on a dark street, and her big laughing "Hello!" before I even entered the room to prevent me from getting upset at the sight. Also, seeing Mema's tiny marker should have made me remember all over again what a big impact she made on me. No, I no longer wanted to live in the past.

That was the first winter of being alone in my real time present. My future was completely uncertain. My past had been destroyed in a way by the divorce and my future altered by the diaspora of the boys. I did not need all of these granite reminders of how set in stone I thought life should go, how these people had created an expectation of unending tradition that died with them. Those adolescent, debilitating questions about life's pointlessness tried to interrupt this moment. I felt myself a ghost. As I approached sixty, I wondered what life was left that was sweet enough to prevent me from just lying down there with these Egertons and letting my son go on home without me. Then from under the one cedar tree shading some other Hicks I didn't recognize, I glanced up at my firstborn son standing in a flood of January sunlight. He had his back to me and was peering down into his cool Yashica camera's viewfinder. Here he was, without ever admitting it, or being able to verbalize it, trying to connect with my past. Maybe. I was then glad we came. Knowing him as I do, I knew at that moment he was creating some form of beauty from this scene. He was photographing the setting, but his fertile imagination was filling with a further declension of the Norlina story, one so far removed from its origin that it would have to be a fiction.

We drove back up through town. Everything was abandoned. The sky was darkening. From the old bus station's driveway we looked across at Mema's house. Gone were the fourteen rocking chairs that rocked so many characters, so many words. I had every intention of getting in the car and going home when my son asked, "Do you want to go see if they are home?" He meant the couple that, miraculously for Mema's final few years of finances in the nursing home, bought that ten-bedroom house on an acre of land for twenty-five thousand dollars. No, I did not want to see if they were home. We had come for the cemetery, to honor the dead; I did not want to see the house emptied of its life, all the things that expressed her quest for beauty in that little forgotten, dying town. It would be too much to bear. It's why I never went in after Mom broke it up. I feared I may have another surreal experience, like the one I had after Mema had moved to the nursing home in Richmond. Mom and I went to Norlina while the house was still intact. Vivid scenes of all the old people from my childhood floated by in a kind of cinematic resurrection. That was hard enough. But, for the sake of the art that I knew was brewing in his head, I relented. We climbed the concrete steps. I held on to the copper railing made smooth in part from the countless times my childhood belly had slid down it. He knocked loudly on the edge of the painted glossy black door.

We could see through the big glass pane a woman about my age with what looked like a loose, teased out perm, bounding to the door. As though she were expecting us, she opened it with a huge grin and a big hello. She was so nice. And Black. Behind her, emerging from the narrow hallway from the kitchen came an older white man using a cane, also smiling broadly. Herbert was a retired high school teacher who had married her, Maria, a Creole woman from New Orleans whose twenty-year-old son was living there with them. I felt a sense of relief that we had already had an uneventful trip to the graveyard. Because no doubt, these new homeowners at the old family place must have regularly sent those Egerton coffins spinning in a mighty upheaval of dirt and presumptions. We introduced ourselves, including that Mattie Lee Hicks was my grandmother who used to own the house. They knew all about her. "Well, come on in!" They were so kind to show us around, but my reaction was like a family returning home after a flood or a hurricane. I was looking for familiar markers like the oversized brocade sofas, cut velvet armchairs, the Hummel figurines, the tinkling candelabras. What I saw was a blur of oversized, faux Lazy Boys, sheets thrown over couches, a series of Goodwill lamps, random cardboard boxes up against the wall, and a big ass TV in the part of the dining room where my throne, that giant red velvet chair, used to be. I almost sensed Maria might have known how I was feeling. We didn't stay long. I couldn't take it. But we talked long enough for Maria to put it together that Mattie Lee was sister to Happy.

"Oh, everybody in town knew Happy! He'd drive his pickup truck to the post office every day."

Herbert interjected, "You know he lost his right leg to diabetes?"

"Yes, my mother and her cousin used to keep me a little informed of his doings towards the end."

"You know he would use his cane to push the gas pedal. It's a wonder he didn't have an accident."

Giggling a little, Maria finished her Happy story. "Oh, yeah. He'd pull up to the post office and just blow on his horn until somebody came up to his window. He'd ask them to go in and get his mail for him. I got it for him a few times. He was always thankful. He was a sweet old man. But what a character."

We thanked them for letting us intrude on them and shared a warm goodbye. It was growing even more cloudy and threatening rain. Before getting back in the car, I got the urge to go look at the railroad tracks behind her house. As children, my brothers and I ran out of the back door sometimes eight or ten times a day to watch the trains go by. Dalton always ignored the adults' dire warnings about going down the slope to secretly put pennies on the track, retrieving them when the caboose passed to show Brian and me Abe Lincoln's distorted head. I didn't want to walk through their backyard, so I guided my son over behind the old appliance store where we could stand on the former train bed. Norlina got on the map because of that track; now it had been bypassed by newer ways to cross the South. The track had even been taken up thirty years earlier. The old bed could have been a narrow path in some eastern North Carolina jungle. It was impossible to imagine the countless huge freight and passenger trains that barreled over those tracks every day, marking time for Mema as precisely as any Swiss watch. That was when Norlina still occupied a place in time. Now that long, flat expanse was filled with grass and scraggly bushes and a few small trees between two small hills that used to hold gravel and rail and creosote ties. The picture it formed reminded me of what I learned long ago in art class. You get a sense of perspective as those lines converge into a vanishing point.

Happy didn't stop getting around Norlina even after being denied a driver's license, despite his prowess with his cane and the gas pedal. Bobby Jean told me that he had accumulated three or four electric wheelchairs that he kept in his old gardening shed. He was fond of taking one out for early morning spins around town. I had no trouble imagining that. Happy, a ninety-something, white haired, old railroad conductor, as oblivious as always to how ridiculously out of place he was, whizzing along Number One highway in the dawn's early light with his pant leg pinned around his stump.

I have nothing left to say, but I'm going to say it anyway.
RANDY NEWMAN, I'M DEAD (BUT I DON'T KNOW IT)

Epilogue

My final spring before retirement, students were given the option to return to the classroom or, because of the lingering fear of Covid, continue remote learning. Only a handful of senior guys in my Theory of Knowledge class took up the offer. During second period on a beautiful, cloudless, sunny day in late May, a continual boom-boom-boom of what sounded like thunder drowned out our conversation. Curious, we left the classroom in a pack and headed towards the center of campus, the big grassy hill I used to roll down fifty-two years earlier. On the hilltop stood a yellow, life-sized Tonka Truck opening its airborne bucket like dinosaur jaws. It was eating the roof of Building Two, my old seventh grade classrooms. It was actually happening.

A couple of years earlier, the county had promised a renovation of the two 1962-vintage high schools, one in the East End and Tucker, as well as my 1956 elementary school. Anything that old could not possibly still function well. I had it all planned out for how we could snazz up Tucker, take care of that pesky asbestos issue, and add central air and heating to replace the noisy old radiators and air conditioning window units (one of mine caught on fire during class once). Most importantly, we would keep Tucker's hippie spirit and beautiful azalea and dogwood grounds intact. But the plans changed on a dime, actually a lot of dimes. The school board decided to forego the fifty-five million dollar renovation of historic old Tucker in favor of a hundred million dollar brand new Tucker. Their plan would reverse the layout. Where the gym and auditorium had stood for sixty years around the open courtyard with massive old trees would now be the new enclosed, train station-esque school. Where all the cool individual classroom buildings had been, a new football field and tennis courts would be built.

The auditorium bit the dust first. From the parking lot, looking beyond the new protective fence, I could see in the pile of rubble partial rows of its upended seats. I surely sat in one of them even back in fifth grade, gazing in awe at my senior next door neighbor who starred in so many plays; my parents would have sat in some of them when I later performed in our variety show; and later still I sat in one to witness the incredible talent of this generation. The gym fell next: the full transition was underway. In this phase, we could stand only a few yards behind another chain link fence on the old cracked sidewalks under the infamous leaky awnings and watch the hermetically-sealed new school with its crazy roof angles and weatherproof interior hallways rise from the dirt. For a short while that spring, past and future stood side by side in a kind of historical limbo. This bifurcated Tucker only delayed the inevitable and compounded my denial of what was coming once summer hit and kids were all gone—the destruction of the rest of the school, the academic buildings, those ten relics of a bygone era, of my bygone era. I felt like that roof on Building Two, resisting the jaws of death, the demise of my own foundation.

My mother and I used to laugh at my great aunt Dizzy's wittily delivered observation about the old Egerton family house in Macon, North Carolina. "Gone . . . gone . . . gone . . . forever." I could say the same about the J. R. Tucker I knew and loved. The memories of that old real estate, of *that* school, ended with that Covid class. Indeed, in August I steeled myself and drove the back way behind school, along the road that used to deliver me to Cafeteria Three's parking lot day after day, year after year, the parking lot where my history changed when Mark and I skipped out on the pep rally. What I saw took my breath away. It was completely disorienting. Open flat expanses of red clay soil filled the area where the classrooms used to be. They had been leveled. Somewhere in the removed rubble lay a few cinderblocks from Room 52 that, if reassembled, would have formed a kind of jig-sawed epitaph that I Sharpied across the wall before making my final exit through my classroom's faded blue metal door. "Lee Knapp taught the children here." Now, that cave of learning, that laboratory of love, that microcosm of my belief in America was the fifty-yard line of the football field. Room 52 . . . gone forever.

As a requirement of a retiree benefit program, I substitute in the new school a few days a year. I admit, my attitude needed a little adjustment the first time I entered and surveyed the new landscape. It was a soulless space, lacking the old (some might say wildly out-dated), charming (some might say unfunctional) traditional setting. I could not help comparing it to what I had known, to *my* school. The *real* Tucker. Perhaps, that was because it was so new; the change seemed so sudden; memories had not formed and attached to those barren walls yet. Nevertheless, it would *never, never* be as special as the old geography.

Entering a year later, both old memorabilia and new artwork had started to adorn some of the walls. A huge tiger painting stared at me from the main hall. Mingling among that eternal flow of teenagers, hearing them laughing in the halls, asking questions in class, practicing for the musical, or shooting hoops during a massive combined gym period, I felt ashamed of my earlier assessment about its lack of a soul. Even more so after I subbed in a class of eighteen lively, smart seniors in an AP Psych class. As usual, they represented a student body of so many different races and ethnic backgrounds, which by now had seen a transition to a majority minority composition.

At the end of class, one very ebullient young Black woman said to the whole class, "OK. We're playing a game. Let's go around the room and you have to tell everybody what you want to major in and what you want to do in life." In a scene reminiscent of my old students joking around the table in a now vanished Cafeteria Three, Black, white, Asian, Middle Eastern, boys, girls, preppy, nerdy, outgoing, shy, those kids all pronounced their plans for their futures. And, I thought, America's too, really. After each student revealed their hopes and dreams, the others all applauded them in delight. I never thought I would admit it, but this entirely new place started to feel completely familiar.

* * *

It wasn't long before another physical reminder of my past was completely erased. It took forty years, but the massive growth westward from Tucker finally butted up against my parents' property. My father died long ago. Six years after my mother passed, a condo developer bought it, along with the properties of three other neighbors. For so long, those few houses looked grossly out of place sitting across from a Lidl and beside a big Wegman's and Cabela's. Then the bulldozers appeared. Trees came down as more red clay earth rolled out like a carpet across a piece of real estate that had housed my past. But for months when driving by to work, I could still see Mom's old brown saltbox dream house, her life's work. Until one spring day on my way home, it happened. Like with school, another bulldozer was, at that very moment, eating the roof, the heart pine floors, the newel post we salvaged from an old bookstore. I circled back around to find a place to park and watch. All of the life, all of the drama, the arguments, the joy, the food, the conversations, my wedding, birthday parties streamed through my mind. Days later, the entire acreage was just one big orange dirt rectangle, ready for new foundations to be laid for somebody else's life.

* * *

Way back, a couple of girls from the Boys and Girls Home used to stop by my classroom some mornings just to talk about school, and sometimes life. Theirs had been upended lives so far, staying in a group home hoping to be fostered or adopted, a goal that one of them doubted since, as she said, "I'm not sure any white folks would want me, being Black and gay, and all." This child had the sweetest voice to go along with her sturdy frame, soft eyes, and equally sweet disposition. On one brilliant sunny day in the spring, she once pondered, "Ms. Knapp, do you ever think how once you're gone, you know, like all of this—the trees, the sky, the flowers— will still be here, but you won't?" It was another of those moments of bonding that transcends any differences in age or background. She was fifteen; I was in my forties. I probably answered, as I would much more so now in my sixties, "Only all the time!"

It is the helplessness, and the mystery, we all feel at the relent-lessness of time and the aching beauty of this life. I do feel those old Questions, like my student's, haunting me more and more often as I make the coffee each night for the next morning, there in the kitchen of my dream house in the country. I'm still forming memories, still writing my history, still cutting my grass here for a while. And, hope-fully, unlike my old school or Mom's house, it will survive, owned by a stranger after I, too, have been reduced to rubble under a pile of red Virginia clay.

Acknowledgements

M y deepest thanks go to my dear friend Dianne Pierce who has been a constant source of encouragement and inspiration for the past forty years. Her contribution to this tome came in both great insights and edits, as well as keeping me pumped up when the whole thing seemed stupid and pointless.

A lifetime of gratitude to Paige and Steve Whitten, who long ago gave me a model for a genuine way to be smart and a smart way to be funny. Their dedication to students and education made me want to be a teacher.

To all of my students who spent time in that cave of learning, Room 52. Every day you made me laugh and made me think. I hope it was the same for you. It was an honor to be your teacher.

To my colleagues over the years, I am so grateful. You are the unsung heroes of our culture, and some of the smartest and funniest and most loving folks I could have ever known. Your examples challenged and inspired me.

And to one of those former colleagues, my companion Mark Condon, how can I thank you? You have supported me in many practical ways, but also by holding me up when I was a little shaky. You've listened to not only this thing, but, well, everything; you've made me laugh more than I ever thought would be possible again; you've shown me the world. I'm so glad we skipped out on that pep rally.

To Holly Caldwell for her great help in editing, especially regarding that em dash.

Finally, my unending gratitude to my family. Cheston Knapp, your wisdom, encouragement, and professional advice made this thing much better, and made all that birthing pain so worth it. To your sweet family, Alexis and Emerson, for all of the joy and love you give me. And Eric, on your strength I so often rely. Your input redirected this work on to more solid ground; and beautiful Meredith for whom I am continually grateful. Finally, Stephen, your unmitigated support of me as more than just your mother, has empowered me, most recently proven on that late Thanksgiving night when you calmed me down and told me just to write on. For Catherine, my wonderful daughter-in-law and mother superior to little-man Winston, your openness, intelligence, and sense of fun have added so much to our family.